The Book of
Psalms
The Heart of the Word

Titles from Kevin Swanson

Family Bible Study Guides
Genesis: A Family Bible Study Guide
Psalms I: A Family Bible Study Guide
Psalms II: A Family Bible Study Guide
Psalms III & IV: A Family Bible Study Guide
Proverbs I: A Family Bible Study Guide
Proverbs II: A Family Bible Study Guide
Proverbs III: A Family Bible Study Guide

Christian Curriculum Project
Christian Classics Study Guide — Volume I
Great Christian Classics: Five Great Narratives of the Faith
Christian Classics Study Guide — Junior Level

The Second Mayflower
Upgrade: 10 Secrets to the Best Education for Your Child
What Does the Bible Say About That?

Visionary Manhood (MP3 / CD)
Vision for Generations (MP3 / CD)
Reforming the Church in the 21ˢᵗ Century (CD)
Family Economics Conference Audio Series (MP3 / CD)
Family Economics Conference Video Series (DVD)
Vision for Generations (DVD)

The Book of

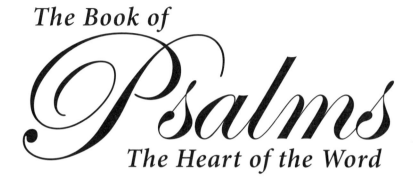

Psalms

The Heart of the Word

BOOK III & IV: PSALMS 73–106

Kevin Swanson

GENERATIONS *WITH* VISION

Scripture quotations are taken from the
King James Version

Published by Generations with Vision
10431 South Parker Road
Parker, Colorado, 80134
www.generationswithvision.com

For more information on this and
other titles from Generations with Vision,
visit www.generationswithvision.com or call 1-888-839-6132.

CONTENTS

INTRODUCTION

"And thou shalt teach [My words] diligently unto thy children, and shalt talk of them when thou sittest in thine house, and when thou walkest by the way, and when thou liest down, and when thou risest up" (Deut. 6:7).

It would be wrong to confine the Bible to a Sunday School class one day a week. That is not what God wants for our children. In the raising of children, parents must teach the Bible to their children every day, throughout the day. Without overstatement, God's revelation in the Bible is the most important textbook in your children's education. In fact, it is the core of your children's education. That is the plain teaching of Deuteronomy 6:7.

This text also requires that *parents* must teach their own children God's Word. Most, if not all, curriculum produced for children today is written with Sunday School teachers in mind. Even educational materials used in homes and homeschools are usually written for generic teachers, not for fathers and mothers. Because we have drifted far from a biblical methodology in the education of children, little curriculum is provided for a Deuteronomy 6:7, Ephesians 6:4, and Proverbs context of learning. That is why this Bible curriculum is provided specifically for parents. These manuals are intended to facilitate teaching directly from a parent to a child. This teaching will always prove to be more effective and more powerful than any other form of discipleship used in any context.

Where Do You Find Family Worship in the Bible?

The practice of family worship is variously described as "family devotions" or "family Bible study." When our children were young we would call it "Bible time." Whatever families call it, the practice itself is rare today. One researcher who has studied

Christian trends for several decades reports that only one family in one hundred has ever tried it. Yet the Bible clearly requires it.

The Book of Hebrews is full of warnings for those who are not careful and consistent in their Christian walk. Two things are prescribed by the writer of Hebrews to save us from slipping into spiritual decline. First, do not neglect the assembling of ourselves together as a church body (Heb. 10:25). Second, do not neglect a daily edifying. "But exhort one another daily, while it is called Today: lest any of you be hardened through the deceitfulness of sin" (Heb. 3:13). Clearly, God wants us exhorting one another on a daily basis. For most people, it is inconvenient to schedule a daily Bible study with other folks from the church. Given the Deuteronomy 6:7 principle, it would make sense that this daily exhortation should come within the context of the home. Exhortation literally means a call to obedience; what we obey is the Word of God. Therefore, one should include both something about the Word of God and a practical, direct application—an encouragement to obedience in that time together. The lessons in this manual are based on this biblical model.

How Children Will Get Our Faith

God's prescribed, normative method for the discipleship of children is by means of their very own parents. The biblical principle relating to the training of children is beautifully summarized in Deuteronomy 6:6–9, here restated in full:

"And these words, which I command thee this day, shall be in thine heart: And thou shalt teach them diligently unto thy children, and shalt talk of them when thou sittest in thine house, and when thou walkest by the way, and when thou liest down, and when thou risest up. And thou shalt bind them for a sign upon thine hand, and they shall be as frontlets between thine eyes. And thou shalt write them upon the posts of thy house, and on thy gates."

It is instructive, first, to note that this command comes right on the heels of the *Shema,* "You shall love the Lord your God with all your heart, with all your soul, with all your mind and with all your strength." Immediately following this—the greatest commandment of all—comes the preeminent application of that love: "Teach My words diligently to your children." A similar pattern is found in John 21:15. Here Jesus asks Peter, "Do you love Me?" Peter answers emphatically in the affirmative, "Of course I love You." Jesus immediately gives him an objective way to apply that love, "Feed My lambs." The quintessential proof of any love you have for your Saviour—for your God—will be found in your desire for and your effort expended in feeding the lambs that He has entrusted to you.

Several other principles can be drawn from the Deuteronomy 6:6–9 passage. First, the teaching is to be thorough. According to verse 2, it is the Lord's interest that the message of God's revelation, all aspects to the biblical worldview, be passed on to our children and children's children so that they might "keep all of the commandments, all of the days of their lives."

Moreover, this teaching must be daily, diligent, and consistent. The Hebrew word *shinantam* is taken from the word used for sharpening a sword. The only way that there will be a successful transfer of God's Word from one generation to the next is by regular, consistent, repeated teaching of that Word. The opposition to the biblical worldview is intense and ubiquitous in the world around us. The human mind by nature is reluctant to receive it. One does not by nature think correctly about God, man, sin, or redemption.

As already mentioned, this teaching is *parental*. The command to teach the children is not assigned to the village, the community, or the civil or church authorities. It is assigned to parents—primarily to fathers. The command is in the masculine singular (see also Eph. 6:4). This mandate is not an isolated command. It is found throughout Scripture, although it is rarely emphasized and practiced in the Christian church today.

Consider several other passages:

Exodus 10:2—And that thou mayest tell in the ears of thy son, and of thy son's son, what things I have wrought in Egypt, and My signs which I have done among them: that ye may know how that I am the LORD.

Proverbs 1:8—My son, hear the instruction of thy father, and forsake not the law of thy mother.

Proverbs 3:1—My son, forget not my law: but let thine heart keep my commandments:

Proverbs 4:3–5—For I was my father's son, tender and only beloved in the sight of my mother. He taught me also, and said unto me, Let thine heart retain my words: keep my commandments, and live. Get wisdom, get understanding: forget it not: neither decline from the words of my mouth.

Proverbs 4:20–21—My son, attend to my words: incline thine ear unto my sayings. Let them not depart from thine eyes: keep them in the midst of thine heart.

Proverbs 5:1—My son, attend unto my wisdom, and bow thine ear to my understanding.

Proverbs 6:20–21—My son, keep thy father's commandment, and forsake not the law of thy mother: Bind them continually upon thine heart, and tie them about thy neck.

Proverbs 7:1–3—My son, keep my words, and lay up my commandments with thee. Keep my commandments, and live: and my law as the apple of thine eye. Bind them upon thy fingers, write them upon the table of thine heart.

Proverbs 23:24–26—The father of the righteous shall greatly rejoice: and he that begetteth a wise child shall have joy of him. Thy father and thy mother shall be glad, and she that bare thee shall rejoice. My son, give me thine heart, and let thine eyes observe my ways.

Proverbs 31:1–2—The words of king Lemuel, the prophecy that his mother taught him. What, my son? and what, the son of my womb? and what, the son of my vows?

The entire Book of Proverbs is dedicated to the theme of the careful discipleship of a son by his father, with the exception of the last chapter which brings in the lessons that a mother taught her son. The discipleship scenario modeled in the Proverbs is a father walking with his son in a close, organic relationship—instructing, pleading, warning, commanding, rebuking, imploring, and challenging. Biblical discipleship is always based in relationship, and there is no more powerful way of discipleship available to us than this one. The God-designed relationship of father and son is precisely built for this God-designed discipleship. May God give us the courage and the wisdom to use it for maximum impact in His kingdom for many generations to come!

Paul also assumes this form of discipleship as the norm in 1 Thessalonians 2:11: "As ye know how we exhorted and comforted and charged every one of you, as a father doth his children." The sort of discipleship the Apostle uses in the church is patterned after this tender, relationship-oriented model in the home!

When Paul turns to the consideration of children in his epistles (Eph. 6:1–4; Col. 3:20–21), his youth program is very simple and inexpensive. He turns to the fathers and says, "And, ye fathers, provoke not your children to wrath: but bring them up in the nurture and admonition of the Lord." Then he turns to the children with, "*Honor that man.* Obey him. Listen to him. Incline your ear to him. Bind those words to your heart. Fasten them about your neck." We are expected to know this powerful, biblical method of discipleship and use it.

There is nothing new in this message. This message was strong for the first several centuries of the church, taught by the early church fathers such as Ignatius, Clement of Alexandria, and Chrystostom. "Fathers, bring up your children in the nurture and admonition of the Lord: and teach them the holy Scriptures, and also trades, that they may not indulge in idleness. Now the Scripture says, A righteous father educates his children well: his heart shall rejoice in a wise son" (Ignatius, A.D. 30–107). It was only with the rise of monasticism and a celibate clergy (as well as the inaccessibility of the Scriptures in the common language) that the use of family worship and discipleship within the familial context faded. The practice revived for a time between 1520 and 1820 in Geneva, Scotland, and England because of the reformation of the Scriptures in the lives of believers, but then it disappeared again. By 1844, J. A. Alexander wrote a book lamenting the decline of family worship and the lack of involvement of parents in the spiritual nurture of their children.

From the succeeding verses of Deuteronomy 6, it is clear that God's Word must be pervasive in the education of a child. If God is the ultimate authority in truth, and if God is the ultimate authority in ethics, certainly His truth must be a consideration in the training and education of children. When children are not trained to look to the Bible as the fount of truth in their understanding of God, man, creation, and redemption, they will begin to think like humanists in their education.

"And these words, which I command thee this day, shall be in thine heart: And thou shalt teach them diligently unto thy children, and shalt talk of them when thou sittest in thine house, and when thou walkest by the way, and when thou liest down, and when thou risest up. And thou shalt bind them for a sign upon thine hand, and they shall be as frontlets between thine eyes. And thou shalt write them upon the posts of thy house, and on thy gates" (Deut. 6:7–9)

This teaching of God's Word must permeate every area of the child's life, including every possible bodily position (sitting, walking, lying down, and rising up). There must be no area in the child's life that is separated from the Word of God. He is not to think that God is connected to church but disconnected from his academics, his entertainment, and the rest of his life.

When a child has the impression that God is appropriate for Sunday but has no business in the geography textbook, the movie theater, or in his play, he has not been trained to think properly about God. Moreover, this teaching of God's Word is to be intimately and readily accessible to the child all of the time. Everywhere he goes throughout his childhood training, he is to be confronted by the living and true God, and it is the parent's responsibility to see to it that this happens. They are to exercise this God-ordained method of Christian training in as varied and sundry circumstances as any average family might find themselves. They should "run into" God on the doorposts of the house. His Word is to be as close to them as something bound on their hands and as obvious to them as an object hanging in front of their faces. In short, they should be thoroughly soaked in a God-centered training. This principle is reiterated in Proverbs 6:20–22:

"My son, keep your father's command, and do not forsake the law of your mother. Bind them continually upon your heart: Tie them around your neck. When you roam, they will lead you: When you sleep, they will keep you: And when you awake, they will speak with you. For the commandment is a lamp and the law is light: Reproofs of instruction are the way of life."

Consider the reality of what we believe. The reality of God—His authority, His law, and His redemption—is far too significant to not take a central, controlling position in the training of the child and in the molding of his mind and his thought patterns. The reality of God and His redemption must be pervasive in the *paideia*, the training and formation of a child of God.

Churches in this country and across most of the Christianized world have funneled tremendous resources into Sunday Schools, youth groups, youth camps, divorce recovery workshops, extensive counseling programs, and an innumerable number of other programs—all of which are solidly rooted in good intentions. Their intention is to evangelize and disciple children or to repair the damage wrought by a society full of fragmented families.

But what kind of programs have we instituted to maximize the methods that God has ordained for the evangelism and discipleship of children? What are we doing to encourage men to be godly leaders in their homes? If the church were to put an ounce of effort into the training of parents to engage in faithful discipleship of their own children, I warrant it would go farther than a pound of effort directed towards salvaging those children that have little or no discipleship contact from godly parents. As the old saying goes, an ounce of prevention is worth a pound of cure.

Churches must begin to work with and through the biblical means that God has ordained to effect the conversion and discipleship of children. Why should we direct such a significant proportion of effort to working where God has not issued a clear command while families know little of what it means to teach the Word of God to their children while they walk by the way, drive in their car, give them baths, put them to bed, and sit down to meals? Why should we be content with the lack of godly instruction in homes, as if our Sunday School classes could some how compensate for this lack?

I know a family who raised their children with daily family devotions, daily taped sermons, psalm singing in the car, regular, fervent prayer, disciplined Sabbath-keeping filled up with the public and private exercises of God's Word, teenaged children trained to lead the Bible studies, and a thousand other exercises of the Deuteronomy six mandate. All six of these children have grown up now and are serving the Lord in churches around the world. I know of other families who exercised the same disciplines and yielded the same results. On the other hand, I know dozens of other families who sent their children to Sunday School but knew little or nothing about a rigorous family discipleship program. In most cases their children, in part or in whole, fell away from the faith. I understand that these stories are anecdotal. However, the principle of Proverbs 22:6 cannot be denied. The verse is interpreted in several ways, but it is generally accepted to say that the instruction and discipline given to a child will make a difference in the way that he goes. The covenantal promises are clear that we are blessed if we obey God's mandates and cursed if we do not (Deut. 27–28). Furthermore, the Lord promises blessings on future generations as we obey His commandments (Exod. 20:6; Deut. 6:2), including those repeated commandments that direct fathers and mothers to teach the Word of God insistently and consistently to their children in all situations of life (Deut. 6:7–9; Eph. 6:4).

The most powerful form of evangelism is God's recommended form because He always blesses obedience to His commands. Indeed, the most effective form of evangelism is that which happens when a father takes the hand of his son or daughter and says, "Let me show you Jesus. Let me show you how to walk in the ways of the Lord by my daily words and living example." Covenantal faithfulness from generation to generation is God's intended design for His people (Gen. 17:10–12; Deut. 7:9; Acts 2:38–39; Is. 59:20–21; Ezek. 37:24–27; Mal. 2:15). Rebellion should be the exception, not the rule. But the means that He has designed for our use to bring about covenantal continuity is contained in Deuteronomy 6:7–9, Psalms 78:4–6, the book of Proverbs, and Ephesians 6:4. Our abandonment of His designed means, or our displacement of it with other programs devised by the minds of men, will produce meager results. Maximize on the means that God has designed, and we will be truly blessed. Ignore it and we will be at a loss. Would that we see a reformation grow into a fulfillment of Isaiah's prophecy in our own generation.

"My Spirit which is upon you, and My words which I have put in your mouth, shall not depart from your mouth, nor from the mouth of your offspring, nor from the mouth of your offspring's offspring, says the Lord, from now and forever" (Isaiah 59:21).

Amen.

Depth vs. Distance

Many family worship programs endorse a straight-through reading of the Bible. Some even provide for a read-through-the-Bible-in-a-year reading program. While this may be good from time to time, I have noticed that our children do not retain much of what is read unless it is explained to them. The Word of God encourages a father to teach "His commandments." Paul sees the father as one who is faithfully exhorting, comforting, and charging his children (1 Thess. 2:11). This is far more than simply reading the Word of God. This study series provides opportunity for discussion, exhortations (calls to obedience), warning, and comfort. By the time your children have completed this book, they will have engaged the material on many levels. They will have learned what every chapter in the Book of Psalms teaches. They will see how the book applies to them personally. This is essential in discipleship.

I would suggest that, from time to time, a year should be taken in family worship to read the Bible through in its entirety. You might do this three or four times in eighteen years of family worship. However, good shepherds will more often take the time to explain the sense or the meaning of the passage and the application of it for the sheep God has brought to them.

"So they read in the book in the law of God distinctly, and gave the sense, and caused them to understand the reading"
(Nehemiah 8:8).

Teaching and Application

I mentioned already that these lessons are written for shepherds. It may surprise some parents reading this that I would call them shepherds or pastors. But that is exactly what we are. Jesus tells us, through His appeal to Peter, to "feed my lambs." These little children are lambs, and we are feeding them God's Word.

Every pastor knows that a text of the Bible must be understood, and it must be exercised in the life of the hearer. We must break down the food so it can be digested. But we must then encourage the lambs to eat. They need to make relevant application of the Word. It must be believed and obeyed. Hence, these lessons are written as a pastor would bring the Word to his flock. First we ask the question, "What does this chapter teach us?" Then we ask, "How does this chapter encourage us to believe and obey God in our lives?" The application of one text to children in the 21st century might be different than for adults in the 21st century. The application might be different in different families. The application sections and the family discussion questions are only meant to inspire further discussion for each family.

How to Use This Study Manual

This Study Manual maintains the unity of Scripture. In fact, the primary interpretation tool is the one that Scripture itself endorses. Use Scripture to interpret Scripture. Where there are challenging texts, classic commentaries by Matthew Henry, Charles Spurgeon, Keil and Delitzsch, and John Calvin have been researched carefully.

In the use of this Study Manual, the following suggested guidelines may be found helpful. These are only suggestions. Families may find their own use for these manuals in other homeschooling arrangements.

1. Obtain enough copies of the study manual for each child who can read. Encourage the children to write their own notes in the manual.

Children under eight or nine years of age may have a hard time understanding some of the material contained in these lessons. You might take a little extra time to explain the lessons to the younger ones. Any experienced parent knows that it is never harmful for younger children to be present when material is taught that exceeds their ability to understand. You never know what children hear and what they will understand. Always aim high in your family worship. As you do this, you will encourage a maturity in the knowledge and discernment of each of the children.

Nevertheless, do not entirely neglect the little ones. In our family, we like to include one Bible story written for little ones from one year up to six or seven years old in our worship. We also like to direct a simple question or a simple application to the little ones.

2. Establish a regular order of your worship time. I would suggest something like the following. This is the pattern that our family has found most edifying.

Singing. Open with the singing of hymns, psalms, and simple choruses. This is a good way to call everybody together and get them involved.

Scripture. Read the Scripture together. Have each child that can read participate by reading several verses. You may wish to split the chapter in two, as well as the exposition.

Memory Work. Have the children recite memory verses or catechism answers they have been learning.

Bible Story. You may assign one of the older children to read a Bible story to the younger children.

Extra Reading. Read an additional devotional book like *Pilgrim's Progress, Foxe's Book of Martyrs,* or a book on church history.

Prayer. Close in prayer. You may wish to tie in aspects of the exhortations in the prayer. Include confession of family sin and as many elements of the Lord's Prayer as possible. If your church provides a list of prayer needs, this would be a good time to address these needs in family prayer.

3. Conduct this time of family worship at least once per day, at least six times every week. That is the Hebrews 3:13 principle. If you have never established the discipline of a regular family worship time, begin with a small, manageable chunk. Consistency is the primary concern. If you can only schedule

a consistent time of family worship for five minutes each day, that would be better than a thirty minute session twice a week. At the very least, make sure you have enough time to read the Word, develop at least one application, and pray.

4. Do your best to maintain an enthusiasm for God and a rich enjoyment for the deep truths of His Word during this time. If Dad, who is leading worship, isn't into it, it is doubtful the children will be into it either. Make this a matter of fervent prayer. It is easy to lose a sense for the importance of this time in the Word. But remember that this is your lifeblood. It is the lifeblood of the family, as important as bread and water for the stomach. In the words of that true disciple of Christ, "To whom would we go? You only have the words of eternal life!" We must take God's Word as personal revelation. This is God speaking to me. This is God speaking to my family. Our relationship with Christ grows as we hold personally communication with Him in His Word. The more personal we take the message, the application, and our prayers, the more intimate the relationship we will have with our God.

Psalms Book 3

Psalm 73

Category: Faith ～ Occasion: Envying the Wicked

Author: Asaph

1 Truly God is good to Israel, even to such as are of a clean heart.

2 But as for me, my feet were almost gone; my steps had well nigh slipped.

3 For I was envious at the foolish, when I saw the prosperity of the wicked.

4 For there are no bands in their death: but their strength is firm.

5 They are not in trouble as other men; neither are they plagued like other men.

6 Therefore pride compasseth them about as a chain; violence covereth them as a garment.

7 Their eyes stand out with fatness: they have more than heart could wish.

8 They are corrupt, and speak wickedly concerning oppression: they speak loftily.

9 They set their mouth against the heavens, and their tongue walketh through the earth.

10 Therefore his people return hither: and waters of a full cup are wrung out to them.

11 And they say, How doth God know? and is there knowledge in the most High?

12 Behold, these are the ungodly, who prosper in the world; they increase in riches.

13 Verily I have cleansed my heart in vain, and washed my hands in innocency.

14 For all the day long have I been plagued, and chastened every morning.

15 If I say, I will speak thus; behold, I should offend against the generation of thy children.

16 When I thought to know this, it was too painful for me;

17 Until I went into the sanctuary of God; then understood I their end.

18 Surely thou didst set them in slippery places: thou castedst them down into destruction.

19 How are they brought into desolation, as in a moment! they are utterly consumed with terrors.

20 As a dream when one awaketh; so, O Lord, when thou awakest, thou shalt despise their image.

21 Thus my heart was grieved, and I was pricked in my reins.

22 So foolish was I, and ignorant: I was as a beast before thee.

23 Nevertheless I am continually with thee: thou hast holden me by my right hand.

24 Thou shalt guide me with thy counsel, and afterward receive me to glory.

25 Whom have I in heaven but thee? and there is none upon earth that I desire beside thee.

26 My flesh and my heart faileth: but God is the strength of my heart, and my portion for ever.

27 For, lo, they that are far from thee shall perish: thou hast destroyed all them that go a whoring from thee.

28 But it is good for me to draw near to God: I have put my trust in the Lord GOD, that I may declare all thy works.

The Point:

The goodness of God sometimes fades in our minds when we are confronted with the success of evil. But then we look through eyes of faith and see the redemption of God and His judgment on the wicked.

How do we feel in the recitation of this psalm?

Our hearts are in turmoil as our eyes fixate on the evil power of the wicked. Suppose for a moment that you are swimming in shark-infested waters. As a gigantic, twenty-foot great white bumps your leg, you feel small and vulnerable. But would fear overwhelm you? Or would you be more impressed with the power of God who made such a magnificent animal? Are you more likely to glorify the big shark, or glorify the big God who made the shark? Very often, our moods and perspectives are fear-based, being controlled by the actions and achievements of the wicked around us. When this happens, we lose our focus on God, Who sometimes does give wicked men temporary success in order that He might perfect His judgment upon them. By the end of the psalm, we refocus our eyes upon God, acknowledge His protection and salvation, and realize His absolute justice.

What does this psalm teach us?

Verse 1. The psalm begins with a gracious recognition of God's goodness to Israel, the body of the church, and the assembly of the saints. As we take in the big picture of God's work with the church in history, throughout the world, and in our own local church, we get a clear picture of the rich blessings God has poured out on us, and we begin to see the sharp difference between the church and the world around us. In the church there is more holiness, sanctification, joy, and blessing than what we find in the wide world surrounding the church.

Those who make up the church should be the "pure in heart." Purity of heart is a singleness of vision. When a foreign substance like dirt is mixed into clear water, it becomes impure. Another example of impurity is the impure eye of an unfaithful man who is quickly taken with other women besides his own wife. Similarly, the impure heart is a double-minded heart (James 1:8). It is unstable and lacking in faith because it fails to keep God in its sights. And this is precisely where the psalmist is failing—this will become clear in the succeeding verses.

Verses 2–16. It was the point at which Asaph's attention was drawn to the prosperity and power of the wicked that he almost slipped. How often do we see the wicked prosper? At times in human history, as human empires grow over hundreds of years, we see a steady growth in the power of the wicked. We watch them as they abandon God's law, endorse abortion and infanticide, and continually teach less and less fear of God in their schools. In the face of the massive expansion of evil, it is easy to be overwhelmed with discouragement. Sometimes the wicked do enjoy more resources, more power, and better health than those who faithfully serve God. This only further fortifies the wicked in their prideful state. As the years go by, they are less and less concerned with the possibility of God's existence or His displeasure with them. As Asaph considers these things, he bitterly confesses, "Surely in vain have I kept my heart pure; in vain have I washed my hands in innocence."

For a moment, Asaph gives way to depression. His spirit falters when he walks over the slippery ice field of disbelief because his eyes are removed from the goodness and justice of the living God. This is what happens to the double-minded man of whom James speaks. When the eyes of the saint begin to wander from God and then focus upon the works of men, his faith in God will languish. The problem with Asaph is that he is distracted. Without the backdrop of the law of God, any believer may be distracted by the delights, activities, and temptations of this world. Or, without the backdrop of the sovereign will of God, he may be distracted by the oppressive acts of the wicked as they sin with apparent impunity. This distraction can press our souls to the ground, causing us to think of nothing but the machinations of the wicked. These distractions distort our perspective.

Verses 17–20. The resolution to these tormenting thoughts comes promptly in verse 17. All Asaph has to do is to step into the congregation of God's saints, and instantly his vision is restored and he sees the end of the wicked as clear as day. For Asaph, this clearer vision led him to interpret reality in these two possible ways. He understands that God would not vindicate those who love Him by punishing His enemies— and He doesn't care a thing about justice. Or He is saving the wicked for a dreadful day of judgment in which He will wipe them away in terrifying and sudden destruction—and justice is highly important to Him. It can only be one or the other, and a man of true faith will conclude that the latter case is the true one. Two hundred years can seem like a very long time when there is nothing but vile oppression and evil power working against the people of God. But if you can see it from God's perspective, you will see that the legacy of the wicked will be nothing but a dream soon forgotten. The evil of the wicked is but for a moment, while their destruction is forever.

Verses 21–24. Now as Asaph sits in public worship, he is better able to see himself from the vantage point of God's reality. Now he can see that he was ignorant and blind to the truth. His heart was grieved and embittered until he saw the hand of God holding him up. As the fog cleared ever so slightly, the focus upon God sharpened even more. Hope returned, and now he knows for certain that one day God will receive him into glory. With this perspective in view, he can hardly be bothered any more by the wicked and their evil progress. God is sovereign; God will judge the wicked, and Asaph is going to heaven and eternal glory. Why should he be bothered with what the wicked are doing?

Verses 25–28. The psalm ends with words that nourish the heart of every man, woman, and child of faith. Truly, there is nothing in heaven and earth that could satisfy the believer besides God Himself. All of our hopes, desires, and purposes hang upon God alone. For the Christian, it is an all or nothing proposition. Either men will find in God the fulfillment of their every hope and desire, their very purpose for living, their salvation from the corruption of sin and temptation, and final justice for every cruel injustice wrought on earth, or they will not. True believers will seek for these things in God and God alone.

When we focus upon the tyranny of evil governments, the deceitful scams, the tragedy of families broken up by sin, and the domination of men who do not fear God in media, entertainment, and education, we are quickly overwhelmed. When we face our own flesh and see how easily we are led into temptation, we are weakened at the very prospect of taking up the battle against it. "My flesh and my heart fail." But in our weakness we have just enough strength to say, "God is my strength and my portion forever!" We have just enough strength to acknowledge God as Savior because we know that strength comes from God Himself.

How do we apply this psalm?

1. Distraction is a joyless business for the Christian. When we are constantly surrounding ourselves with news reports or fictional stories about wicked men who continually break God's commandments without receiving consequences but do not have the vision of God's righteousness, justice, and redemption, we will be disheartened in our faith. Therefore, we should be careful how much we immerse ourselves in godless education, media, and entertainment. Whatever we do, we need to engage in regular prayer and the reading of the Word such that we are able to see the backdrop of God and His truth around us and behind everything we experience.

2. Let us be careful not to allow feelings of defeat or bitterness to consume us as we view the success of wicked men in the workplace or in the political realm. Some Christians and their ministries over-emphasize the conspiracies of godless men against God's law and His liberty. They lose the proper perspective because they themselves are not living in the fear of God and do not have an understanding of His sovereignty, power, and love for His people.

How does this psalm teach us to worship God?

1. There is something about public worship and the assembly of the church that clarifies our vision, enabling us to see the world around us from the right perspective. Those who are absent from the public assemblies of worship will constantly slip and slide in the ice fields of wrong perspectives and discouragement.

2. It is appropriate to mention the wicked and their activities during our public worship of God, but it must only be a brief mention. Godly worship is always to be focused upon God in His redemption, His final and perfect judgment, and His

goodness to His church. That is the vision that we must capture every time we worship God in our families and churches.

Questions:

1. Give several examples of Faith Psalms.

2. What is it to be pure in heart?

3. According to James, what sort of man is unstable in all his ways?

4. Why did Asaph's foot almost slip?

5. How did Asaph regain a vision for God?

Family Discussion Questions:

1. What happens to you when you focus a little too much on what the enemy is doing?

2. Are you a different person after Sunday worship? When you stop the work and entertainment that you do on every other day and focus upon God in the assembly of the saints on Sundays, do you find this changes your attitude and perspective?

PSALM 74

Category: Deliverance ~ Occasion: A Decimated Church

Author: Asaph

1 O God, why hast thou cast us off for ever? why doth thine anger smoke against the sheep of thy pasture?
2 Remember thy congregation, which thou hast purchased of old; the rod of thine inheritance, which thou hast redeemed; this mount Zion, wherein thou hast dwelt.
3 Lift up thy feet unto the perpetual desolations; even all that the enemy hath done wickedly in the sanctuary.
4 Thine enemies roar in the midst of thy congregations; they set up their ensigns for signs.
5 A man was famous according as he had lifted up axes upon the thick trees.

6 But now they break down the carved work thereof at once with axes and hammers.

7 They have cast fire into thy sanctuary, they have defiled by casting down the dwelling place of thy name to the ground.

8 They said in their hearts, Let us destroy them together: they have burned up all the synagogues of God in the land.

9 We see not our signs: there is no more any prophet: neither is there among us any that knoweth how long.

10 O God, how long shall the adversary reproach? shall the enemy blaspheme thy name for ever?

11 Why withdrawest thou thy hand, even thy right hand? pluck it out of thy bosom.

12 For God is my King of old, working salvation in the midst of the earth.

13 Thou didst divide the sea by thy strength: thou brakest the heads of the dragons in the waters.

14 Thou brakest the heads of leviathan in pieces, and gavest him to be meat to the people inhabiting the wilderness.

15 Thou didst cleave the fountain and the flood: thou driedst up mighty rivers.

16 The day is thine, the night also is thine: thou hast prepared the light and the sun.

17 Thou hast set all the borders of the earth: thou hast made summer and winter.

18 Remember this, that the enemy hath reproached, O LORD, and that the foolish people have blasphemed thy name.

19 O deliver not the soul of thy turtledove unto the multitude of the wicked: forget not the congregation of thy poor for ever.

20 Have respect unto the covenant: for the dark places of the earth are full of the habitations of cruelty.

21 O let not the oppressed return ashamed: let the poor and needy praise thy name.

22 Arise, O God, plead thine own cause: remember how the foolish man reproacheth thee daily.

23 Forget not the voice of thine enemies: the tumult of those that rise up against thee increaseth continually.

The Point:

As the people of God face great desolation and ruin at the hands of the wicked, they are still impressed with the sovereignty of God, and cry out for his deliverance.

How do we feel in the recitation of this psalm? The desolation of war is devastating. If we were to walk through war-torn streets strewn with dead bodies and lined by blown-apart buildings, our minds would grow numb, and we would barely be able to comprehend what had happened. This is how the psalmist feels as he views the "sanctuary" of the people of God. We understand "sanctuary" to mean the church or assembly of God, and it applies just as much to the church in the New Testament as it did to the church in the Old Testament. With the church in shambles around us, we turn to God Who is the omnipotent Sovereign of heaven and earth. For a brief moment, we wonder if He cares about His beloved people. By the end of this contemplation we are certain that He most certainly will do something about the tragic state of the church.

What does this psalm teach us?

Verses 1–11. How could God do this to us? This question pierces to the very soul of the believer who sees the devastation of the church before him. Of course, the psalmist attributes the destruction to the enemy in verses 3–8, but it would not have happened had it not been for God's ·sovereign purpose. God is in control, and if the church has been utterly decimated by the enemy, it could not have happened had not God purposed it. Therefore, Asaph is convinced that God is displeased with his people, and, as a son who appeals to his father on the basis of his relationship, he cries out, "Why have you rejected us forever, O God?" He cries out on the basis of the investment God has put into His people. After all, God redeemed His people from slavery in Egypt—not to mention redeeming them by means of the death of His own Son. Why should He neglect the investment that cost Him the death of His eternally begotten Son?

But the church sits in ruin, and those who cannot see the corruption and the weakness of the church will never feel the true import of this psalm. This psalm speaks powerfully to the church in every age. Consider the ruin of the church in the Middle East and North Africa as the Muslims overwhelmed the initial breadbasket of the faith in the 7th and 8th centuries. Or think about the almost complete ruin of the Christian church in Germany, France, England, and Scotland today. What about the many challenges the church faces in this country? We see modernism's rejection of supernaturalism and evangelicalism's compromise with man-centered ways of thought and life. There is chaos in the local church, with discontentment among the members, frequent church splits, and pastors who have to resign from office after they are discovered to have been living in adultery or homosexuality for twenty to thirty years. Practically every sincere believer alive today can repeat the words of this psalm as one who has firsthand experience with these circumstances. He prays these words through the tears that pour out of his aching heart, knowing that the old Christian church is dying in the Western world. Almost every mainline denomination has capitulated to the ordination of homosexuals. Among the faithful few left, there is constant schism, mistrust, academic pride, and confusion. The layers of decay, corruption, and weakness are too many to count.

So the Psalmist cries out to God, "Take a look at it! Dear God, pick through the ruins of the razed sanctuary and look at what your enemies have done!" The intent of the following verses is to incite God to love His people and to take vengeance upon the enemy who has destroyed the church. The psalmist interprets what he sees in the body of the church by way of metaphor, and his descriptions are poignant and painful: malicious vandals are viciously attacking the church, smashing the furniture, the walls, and the décor. They are burning the whole structure to the ground. In the same way, evil forces have broken the church of Jesus Christ to pieces. In such a weakened state, the church is utterly incapable of proclaiming the truth of God's Word against the antithesis of the world; it is a church that is split a thousand ways by internal dissension and filled with leaders without character who are taken by homosexuality and other vile sins. The ideas and institutions of men destroy the church by corrupting it and compromising it from the inside. What destroys the church is the orthodox and orthopraxic compromise that begins in the personal lives of those who come from within the church.

In verses 10 and 11, the psalmist appeals to God on the basis of His love for His people and His antipathy towards His enemies. "How long are you going to let the enemy mock you?" Asaph asks. He could hardly be more insistent. He verges on audaciousness in his appeal.

Verses 12–17. This second part of the psalm turns to a contemplation of God's greatness in creation, providence, judgment, and redemption. These are comforting words indeed, as we recall that God is both our King and Savior. The Old Testament saints have a vivid mental image of God parting the Red Sea and destroying the enemy. But salvation is far more than the destruction of Pharaoh and the great and powerful Egyptian empire. Verse 14 says that God destroys the leviathan, the dreadful serpent in the waters. We see that this prophecy was fulfilled when Jesus crushed the head of all evil principalities and powers at the cross.

Verses 15–17 speak of God's providential control over the weather patterns, the rivers and oceans, the sun and moon, and the seasons. Such language is comforting to those of us who find ourselves sitting in the ruins of His precious church. If God were not all-powerful over this world in all of history, then there would be no hope for us in these ruins.

Verses 18–23. Now Asaph appeals to God again on the basis of His justice and mercy. Would not a just God wish to deal with those who are destroying His church? Would not a merciful God care for His tender dove as she is being ripped to shreds by a wild beast? Asaph's words show that he is assuming that God can be provoked to action and that the fervent prayers of a righteous man do avail much. These prayers may be emotional pleadings, but they are based in truth and come as a result of our confidence in God's covenant relation with us, for we know His commitment to mercy and justice. If a father happened to see a horrible ruffian on the street attacking his precious child, don't you think he would be anxious to save her from the man's hands? "Do not hand over your tender dove to the wild beasts," says Asaph to our Father in heaven.

In verse 20, Asaph adds yet another appeal, calling God to act on the basis of His long-standing covenant with His people. A covenant is an agreement and a promise, and it is sealed in blood. If God has promised to Himself and to us that He will have a people for Himself and that He will be a God to us and we will be His people, then we can hold Him to that promise. Of course, the promise itself is a gracious promise. But it is still a promise.

The final verses of the psalm encourage us to boldly draw near to God as poor and needy because God resists the proud but draws near to the humble. Therefore, as we acknowledge our weakness and our need, and as we call God to help us in our disgrace and oppression at the hands of the enemy, we can count on His deliverance.

How does this psalm teach us to obey God?

1. Now we are in the early years of the 21st century, and Muslims are purchasing church properties in Europe to build their mosques. Yet it is not the Muslims who have destroyed the church in Europe. Christian churches were destroyed long before the Muslims came—when the church leaders stopped loving God and His holy law and turned to serve other gods, the chief of which were the gods of self and materials. This is the enemy we ask God to destroy! It is anything and everything that tempts us away from God whether it be our own flesh, false teachers within the church, or forces outside of the church such as ungodly education, media, or government.

2. This psalm also assumes a love for the church of Christ. We cannot read this precious psalm with passion and fervor unless our hearts are first broken by how pitiful and weak the church is in our own times.

How does this psalm teach us to worship God?

Fervent prayers are essential in worship, and this psalm is an excellent example of that. These prayers begin with a deep sense of our need and our helplessness without God's intervention. Fervent praying is also persuasive praying. We persuade God in worship when we form arguments based on our knowledge of the nature of God and His covenant with us.

Questions:

1. Give several examples of Deliverance Psalms.

2. What is the psalmist concerned about in this psalm?

3. What does he want God to do?

4. How does he attempt to persuade God to action?

5. How does he describe God's sovereignty and power in verses 12–17?

6. Who or what is the leviathan?

Family Discussion Questions:

1. Do we love the church of Jesus Christ? Are we deeply concerned with the decline of the church in our country? How might we pray to God concerning this?

2. How fervent are we in our prayers? Do we just say things we have memorized without thinking about what we are saying? Do we really desire the things that we pray for, and are we sensitive to our own great need before we begin to pray?

PSALM 75

Category: Praise ～ Occasion: Pride ～ Author: Asaph

*1 Unto thee, O God, do we give thanks, unto thee do we give thanks:
for that thy name is near thy wondrous works declare.*
2 When I shall receive the congregation I will judge uprightly.
*3 The earth and all the inhabitants thereof are dissolved: I bear up
the pillars of it. Selah.*
*4 I said unto the fools, Deal not foolishly: and to the wicked, Lift not
up the horn:*
5 Lift not up your horn on high: speak not with a stiff neck.
*6 For promotion cometh neither from the east, nor from the west, nor
from the south.*
7 But God is the judge: he putteth down one, and setteth up another.
*8 For in the hand of the LORD there is a cup, and the wine is red;
it is full of mixture; and he poureth out of the same: but the dregs
thereof, all the wicked of the earth shall wring them out, and drink
them.*
9 But I will declare for ever; I will sing praises to the God of Jacob.
*10 All the horns of the wicked also will I cut off; but the horns of the
righteous shall be exalted.*

The Point:

Men who exalt themselves will be brought down, and God will
exalt whomever He will.

How do we feel in the recitation of this psalm?

How do you feel when you hear that God is in absolute and
total control over this world and over every single person
on it? First, do you believe that this is true? Second, are you
comforted to know this? Suppose you are sitting in a classroom
when your atheist professor challenges God to strike him dead
on the spot. Or suppose you are listening to a governor's "State
of the State Speech" in the halls of the civil magistrate, and
the man proudly announces his support for more funding of
abortion or infanticide, receiving a standing ovation from the

entire room. In these sorts of real-life circumstances, you must ask yourself, "Do I really believe the words of this psalm?" If you knew for certain that God always brings these wicked men down in His time, how would that change your perspective of the situation? This is what would happen. The fear of God would take the place of the fear of man, and great confidence in God's sovereignty would overwhelm you. Such psalms as these encourage us to humbly bow before God and declare His total sovereignty. This world is filled with people who praise themselves, but that is not the case with us! We are unashamed to praise the God of heaven for His perfect justice, faithful mercy, and absolute sovereignty.

What does this psalm teach us?

Verses 1–3. Twice the psalmist says in the opening verses, "We give thanks to you, O God!" Asaph praises God for revealing His Name to His people. When the God of heaven chooses to reveal His personal name to His people, He draws near to His people. When we call ourselves "Christians," we identify ourselves with the Name of God. In faith, we appropriate everything that God Himself has associated with His name. He is our omnipotent Deliverer. He will defend the glory and reputation of His Name by forgiving our sins because He has introduced Himself to us as the merciful Savior (Ps. 79:9).

God is in control over all things, especially the salvation of His people and the judgment of the world. Things may appear out of sorts while the wicked are running wild, but God has a handle on the foundations of the earth. His justice is perfect and He will sort things out in His time. If God is truly in absolute control over what happens, He will choose, in justice and mercy, the precise time in which all things come to pass. If some certain thing that He has purposed to happen fails to play out, then God would not be sovereign at all. The psalmist asserts his complete confidence in God's sovereign oversight over all things.

Verses 4–8. Now the psalmist turns to the arrogant and calls for him to stop his boasting. "Lifting up of the horn," in verse 4 is a reference to a practice in battle where the generals would raise a horn to signify their victory and power over the enemy. In this way, the ungodly are warned not to lift up their horn against the God of heaven. For a time they exalt themselves above God and His holy law, refusing to render Him the worship due His Name. Indeed, this heart condition perfectly describes many who are walking the streets in the present day. These men think that their prosperity has come from the works of their own hands. Instead of worshiping the true God, they render their adoration and praise to mere men such as athletes, politicians, and movie stars. But the irony of it all is that God is the Sovereign who brings one man down and sets another man up. When men refuse to acknowledge that sovereignty (as in the case of King Nebuchadnezzar), they subject themselves to God's judgment (Dan. 4:34–35). Pride is refusing to acknowledge the sovereignty of God. Achieving a position of wealth and status must not be equated to pride. No, pride is rather the failure to recognize and worship the God Who is the source of all power and wealth.

Verse 8 describes in frightful terms what happens to the proud who refuse to acknowledge God's sovereignty. Similar language is used in Revelation 14 when referring to the judgment of the wicked in hell: "The same shall drink of the wine of the wrath of God, which is poured out without mixture into the cup of his indignation; and he shall be tormented with fire and brimstone in the presence of the holy angels, and in the presence of the Lamb." In biblical times, the most concentrated part of a cup of wine was found in the dregs at the bottom. Therefore, when Asaph speaks of the wicked drinking of the cup of Yahweh down to the very dregs, he means that the judgment God brings on the proud will be both intense and thorough. They will be forced to drink up God's most severe judgment down to the very last drop.

Verses 9–10. The psalm now ends with a commitment to sing God's praises forever. In contrast to the proud, Asaph takes his place on his knees before God, lifts his hands, and exalts the God worthy of all praise. Then he commits to bringing down the proud wicked by cutting off the horns of their power and influence. All righteous men will commit to bringing down the proud by doing their level best to keep men who refuse to fear God out of positions of influence in the church or civil government. If Christians have the power of the vote, they will insist on electing righteous men who fear God and keep His commandments.

How do we apply this psalm?

This short psalm provides us with two choices or two approaches to life. Either we will give way to pride and fail to give God the praise due His Name, or we will acknowledge God's sovereignty and constantly refer back to it in prayer and praise. Let us all humble ourselves under the mighty hand of God today. Whenever we receive commendations, rewards, and promotions, it would be well for us to immediately render gratitude to God as the source of that blessing.

How does this psalm teach us to worship God?

Occasionally, there will be an intensity in the words of our songs in true godly worship. If God is real, and judgment is real, and redemption is real, these are the most intense realities in the universe. Therefore, we should not shy away from lyrics that speak of the wicked suffering God's severe judgment. When a church refuses to sing of the judgment of God, we can conclude that it is probably blurring the distinction between belief and unbelief, pride and humility, and sin and righteousness.

Questions:

1. What does the phrase "Lifting up the horn" mean?
2. Who is in control of all things? What does it mean to be in control of all things?
3. How does this psalm define a proud man?

4. What will God do to the proud man who refuses to repent and humble himself before the Lord?

5. What does it mean to drink the dregs of the cup of the Lord?

6. Give several examples of Praise Psalms.

Family Discussion Questions:

1. Are we a proud family? From this psalm, can you describe how God feels about pride? How could we humble ourselves before the Lord?

2. How do we cut off the horns of the wicked in our day? Is this our commitment?

PSALM 76

Category: Praise ~ Occasion: Warfare ~ Author: Asaph

1 In Judah is God known: his name is great in Israel.
2 In Salem also is his tabernacle, and his dwelling place in Zion.
3 There brake he the arrows of the bow, the shield, and the sword, and the battle. Selah.
4 Thou art more glorious and excellent than the mountains of prey.
5 The stouthearted are spoiled, they have slept their sleep: and none of the men of might have found their hands.
6 At thy rebuke, O God of Jacob, both the chariot and horse are cast into a dead sleep.
7 Thou, even thou, art to be feared: and who may stand in thy sight when once thou art angry?
8 Thou didst cause judgment to be heard from heaven; the earth feared, and was still,
9 When God arose to judgment, to save all the meek of the earth. Selah.
10 Surely the wrath of man shall praise thee: the remainder of wrath shalt thou restrain.
11 Vow, and pay unto the LORD your God: let all that be round about him bring presents unto him that ought to be feared.
12 He shall cut off the spirit of princes: he is terrible to the kings of the earth.

The Point:

God works his terrifying justice and thereby saves the meek.

How do we feel in the recitation of this psalm?

We feel every sentiment that accompanies a fighting man riding into a battle to wage a just war and gain the victory. There the dragon lies in a pool of blood while the knight carries the fair maiden away to safety. How do you feel as you gaze at this scene of ferocious justice and salvific mercy? The deepest commitments of the human heart cry out for retribution upon evil and deliverance for the helpless loved one. When it becomes plain that these longings in the human soul are met, great relief, exhilaration, and exaltation sweeps over the soul.

What does this psalm teach us?

Verses 1–3. The world has its heroes. Today people put pictures of their heroes—movie stars, singers, and sports figures—on their bedroom walls. This is not unusual at all; it is completely natural for people to make a hero out of somebody. Historically, the greatest heroes have always been military leaders who exhibited great courage and prowess on the battlefield. They are famous for their feats in battle, and, as this psalm would put it, "Their names are great!" In Judah among God's people, the most famous of all would be God Himself. Others may speak of the president of the country, some great military captain in World War II, or a ball player with a batting average of .500, but our conversations will be filled with references to the God of Israel. His tent is in Jerusalem, which means that He has already chosen to live with His special people, the "called out" ones, or the "church of the firstborn" (Heb. 12:22). And when the enemy came against His people in Jerusalem, our Military Champion broke their arrows, shields, and swords to pieces. This psalm praises God for His great feats in battle.

Verses 4–9. The praise contained in these verses is praise given to a military hero. When the psalmist calls God glorious and excellent, he speaks of God's omnipotent power and His great conquests over mountains of opposition. He renders the most powerful dictators on this globe incapable of opposing Him. He defuses their initiative, confuses their purposes, and weakens their commitment to the war. Even those empires whose armies are outfitted with the highest technology available (which at that time were horses and chariots) are no competition for the Lord of lords and King of kings! For at some point these empires always lose the will to continue on in opposition to the living Christ. One thinks of the Roman Empire that simply lost the will to survive as the citizenry lost the will to work and defend themselves against the marauding hordes. Any empire that is more interested in building its own wealth and power base than serving Christ will eventually fade away.

What business do we have fearing these so-called great empires and their presidents and dictators? Should we tremble at the power of the great empires and the wrath of men, or should we rather fear the One Who takes these empires down and sends the wicked, both body and soul, to hell forever?

As you can see from verses 8 and 9, we cannot separate God's judgment from His salvation. God brings His judgment in order that He might save the humble on the earth. If God is going to save His people, then somebody is going to get killed. There are many applications to this single principle, the foremost example of which was our Lord Jesus Christ Himself who took the cup of God's wrath and suffered and died that we might live, but also so that He could conquer principalities and powers. He spoiled these powers, "making a show of them openly" on the cross (Col. 2:15). And, in the wake of all this bloody warfare, God was saving the meek.

Verses 10–12. Verse 10 speaks of God's absolute sovereignty over the kings of the earth who wage war and bring their own wrath and judgment upon thousands. Such men of might are powerful dictators and kings, many of whom have killed millions of people—men like Adolf Hitler or Josef Stalin. But these men are still well within the control of the sovereign God of heaven and earth. Nebuchadnezzar learned this lesson well. God put him out to pasture until he admitted God's sovereignty in these memorable words: "He does whatsoever He wills in the armies of heaven and among the inhabitants of the earth, and none can stay His hand or say, 'What are you doing?'" (Dan. 4:35). In fact, the most violent and wicked acts of men will always glorify God in some way. If men were to attempt to do even more wickedness, God would restrain them from it. Remember that the arch-crime of all history occurred when men put the Son of God to death by wicked hands at the cross of Calvary. But this was also done by the explicit determinate plan and foreknowledge of God (Acts 2:23), and the redemption of Christ is and will be to the praise of the glory of his grace forever and ever (Eph. 1:6)!

The point made here is that God's work of judgment and mercy is a fearful thing. He ought to be feared. When you sit before the judgment seat of almighty God and see the earth grow dark, feel the earth quake, and watch the Son of God become the propitiatory sacrifice, taking the wrath of God for you, shouldn't you fear? As you see the carcasses of principalities and powers strewing the plains around the cross, and you hear those words, "Not Guilty," declared from the throne room of heaven, shouldn't you tremble just a little? Shouldn't you fear the judgment and mercy of God and perhaps bring Him your tithes and gifts? That is the point of this psalm.

How do we apply this psalm?

1. Surely we ought to fear such a God Who, in the midst of His dreadful judgment, saves the humble meek of the earth. This fear of God must be rooted in a deep understanding of God's law and a deep conviction of our own sin. It is also important that we see God's acts of judgment in history, from Sodom and Gomorrah to the armies of Pharaoh—from the principalities and powers that were overcome at the cross to the final destination of the wicked. You must fear the God of the law before you can love the God who killed His Son for you.

2. If we will be saved, something must die. Something must die in order that something might live. The Apostle Paul speaks of the world being crucified unto himself in Galatians 6:14, and every true Christian over time will see the world fade in its power to tempt him and lure him away from Christ. Every time we confess our sin and repent of that sin, we mortify or put to death the flesh.

How does this psalm teach us to worship God?

We do not always speak of God's salvation in terms of warfare and violence, but this is precisely how God speaks of it. Words like "war," "fighting," "killing," and "wrath" are essential if we are to understand God's salvation.

Questions:

1. Why is God famous in Zion?

2. According to this psalm, how does God save the meek?

3. Give several examples of Praise Psalms.

4. What can we say about the wrath of men who do terrible things, such as Adolf Hitler or Nero?

5. What happens to powerful empires that refuse to acknowledge Christ as Lord?

6. What are some of God's acts of judgment in history?

Family Discussion Questions:

1. Who are our heroes? Are there pictures of our heroes on our walls? Do we have biographies of heroes on our bookshelves? What makes these people our heroes?

2. Are we putting to death the flesh in our lives? Is the world becoming less attractive to us all the time?

Psalm 77

Category: Faith ～ Occasion: Overwhelming Trouble ～ Author: Asaph

1 I cried unto God with my voice, even unto God with my voice; and he gave ear unto me.

2 In the day of my trouble I sought the Lord: my sore ran in the night, and ceased not: my soul refused to be comforted.

3 I remembered God, and was troubled: I complained, and my spirit was overwhelmed. Selah.

4 Thou holdest mine eyes waking: I am so troubled that I cannot speak.

5 I have considered the days of old, the years of ancient times.

6 I call to remembrance my song in the night: I commune with mine own heart: and my spirit made diligent search.

7 Will the Lord cast off for ever? and will he be favourable no more?

8 Is his mercy clean gone for ever? doth his promise fail for evermore?

9 Hath God forgotten to be gracious? hath he in anger shut up his tender mercies? Selah.

10 And I said, This is my infirmity: but I will remember the years of the right hand of the most High.

11 I will remember the works of the LORD: surely I will remember thy wonders of old.

12 I will meditate also of all thy work, and talk of thy doings.

13 Thy way, O God, is in the sanctuary: who is so great a God as our God?

14 Thou art the God that doest wonders: thou hast declared thy strength among the people.

15 Thou hast with thine arm redeemed thy people, the sons of Jacob and Joseph. Selah.

16 The waters saw thee, O God, the waters saw thee; they were afraid: the depths also were troubled.

17 The clouds poured out water: the skies sent out a sound: thine arrows also went abroad.

18 The voice of thy thunder was in the heaven: the lightnings lightened the world: the earth trembled and shook.

19 Thy way is in the sea, and thy path in the great waters, and thy footsteps are not known.

20 Thou leddest thy people like a flock by the hand of Moses and Aaron.

The Point:

While in the throes of deep trouble, we may toss on our beds at night, but we will find comfort when we meditate upon the mighty works of God in history.

How do we feel in the recitation of this psalm?

Trouble is an inevitability of life, and for some reason we tend to reflect on our troubles at night when we are trying to sleep. It is at that time that we can sense the desperation of our condition and turn to God for help. But it seems that God is very distant from us, and our prayers receive no answer. Where do we turn when many hours of prayer and meditation do nothing to comfort the soul? Our minds instinctively reflect upon the mighty works of God in the past. Our attention is drawn away from our present state of trouble to the power, holiness, and love of God for His people. After the third verse, we will completely forget our own condition as we lose ourselves in deep meditation upon the character and work of God.

What does this psalm teach us?

Verses 1–3. The greatest men can face the deepest discouragements. Even men like Elijah, Jeremiah, and John the Baptist fought discouragement and struggled with lapses in faith! As they lay in the cave, prison cell, or at the bottom of a deep well in the dark of the night, they spoke their heart-troubles to God. But, even in these prayers and meditations, their souls received no comfort. We see the same scenario in this psalm as the psalmist stretches out his hands to receive God's comfort and blessing but receives nothing. This discouragement is deep. As his thoughts turn back to God, his distress only intensifies. It is usually at this point that the faithless give up on God and rely on cheap worldly comforts like food, drink, or drugs to make it through their troubles. But Asaph steadfastly continues his meditation and prayer.

Verses 4–9. He turns to memories of better days gone by when he could sing a song in the night. Under normal circumstances, singing is effectual for renewing the spirit and bringing us closer to God as we walk through the trials of our lives. But this time is different. Asaph won't be singing any songs tonight.

So he asks whether God will cast him off forever. Will this present darkness ever break? The morose, dark language he uses approaches faithlessness. But he only asks the questions: will God be true to His promises? Is His unfailing love going to fail? If he proceeds to answer the questions wrongly, he may experience a fatal breach of faith. However, the true believer will not "go there." He may ask these questions, but he will never go so far as to say that God will fail the covenant.

The root of the problem is noted in verse 9. God is angry with His people. Verse 7 makes the subtle shift from the individual's relationship with God to the corporate (group) relationship with God. The psalmist now speaks of Israel (or the corporate body of the church). Life in the church, in the "candlesticks" (Rev. 1:13; 2:5), or in the vine is relational. Both the individual and corporate relationships with God are real and personal relationships, often characterized by emotions similar to what we experience with our own family members—sometimes affection, sometimes sadness, or sometimes coldness that can lead to distance and disowning. Occasionally, a man of God realizes what is happening to the people of God. He looks around him and the hard, cold reality of a dying church dawns upon him. Vines shrivel. Candlesticks are removed. Whether it be this or that local church, the evangelical denominations, or the entire Western church, the bride of Christ struggles mightily for mere survival in the present day. It may be that God is abandoning the church in the Western world. If He abandons our churches, will He abandon us? Asaph is traumatized by these considerations.

Verses 10–20. Now the psalmist thinks back on the powerful works of God in history, and he identifies with these events. The man of faith associates himself with the church in history, whether it be the church of the Old Testament saints or that of the New Testament Apostles. Although he may not see God's intervention in the immediate circumstances, there is no question that God has intervened in the past by working great miracles for His people. From the crossing of the Red Sea and the destruction of Pharaoh's armies to Gideon's mighty victory, and from the creation of the world to the resurrection of the Son of God from the dead, there is much to remember. In Asaph's dark depression, his attention is held by the power of God rather than by his own weaknesses. Though God may not be helping him immediately, he can at least rest himself in God's mighty works in the past, trusting that God will work again in the future.

Verse 13 is a corrective to the earlier statements that might have implicated God with wrongdoing. Asaph reminds himself that God's works are impeccably holy. His motives are pure and His actions are right; He brings about that which is good for Himself and for His people. Even His acts of judgment bring about the purification and the establishment of His holy church. In the New Testament Paul declares that Christ is preparing for Himself a "glorious church, not having spot or wrinkle… that it should be holy and without blemish" (Eph. 5:27). Therefore, God's work in the earth is for the benefit of His precious church, made up of the "saints" or the holy ones, and He will sanctify that church in the end. Even the great empires of the earth will serve the living God for the benefit of His church.

The psalm ends with a poetic description of the power of God displayed at the Red Sea, when God separated the mighty waters to deliver His people from the armies of the greatest empire on earth. All of the elements are under His control—the mighty oceans, clouds, thunder and lightning, and earthquakes. They belong to Him and they are at His beck and call. Yet, He used these powerful elements to make a pathway for His people, gently leading them to salvation. What a picture of God's power and mercy is wonderfully brought together in a single motif!

How do we apply this psalm?

Small children usually do not understand what it is to be discouraged or depressed. But as our children mature into adulthood, they will have to wage war on the battlefield of the mind. Doubts and discouragement will come. How will they react to tragedy in their own lives? Will they abandon God as many do in the present day? Or will they be the ones crying out to God in order that He does not abandon His people?

When waves of doubt and discouragement roll in, our children must learn the discipline of godly meditation. Although it may not be a sin to have discouraging thoughts, what you do with those thoughts is critical. Will your heart turn inward or outward? Will it turn towards meditation on God's faithfulness and holiness in His works, or will it harbor bitterness towards Him? The man of faith identifies himself with God and His people, losing himself in meditating on God's powerful salvation.

How does this psalm teach us to worship God?

Worship includes picturing the mighty acts of God in history. The word pictures provided in the psalms should help us to "feel" the power of God's great works in history. The lightning flashes. The thunder crashes. The power of God is palpable in our midst. There it is: the hand of God is holding back six trillion tons of water as His people walk on dry ground to safety. Such descriptions take you into the story and help you experience the miracle one more time.

Questions:
1. What is Asaph's mood at the beginning of the psalm?
2. How would you characterize God's relationship with His people, according to verse 9?
3. Where does Asaph direct his attention for the last half of the psalm?

4. How does Asaph describe the works of God?

5. What great saving act of God is referred to in the final verses of the psalm?

6. Give several examples of Faith Psalms.

Family Discussion Questions:

1. How well do we discipline our minds when we are tempted to discouragement and doubts? Would it be helpful to memorize psalms like this one?

2. Do we instinctively turn to food, chocolate, or sweets to lift our spirits when we are discouraged? How do these things fail to get to the root issue in our discouragements and depressions?

3. Why would the story of Israel's deliverance from Egypt be an encouragement to us, since we were not the ones delivered?

PSALM 78

Category: Didactic ~ Occasion: Family Discipleship ~ Author: Asaph

1 Give ear, O my people, to my law: incline your ears to the words of my mouth.
2 I will open my mouth in a parable: I will utter dark sayings of old:
3 Which we have heard and known, and our fathers have told us.
4 We will not hide them from their children, shewing to the generation to come the praises of the LORD, and his strength, and his wonderful works that he hath done.
5 For he established a testimony in Jacob, and appointed a law in Israel, which he commanded our fathers, that they should make them known to their children:
6 That the generation to come might know them, even the children which should be born; who should arise and declare them to their children:
7 That they might set their hope in God, and not forget the works of God, but keep his commandments:

8 And might not be as their fathers, a stubborn and rebellious generation; a generation that set not their heart aright, and whose spirit was not steadfast with God.

9 The children of Ephraim, being armed, and carrying bows, turned back in the day of battle.

10 They kept not the covenant of God, and refused to walk in his law;

11 And forgat his works, and his wonders that he had shewed them.

12 Marvellous things did he in the sight of their fathers, in the land of Egypt, in the field of Zoan.

13 He divided the sea, and caused them to pass through; and he made the waters to stand as an heap.

14 In the daytime also he led them with a cloud, and all the night with a light of fire.

15 He clave the rocks in the wilderness, and gave them drink as out of the great depths.

16 He brought streams also out of the rock, and caused waters to run down like rivers.

17 And they sinned yet more against him by provoking the most High in the wilderness.

18 And they tempted God in their heart by asking meat for their lust.

19 Yea, they spake against God; they said, Can God furnish a table in the wilderness?

20 Behold, he smote the rock, that the waters gushed out, and the streams overflowed; can he give bread also? can he provide flesh for his people?

21 Therefore the LORD heard this, and was wroth: so a fire was kindled against Jacob, and anger also came up against Israel;

22 Because they believed not in God, and trusted not in his salvation:

23 Though he had commanded the clouds from above, and opened the doors of heaven,

24 And had rained down manna upon them to eat, and had given them of the corn of heaven.

25 Man did eat angels' food: he sent them meat to the full.

26 He caused an east wind to blow in the heaven: and by his power he brought in the south wind.

27 He rained flesh also upon them as dust, and feathered fowls like as the sand of the sea:

28 And he let it fall in the midst of their camp, round about their habitations.

29 So they did eat, and were well filled: for he gave them their own desire;

30 They were not estranged from their lust. But while their meat was yet in their mouths,

31 The wrath of God came upon them, and slew the fattest of them, and smote down the chosen men of Israel.

32 For all this they sinned still, and believed not for his wondrous works.

33 Therefore their days did he consume in vanity, and their years in trouble.

34 When he slew them, then they sought him: and they returned and enquired early after God.

35 And they remembered that God was their rock, and the high God their redeemer.

36 Nevertheless they did flatter him with their mouth, and they lied unto him with their tongues.

37 For their heart was not right with him, neither were they stedfast in his covenant.

38 But he, being full of compassion, forgave their iniquity, and destroyed them not: yea, many a time turned he his anger away, and did not stir up all his wrath.

39 For he remembered that they were but flesh; a wind that passeth away, and cometh not again.

40 How oft did they provoke him in the wilderness, and grieve him in the desert!

41 Yea, they turned back and tempted God, and limited the Holy One of Israel.

42 They remembered not his hand, nor the day when he delivered them from the enemy.

43 How he had wrought his signs in Egypt, and his wonders in the field of Zoan.

44 And had turned their rivers into blood; and their floods, that they could not drink.

45 He sent divers sorts of flies among them, which devoured them; and frogs, which destroyed them.

46 He gave also their increase unto the caterpiller, and their labour unto the locust.

47 He destroyed their vines with hail, and their sycomore trees with frost.

48 He gave up their cattle also to the hail, and their flocks to hot thunderbolts.

49 He cast upon them the fierceness of his anger, wrath, and indignation, and trouble, by sending evil angels among them.

50 He made a way to his anger; he spared not their soul from death, but gave their life over to the pestilence;

51 And smote all the firstborn in Egypt; the chief of their strength in the tabernacles of Ham:

52 But made his own people to go forth like sheep, and guided them in the wilderness like a flock.

53 And he led them on safely, so that they feared not: but the sea overwhelmed their enemies.

54 And he brought them to the border of his sanctuary, even to this mountain, which his right hand had purchased.

55 He cast out the heathen also before them, and divided them an inheritance by line, and made the tribes of Israel to dwell in their tents.

56 Yet they tempted and provoked the most high God, and kept not his testimonies:

57 But turned back, and dealt unfaithfully like their fathers: they were turned aside like a deceitful bow.

58 For they provoked him to anger with their high places, and moved him to jealousy with their graven images.

59 When God heard this, he was wroth, and greatly abhorred Israel:

60 So that he forsook the tabernacle of Shiloh, the tent which he placed among men;

61 And delivered his strength into captivity, and his glory into the enemy's hand.

62 He gave his people over also unto the sword; and was wroth with his inheritance.

63 The fire consumed their young men; and their maidens were not given to marriage.

64 Their priests fell by the sword; and their widows made no lamentation.

65 Then the LORD awaked as one out of sleep, and like a mighty man that shouteth by reason of wine.

66 And he smote his enemies in the hinder parts: he put them to a perpetual reproach.

67 Moreover he refused the tabernacle of Joseph, and chose not the tribe of Ephraim:

68 But chose the tribe of Judah, the mount Zion which he loved.

69 And he built his sanctuary like high palaces, like the earth which he hath established for ever.

70 He chose David also his servant, and took him from the sheepfolds:

71 From following the ewes great with young he brought him to feed Jacob his people, and Israel his inheritance.

72 So he fed them according to the integrity of his heart; and guided them by the skilfulness of his hands.

The Point:

History presents an important lesson for our children. We should teach them about the redemptive work of God in spite of the faithlessness of men.

How do we feel in the recitation of this psalm?

Terrible things happen when men forget the providential, miraculous works of God in history. This memory lapse is a result of fathers failing to relate the great stories of God's redemptive works to their children. Such flagrant and irresponsible dereliction of duty is terribly common in our day. Therefore, the testimony of this psalm should fire a conviction in the hearts of all of us regarding the crucial importance of family worship. Future generations rely on this testimony. At points throughout the psalm, we should be incensed at the foul ingratitude and blind rebellion of men, for these men saw the mighty acts of God in the destruction of the mightiest armies on earth, and then they complained about the food fare only a few weeks later. The last thing in the world we want is for our children to turn out to be like these ingrates.

What does this psalm teach us?

Verses 1–2 introduce this didactic psalm. A didactic psalm is much like a sermon you would hear on the Lord's Day, so Asaph directs the people to incline their ears to these words. Listening is the first indication of true faith. If you will not listen to the message the pastor brings to you, or if you cannot listen during family worship, then it is doubtful that the Word of God will ever take root in your heart.

The message preached is a history lesson from days gone by. Our faith is rooted in history. Without the historical record of Abraham, Moses, David, and Christ, we would have no faith at all. We would know nothing of God's creation, God's promises, and God's redemption. Unless the events of the past are carefully recounted over and over again, they will fade away in the minds of our children and grandchildren like memories that disappear into the fog of yesteryear. They will become the "dark sayings of old."

Verses 3–11. The secret to keeping the stories alive in the hearts of future generations is found in these verses. We must teach them to our children and to our grandchildren. If grandparents and parents together commit to teaching God's Word and His works to their children, this will provide a double link in the chain, assuring covenantal continuity from generation to generation. Should either parents or grandparents fail in this regard, we will see increasing numbers of children abandon the faith of their forefathers. Sadly, this is what we have seen over the last two hundred years in many nations around the world. America is no exception to this general trend towards apostasy. After very promising beginnings and rich Christian roots, the nation now is almost entirely anti-Christian in its institutional commitments. It is hard for some to believe today that Bibles and hymnals were Thomas Jefferson's recommended curriculum in the schools of Washington D.C. some two hundred years ago. The New England Primer was the basic curriculum used for the first several generations. The little book began with "A. In Adam's fall, we sinned all." For centuries, the commandments of God were taught in American schools, and God blessed the nation in every imaginable way. Now Bibles and hymnals are no longer used in schools in Washington, D.C. Instead, public schools would rather teach ten-year-old children about homosexuality. What happened between 1800 and 2000? There is only one possible answer to that question: somebody walked away from the historic battle against falsehood and evil. One or several generations were unfaithful to God and turned back in the day of battle. They were armed and ready for battle, thanks to their own great and godly heritage, but they did not keep covenant or walk in His law. We must learn from these historical lessons and be warned not to emulate such heartless and cowardly examples.

If the faith was a relay race, somebody dropped the baton somewhere along the way. Parents and grandparents no longer considered family worship as an important priority. Perhaps they had more important things to do than to save their children from hell. Maybe they didn't believe in hell, or maybe they didn't believe that Jesus came to save them from death and hell. Whatever the case, somebody dropped the ball. But it is never too late to heed the warnings of this psalm. The historical record of God's dealings with men stays alive when fathers are faithful to pass the message on to the next generation. Asaph was such a man who had received the story from his father. Now he commits to pass along four things to his own children: the praises of Yahweh, His power, His awe-inspiring works, and the principles of His holy law.

When God gave the law to Moses, He gave him ten commandments (this story is recorded in Deuteronomy 5). Then He gave Moses an eleventh commandment in Deuteronomy 6:6–9. It was an addendum of sorts but important enough to include on the heels of the ten commandments. God wanted the children of Israel to heed His commandments and pass them on to their children and grandchildren. Their commitment to His commandments would be primarily evident in their willingness to teach the commandments to their children.

Verses 7–9 present several goals for this parent-child discipleship. First, we must desire to see faith in our children, that they would set their hope in God. People will hang their hopes on all sorts of things, such as material wealth, technology, or the heathen gods of the nations. But our hope must rest solidly upon the true and living God. Second, we must want our children not to forget God's works of redemption in history, from the Red Sea to Calvary. This is fundamental to our faith, and this is why we repeat these stories hundreds of times during our children's lives. At the end of our family worship each day, we want our children to keep God's commandments. If we teach our children for thousands and thousands of hours but never see them living out the truths we teach them, all that teaching is in vain! We do not want just hearers of the Word but doers also! Finally, according to verses 8 and 9, we want our children to take a hard right turn away from the direction set by the last few unfaithful generations—especially by the recent apostate generations in nations like England and America. We don't want our children repeating the sinful patterns and directions set by their grandparents and great-grandparents. There have been generations, even in our own times, who "were not steadfast with God." These were the men who flinched in the day of battle.

How could anybody be so faithless and so lifeless in the time of battle? Again verse 11 explains this failure by the fact that the children of Ephraim simply forgot God's works. To forget God's victories in battle, whether at the cross of Christ or at the beachhead of the Red Sea, is to lose interest in the entire war. God took care of the Egyptian empire, but He left it to His people to clean up the side skirmishes with the Philistines and the Amorites in Canaan. He does the same with us. But when we forget about Christ's victory against the great power of sin and death on the cross, we will forfeit the side skirmishes we are called to fight in our own lives.

Verses 12–72. The remainder of the psalm sets forth the general pattern whereby God works with His people in history. Almost always, we will see some variation of this pattern repeating itself, even with our own churches. It is the pattern of deliverance, sin, judgment, repentance, and mercy.

This psalm confines itself to the period of Israel's history, extending from the Exodus to the ascension of David to the throne. In a similar vein, Psalm 106 will continue the story into the period of the kings and the exile.

Verses 12–16. Deliverance. God delivered His people from Egypt with a mighty hand and provided water from a rock. All these are symbols and signs of God's redemptive work. In the New Testament He delivers His people from the power of sin by the cross of Christ, providing them with living water from the Rock, which is Christ.

Verses 17–19. Sin. Even after this mighty deliverance, His people sinned against Him by doubting His goodness and refusing to be grateful.

Verses 20–22. Judgment. God punished His people with fire because they refused to believe in Him despite His faithful demonstration of His saving power (verse 22). The same problem occurs today as it did then. Unless men and women believe in the Lord Jesus Christ who saves them from their sins (Acts 16:31; Matt. 1:21), they will never be saved. There is no substantial difference between the salvation plan for Old Testament saints and the one for New Testament believers. All alike must believe that God is their Savior if they will be saved. If they do not trust in God for their salvation, or if they do not want to be saved from evil and sin, they will never be saved. This is the basic problem with all of the merit-based religions and man-centered systems of belief in the world today.

Verses 23–29. Mercy. Despite their ungrateful spirit, God still provided them with quail and manna in the wilderness.

Verses 30–33. Sin and Judgment. Again, they sinned against God and refused to believe that God would save them, despite all the mighty works He had performed right before their eyes. Those who do not believe God will not obey Him. Faith and works always come together as distinct elements, but they are not separate from each other. So God punished them for their faithlessness by killing a number of the "fattest of them," while they were still chewing the food that He had given them.

Verses 34–39. Repentance. For a while they demonstrated something of a penitent spirit and "remembered the God of their salvation." But the repentance was half-hearted and short-lived. Nevertheless, God was merciful and did not punish them as He could have.

Verses 40–42. More Sin and Rebellion. The psalmist cannot count the number of times these rebellious people provoked God in the wilderness. Whether it was their ungratefulness, their refusal to trust His goodness, their forgetfulness concerning His mighty work of deliverance, or their incessant grumbling, they did everything they could have done to break relationship with God.

Verses 43–55. Mercy. Yet God is still merciful, and again the psalmist reviews the many instances in which God delivered His people from slavery in Egypt and took them all the way to a land flowing with milk and honey.

Verses 56–58. More Sin and Rebellion. Even after inheriting the land, they quickly fell into idolatry during the period of the Judges.

Verses 60–64. Judgment. So God judged them again and turned His people over to their enemies.

Verses 65–72. Mercy. Nevertheless, He did not leave them in this miserable condition. Again, He returned to His people in mercy and raised up a mighty deliverer who established a kingdom foothold for the nation. However brief a period it was, David ushered in a golden age for the people of Israel which lasted through the reign of his son, Solomon. Importantly, it was the tribe of Judah, and not Ephraim, through which God chose to work. A simple shepherd and a wise and capable king,

David served as a prefigurement of Jesus Christ Who would be the ultimate Shepherd and King for His people.

In conclusion, we see that the impossible task of saving a rebellious and wicked people is recounted here in this psalm. Saving Israel from Egypt is one thing, but saving them from their sins is far more challenging! But God is not about to give up on this breathtaking, seemingly impossible task. He will find a way to save His people from their sins. Surely, the only hope for salvation will come by the way of the tribe of Judah and by way of a Shepherd Who can only be our Lord Jesus Christ (John 10:11).

How do we apply this psalm?

1. Hopefully, this psalm will underscore for all of us the critical importance of family discipleship. We must impress these stories on the minds of our children if the faith will survive from generation to generation. Of all the things that we do as a family, it is safe to say this is the most important activity. Parents must pass on their faith to their children, and children must listen carefully so that they won't drop the baton in the spiritual relay race that spans the generations. We must take this task seriously.

We must also prepare our children to teach their children the story of God's redemption and the laws of God. But first, our children must internalize these things themselves. The truths of Scripture should work into the very center of their hearts. Also, if our children are to be prepared to pass these stories on to their children, it would be beneficial if they practiced with their younger siblings in the home. Of course, they should at least be able to read the Bible aloud to their younger siblings, but as they approach their later teen years, they should be able to explain the truths and apply them in relevant ways.

2. Our responsibility remains the same as Israel's in the wilderness. We must simply trust in the God of our salvation! As we read and hear the stories of God's redemption in the Old and

New Testaments, we are obligated to believe them! We must both believe the stories and believe the God who is behind them. Without faith in God as Savior, we will never be saved, and we will never fight our skirmishes in this gigantic war of the worlds.

How does this psalm teach us to worship God?

1. When we worship God, we should relate the redemptive works of God in history to those around us. These historical accounts are not make-believe stories, nor are they bare historical facts without meaning and real significance. Some will believe these things for their comfort and for the saving of their souls, and some will not. Those with true faith will always be greatly impressed with these stories as the very acts of God that really accomplished redemption for His people. True believers will recognize God's hand working in these amazing stories and will believe them in simple, childlike faith.

2. We can also learn from the examples of a rebellious people. As we hear these stories of rebellion, we should instantly recognize remnants of that spirit within all of us, which should lead us to repentance.

Questions:

1. Give several examples of Didactic Psalms.

2. What are the things we should pass along to our children as we disciple them?

3. Why did the children of Ephraim turn back in the day of battle?

4. What is the historical pattern outlined in verses 12–72?

5. How did the children of Israel express their rebellion against God?

6. In what ways does God bring judgment upon His people?

7. How does God show His mercy?

8. According to the last verse, whom did God finally use to save His people? Whom does God use to save His people from their sins?

Family Discussion Questions:

1. Will our children be able to disciple their own children in the Word of God, or will they drop the ball? Are they able to communicate God's Word to other children now? When will they be ready to do this?

2. Do we see any of the behavior patterns outlined in this chapter in our own lives? Do we sin against God? Are we ungrateful, or do we complain against him despite his many blessings? Do we turn materials into idols and then ignore the God that gave us these things?

PSALM 79

Category: Deliverance ~ Occasion: Persecuted Saints ~ Author: Asaph

1 O God, the heathen are come into thine inheritance; thy holy temple have they defiled; they have laid Jerusalem on heaps.
2 The dead bodies of thy servants have they given to be meat unto the fowls of the heaven, the flesh of thy saints unto the beasts of the earth.
3 Their blood have they shed like water round about Jerusalem; and there was none to bury them.
4 We are become a reproach to our neighbours, a scorn and derision to them that are round about us.
5 How long, LORD? wilt thou be angry for ever? shall thy jealousy burn like fire?
6 Pour out thy wrath upon the heathen that have not known thee, and upon the kingdoms that have not called upon thy name.
7 For they have devoured Jacob, and laid waste his dwelling place.
8 O remember not against us former iniquities: let thy tender mercies speedily prevent us: for we are brought very low.
9 Help us, O God of our salvation, for the glory of thy name: and deliver us, and purge away our sins, for thy name's sake.
10 Wherefore should the heathen say, Where is their God? let him be known among the heathen in our sight by the revenging of the blood of thy servants which is shed.
11 Let the sighing of the prisoner come before thee; according to the greatness of thy power preserve thou those that are appointed to die;

12 And render unto our neighbours sevenfold into their bosom their reproach, wherewith they have reproached thee, O Lord.
13 So we thy people and sheep of thy pasture will give thee thanks for ever: we will shew forth thy praise to all generations.

The Point:

A desolate and morally compromised people of God cry out for deliverance.

How do we feel in the recitation of this psalm?

As you view a battlefield that is strewn with mangled bodies, your heart is torn by the horror of the devastation. You are sickened as you look upon a scene of destruction and loss. It would be one thing if you could view it in a distant, dispassionate, impersonal way. But this is impossible. As you make out the forms of friends and loved ones on the field, the reality of the loss begins to sink into the very core of your being. What makes the scene portrayed in this psalm particularly galling is that the torn and brutalized body before you is the bride of Christ, the precious saints of the living God. How can the enemies of God get away with this horror? Cries for mercy mix with cries for justice in this psalm.

What does this psalm teach us?

Verses 1–4. The first verse sets the context for the entire psalm. Jerusalem is devastated. Whether Asaph speaks prophetically concerning what will happen during the Babylonian conquest or he speaks of some other occasion in Israel's history, we do not know. What is clear is that the temple is defiled and the destruction is complete. Dead bodies are everywhere, and no one is left alive to bury them. So the vultures do the honors. Grief and indignation cause cries of anguish over the fallen people of God, for they have been consumed by heathen nations that do not serve the living and true God.

Jerusalem is a figure of the church of Christ (Heb. 12:22), so this description may be applied appropriately to the Christian church in Europe and America, especially since the 1800s. The world has corrupted the church. The ideas of apostate men who utterly rejected God (Darwin, Nietzsche, Rousseau, Marx, Sartre, and others), now dictate how most Christians think and live. These Christians have attended the pagan schools and universities, and they have drunk deeply of these apostates' ideas—to the point that now both the evangelical and Roman churches have become powerless to impact culture in any meaningful way. One Christian pollster found that the divorce rate among Christians was even higher than that of atheists and agnostics. In Europe, church attendance has fallen to single digits, and the buildings serve well as mosques for the Muslims. Devastation is everywhere! Granted, this is the devastation brought about by ideas that corrupt the church from the inside, but the heathen have done their work. Now the churches die and the buildings lie empty.

Also, the little that remains of the local church is torn apart by the vicious enemies of unresolved conflicts, bitterness, deceit, and poor shepherding. Those who have lived through the pain of angry church splits know something of this devastation. Never in the previous five centuries has the church ever been as weak as it is today, and the enemies—the world, the flesh, and the devil—have taken the upper hand in the recent skirmishes.

Verses 5–7. The psalmist rightly blames this ruinous condition on the heathen nations. Yet at the same time the psalmist can't help but point out that God is also angry with His people. We know that this destruction does not come about apart from God's sovereign purposes. He is chastising His covenant people, and His jealousy burns hot against them when they persist in serving other gods before Him. Nevertheless, that does not attenuate His wrath and just vengeance against those heathen nations that persecute His people. Israel may be a disobedient people, but they are still God's people, and Jerusalem is still His dwelling-place. Knowing full well that God sovereignly ordains the bloody onslaughts of the enemy according to His own purposes, we can still say, "Woe to that nation by whom those onslaughts come!" (Matt. 26:24; Jer. 50:9–11) Every nation that refuses to bow the knee to Christ will be destroyed. Certainly the Roman Empire collided with this reality after many centuries of persecuting the indomitable church of Jesus Christ. At the same time that God chose to save many individual Romans, He brought the empire to its knees because it refused to serve the living Christ. It may seem odd to some that God judges nations temporally, but this is a common theme throughout the Old and New Testaments. "The wicked shall be turned into hell, and all the nations that forget God" (Ps. 9:17).

Verses 8–9. Here is the second cause for the ruin of Jerusalem: Israel has sinned against God. While those heathen influences that corrupt the people of God will bear their own guilt, the ultimate problem lies in the hearts of this people who have rebelled against God. The psalmist pleads for God's forgiveness on behalf of the nation. Since nations are condemned to hell for their sin, it must be nations that have sinned against God and must repent before Him. But how can God forgive the sins of a whole family, an entire church, or a nation? When He destroys those nations, many individuals within the nation go to hell. And when He removes a candlestick from its place as in Revelation 2, the people within the church represented by that candlestick go to hell. Of course, there are exceptions to the rule, where God's special blessing still remains with His elect, as on Shadrach, Meshach, and Abednego in the land of Babylon.

The sins that have weakened the church in our generation are a failure of the pastors to teach the law of God and a failure to shepherd the sheep. The church is overwhelmed with the idolatry of materialism, an unbiblical egalitarianism, a self-oriented existentialism, intellectual pride, and an education that ignores the fear of God. May God grant that pastors everywhere fall on their faces before their congregations and before God, confessing the sins that have rendered the church powerless! The only thing we can do is cry out to God for His forgiveness and deliverance from the sins that have so utterly corrupted us.

Verses 10–12. Now Asaph turns back to the malicious intent of the enemies that have consumed the people of God. There is no fear of God in the eyes of these enemies. They think they can sin with utter impunity. They assume that God is disconnected from His world, that He is not jealous for His own glory, or that He is disinterested in His own people. The psalmist asks for God's vengeance upon those who have trashed His people—not so much for the sake of His people, but because these enemies have reproached the name of God. Asaph's chief concern is the glory of God. So, as he calls down judgment upon the wicked, the psalmist also begs God for mercy upon the last remaining living souls. There they are! Lying in the killing fields are the wounded bodies of the remnant, fighting for every breath and pleading for God's preserving mercy.

Verse 13. The psalm ends with a glimmer of hope that one day God's people will emerge victorious over their enemies, and they will give thanks for that deliverance through all eternity. Though the church may continue to take some serious hits, we can still look back over six thousand years and see God's preserving grace all along—at the Red Sea, during the Babylonian captivity, and through the Roman persecutions and the relentless humanist incursions of the last nine centuries. The pattern of history plainly shows God's preserving grace saving His church through it all.

How do we apply this psalm?

1. Does your heart ache for the plight of the church in the 21st century? Those who see little value in the church of Christ simply will not be able to feel the pain in the words of this psalm. Let us consider each expression of the church of Christ as precious, and, when she is under attack, we should recite psalms like this one.

2. When the wicked attack the righteous, there will always be opportunities for confession of sin. These are not mere

random attacks. We must assume that God is involved and that He convicts the righteous in those areas where they have fallen short of His expectations. Yet this in no way justifies the cruel treatment the wicked bring upon the righteous by their persecutions. It is appropriate for us to condemn the wicked and call God's swift judgment upon them while at the same time humbly acknowledging the sins we have committed against Him.

How does this psalm teach us to worship God?

Worship includes confession of corporate sins as well as individual sins. It is quite appropriate for fathers to ask forgiveness for the sins of their families, even as pastors should ask forgiveness for the specific sins of their churches. In our worship, we should acknowledge that our sins and our enemies are too big for us and cry out for God's saving grace. But the chief desire of our hearts in these prayers must be the glory of God and the vindication of His righteousness in all the earth. Therefore, this psalm ends in thanksgiving, praise, and worship.

Questions:

1. Give several examples of Deliverance Psalms.

2. What are the two causes that brought about the destruction of God's people?

3. Did God intend for His people to be routed by the enemy? Why?

4. With whom is God angry in this psalm?

5. What happens to nations that will not repent?

6. What is the psalmist most concerned about in this psalm?

Family Discussion Questions:

1. What is our heart attitude towards the plight of the church in Europe and America?

2. Give several ways that we could pray for the salvation of our local church.

Psalm 80

Category: Deliverance ⁓ Occasion: Spiritual Declension

Author: Asaph

1 Give ear, O Shepherd of Israel, thou that leadest Joseph like a flock; thou that dwellest between the cherubims, shine forth.

2 Before Ephraim and Benjamin and Manasseh stir up thy strength, and come and save us.

3 Turn us again, O God, and cause thy face to shine; and we shall be saved.

4 O LORD God of hosts, how long wilt thou be angry against the prayer of thy people?

5 Thou feedest them with the bread of tears; and givest them tears to drink in great measure.

6 Thou makest us a strife unto our neighbours: and our enemies laugh among themselves.

7 Turn us again, O God of hosts, and cause thy face to shine; and we shall be saved.

8 Thou hast brought a vine out of Egypt: thou hast cast out the heathen, and planted it.

9 Thou preparedst room before it, and didst cause it to take deep root, and it filled the land.

10 The hills were covered with the shadow of it, and the boughs thereof were like the goodly cedars.

11 She sent out her boughs unto the sea, and her branches unto the river.

12 Why hast thou then broken down her hedges, so that all they which pass by the way do pluck her?

13 The boar out of the wood doth waste it, and the wild beast of the field doth devour it.

14 Return, we beseech thee, O God of hosts: look down from heaven, and behold, and visit this vine;

15 And the vineyard which thy right hand hath planted, and the branch that thou madest strong for thyself.

16 It is burned with fire, it is cut down: they perish at the rebuke of thy countenance.

17 Let thy hand be upon the man of thy right hand, upon the son of man whom thou madest strong for thyself.
18 So will not we go back from thee: quicken us, and we will call upon thy name.
19 Turn us again, O LORD God of hosts, cause thy face to shine; and we shall be saved.

The Point:

Standing in the middle of a demolished church, the faithful pray that God will turn the hearts of His people back to Himself.

How do we feel in the recitation of this psalm?

Whatever faith once marked the people of God has now pretty much disappeared. We look around us and see the devastation brought about by disobedience and faithlessness. The hearts of men in the church have turned to stone, and God Himself has turned His face from His people. Here is an impossible situation. We are left to the oppression of the enemy. We are now defenseless to both the enemy within and the enemy without. We have a keen sense of our helplessness and our utter dependence upon God. Unless God intervenes and turns our hearts toward repentance, the church is destined for obliteration. We are decimated. We are intensely, desperately grieving over the remnants of the church. Three times throughout this psalm, we issue a desperate cry for God's intervention. Three times we cry out for the gift of repentance and the favor of God's grace. Only God could have turned our hearts enough to issue a cry for help like this one!

What does this psalm teach us?

Verses 1–3. The psalmist directs his plea to the Shepherd of Israel. Besides the reference to God as Shepherd in Psalm 23, this is the only other such reference in the Psalms. This psalm constitutes a desperate cry for help, and it is appropriate that this tender and poignant title for God be used in the address. Also,

Asaph refers to Israel as "Joseph" and "Benjamin," who were the favored sons of Jacob. By his use of such wisely-appropriated references, Asaph appeals to the special relationship God has with His people Israel. He brings to mind a godly heritage and tender memories of a better time in Israel's history.

The prayer is a plea for Yahweh to take action. It is essential that God act for the preservation of His people, if His people will be preserved. Throughout the psalm, the core element of Asaph's prayer is repeated three times:

> "Turn us again, O God, and cause thy face to shine; and we shall be saved!"

If the condition of the church will ever turn around, it will only happen when those who make up the church turn their hearts back to God. Asaph knows that this turning will only come by the sovereign and efficacious work of the Spirit of God in the hearts of these people. So three times he prays for God's merciful intervention.

Verses 4–7. To accentuate the miserable condition of the people of God, the psalmist describes Yahweh as being so angry that He is even irritated by the prayers of His people. What confidence then do they have that God will answer this prayer, if He is so angry with His people? The setting of this psalm has Israel suffering at the hands of their enemies, and the psalmist plainly attributes this suffering to God's sovereign purpose. It is God Who has brought them to bitter tears. But their enemies will now take advantage of their weakened condition as they have fallen out of favor with God. As in Israel's history, the relationship of God's people with their unbelieving neighbors and enemies has always been a tenuous thing. There is always the potential for lawsuits, persecutions, and war. Whether we live in a state of relative peace and comfort or we are plagued with constant strife and loss is ultimately determined by God. "When a man's ways please the LORD, he makes even his enemies to be at peace with him" (Prov. 16:7). So when the people of God face resistance from enemies and a disruption of peaceful relationships with neighbors, we conclude that God's hand must be in it. How do we address these unsettled relationships and stop the mouths of derisive enemies? The best thing the psalmist knows to do is to cry out, "Turn us again, O God, and cause your face to shine!" There is only one important relationship that needs fixing, and that is our relationship with God Himself!

Verses 8–19. The remainder of the psalm takes up the allegory of the vine. In both Old and New Testaments the church is compared to a vine, a plant, or a tree; however, most people today do no picture the church in such an organic, connected way. In other words, most people today think of the church as twelve eggs sitting in a carton. But the Bible configures the twelve eggs as cracked and cooked in the frying pan. There is still a distinction between the individual eggs, but they are all connected in a single mass of whites and yolks. By the Bible's constant references to trees and vines, Scripture employs God's organic creation to beautifully portray both the unity and particularity of the covenant body.

As the story is retold in verses 8–11, God took this vine out of Egypt and planted it in the land of Canaan. After 400 years, King David and King Solomon finally consolidated the kingdom, and the nation enjoyed a wonderful time of prosperity and peace. But the hearts of the Israelites turned away from God, and as a consequence they faced attacks, invasion, subjugation, and exile at the hands of enemies.

Again, the psalmist recognizes God as the chief cause for Israel's success. But it is also God's hand that brought severe retribution for their disobedience. After building up this beautiful nation, God proceeded to tear it apart. Asaph compares the destruction of Israel to what happens when wild boars run rough-shod through a neatly-cultivated garden. If you put a few pigs in a garden, it won't take long before they have plowed up the whole yard. Over the years, Israel turned into something similar, largely due to the constant military incursions from Philistia, Moab, Syria, Assyria, and Babylon.

God has torn up His beautiful, fruitful garden. He has turned on his own son (verse 14). Why would He do this? The psalmist pleads that God would return to His vineyard that He had so carefully cultivated over previous generations. He presses for a change in God's countenance towards His own people. When God smiles on His people, they will prosper. But when He frowns, destruction overwhelms them.

What a predicament for the church of God! In this desperately hopeless condition, the psalmist calls out for a Messiah, a Savior in the form of the Son of Man. Surely, verse 17 is a prophetic reference to Jesus Christ, the Son of God, and He will arise from this very same vine. If God does not preserve the vine, there will be no Savior. With no Savior, there will be no Son of man who rises up to deliver the people of God!

Two truths interlock in verse 18 as the psalmist testifies to the perseverance of a remnant and hinges it upon God's quickening, regenerating work. The church will persevere. That is its commitment. But if we did not believe that God will quicken, we could never commit to a lifetime of fidelity to God. This is always the testimony of the godly. We turn to God in faith, while at the very same time we acknowledge God's sovereignty in regeneration.

How do we apply this psalm?

This psalm speaks worlds to the condition of the church today. What can possibly restore the church in England, Scotland, Holland, or America to its former state? The tidal wave of apostasy sweeps each successive generation into a hundred streams of heterodoxy and increasingly egregious forms of unbelief. Israel had its idolatry; our churches are plagued with homosexuality, divorce, and materialism. Israel broke into two nations after Solomon; the church of Christ has fractured into a thousand denominations. The older denominations countenance every form of sin even within the clergy while the "reforming" sects fight within themselves over every minor thing until there is hardly any unity left at all!

What can possibly salvage the church when God has removed His presence from us? Will the mega-church save the body of Christ in our generation? What if we repackage the message with more palatable terms and organizing features? Or what about introducing new programs for the children? Could we make the services more informal? Shall we remove all hierarchy in organization? Or would it be better to increase hierarchy and formality? Perhaps a worship band performing popular music forms would tune these hearts to love God more. Or would it be better to bring the old pipe organ back and introduce a form that might inspire more reverence in worship? And so it goes as well-meaning leaders in the present day church desperately attempt any and all possible solutions to correct the degradation of the faith in the Western world. They have tried everything. But we know that all of these things are vain efforts: they are just superficial solutions to a heart problem.

Unless God turns the hearts of His people back to Him, the church will fade away. Those who cannot see how these psalms apply to the devastating conditions of the churches have a false impression of the church. They are themselves on the road to apostasy, and their hearts are consumed with pride. Truly, the destruction that has wasted the church is breathtaking. What was once a strong church in this country is now a broken, despised, abandoned shell of a church, so weak that it is hardly able to impact any of our own institutions let alone disciple the nations through a vibrant missionary outreach. May God give us eyes to see our broken-down condition! This is a psalm to be prayed on our knees with tears and a sincere, passionate appeal to the Shepherd of the church.

"Turn us again, O God, and cause thy face to shine; and we shall be saved!"

Let us pray that God will turn the hearts of His church to repentance. May God move us from a man-centered orientation to a God-centered view of truth, ethics, worship, and life!

How does this psalm teach us to worship God?

1. This is a psalm calling for corporate repentance within the church. Whether we are talking about the church on a denominational level or some small local church, the message is the same. Some churches may enjoy a little repenting zeal for a while, but so quickly these churches wander from biblical truth and right practice. Hearts drift away from a warm, close relationship with the living Christ. The great psalms and hymns once sung with zeal and knowledge are now sung as an empty ritual. Great pride is taken in mere assent to doctrinal propositions, but it is empty knowledge without life. It is pseudo-faith without works. This church is "reformed," but it sees no need to reform and repent any more. As long as we live in a sinful world, there will never be a time when the church is not in need of repentance, a fresh and new turning back to God. Although most churches today would never refer to themselves as "Repentance Community Church," every true church must at least consider itself as such. Therefore the leaders, pastors, elders, presbyteries, and denominational general assemblies must issue regular calls for repentance, and they should lead in this repentance. This repentance must reframe the preaching, teaching, and practice of the church.

2. Though this Psalm and a few other psalms do employ repetition of a key phrase, this is rare in biblical worship. There is far more repetition in modern hymnody, choruses, and prayers. In fact, Jesus discourages the use of vain repetition in worship. Repetition should therefore be used on occasion for emphasis, reserved for our most desperate pleas for God's help in times of great distress.

Questions:

1. Give several examples of Deliverance Psalms.

2. What sort of metaphor does this psalm use to help us visualize the church? Give several other examples where Scripture uses this metaphor.

3. Who cultivated the garden of Israel, and who sent the boars into the garden to destroy it?

4. What is the fundamental problem with Israel that brought such destruction upon them?

5. How do we solve this problem?

Family Discussion Questions:

1. Can you catch a vision for the needs of our family and our church? Are you aware of the struggles of the body of our local church or even the church as a whole in this country? How does the weakness of the church affect our individual family?

2. What are the sins that are addressed from the pulpit of our church? What is our "repentance agenda"? Does our family need to repent of certain sins from time to time? What sorts of sins could we confess and repent?

PSALM 81

Category: Praise ~ Occasion: Day of Remembrance (Passover)

Author: Asaph

1 Sing aloud unto God our strength: make a joyful noise unto the God of Jacob.
2 Take a psalm, and bring hither the timbrel, the pleasant harp with the psaltery.
3 Blow up the trumpet in the new moon, in the time appointed, on our solemn feast day.
4 For this was a statute for Israel, and a law of the God of Jacob.
5 This he ordained in Joseph for a testimony, when he went out through the land of Egypt: where I heard a language that I understood not.
6 I removed his shoulder from the burden: his hands were delivered from the pots.
7 Thou calledst in trouble, and I delivered thee; I answered thee in the secret place of thunder: I proved thee at the waters of Meribah. Selah.

8 Hear, O my people, and I will testify unto thee: O Israel, if thou wilt hearken unto me;

9 There shall no strange god be in thee; neither shalt thou worship any strange god.

10 I am the LORD thy God, which brought thee out of the land of Egypt: open thy mouth wide, and I will fill it.

11 But my people would not hearken to my voice; and Israel would none of me.

12 So I gave them up unto their own hearts' lust: and they walked in their own counsels.

13 Oh that my people had hearkened unto me, and Israel had walked in my ways!

14 I should soon have subdued their enemies, and turned my hand against their adversaries.

15 The haters of the LORD should have submitted themselves unto him: but their time should have endured for ever.

16 He should have fed them also with the finest of the wheat: and with honey out of the rock should I have satisfied thee.

The Point:

Although God's faithfulness has great historical precedent and is worthy of His people's praise, they have not always appreciated it as such.

How do we feel in the recitation of this psalm?

We feel a shame and indignation for a people who are so thick-headed that they cannot see the goodness of God in His salvation. How often is this the condition of our own hearts? The children of Israel are not the only ones who give way to idolatry and refuse to give God the worship due Him. We are convicted of our own faithlessness as we watch the gross apostasy of others. Even when God shows His goodness and mercy in manifold ways, how quickly the hearts of His people are drawn away to worship the baubles and idols offered to them by the world! What corrupted vision and foul ingratitude exude from these hearts! This unfaithful spirit is sickening, but we are more captured by the kindness and faithfulness of

God than the wickedness of covenant breakers and apostates in the history of the church (whether in the Old or the New Testament).

What does this psalm teach us?

Verses 1–3. This is an unusual psalm in that it commands praise from a people who are about to be shamed for their unfaithfulness. But the psalm speaks about the faithfulness of God in spite of the disobedience of His people. As the faithful remnant focus on God's goodness, they are pressed to cry out in joyful praise while repudiating the unfaithfulness of the rest of the people who have turned away from Him.

Evidently, the psalmist has written this psalm for a solemn feast day that was first instituted in the day when Israel "went out through the land of Egypt." This is referring to the Passover, which was the major event of the year for God's people in the Old Testament. The Passover commemorated the Exodus, when God saved His people out of the clutches of the mighty Egyptian empire. It was a day of remembrance, a time for joyful praise and celebration.

Verses 4–7. The story of God's redemption is a theme that returns again and again in the psalms. Let us never grow tired of telling these stories! Indeed, God's faithfulness is powerfully demonstrated in the salvation of His people from Egypt. For the next few verses, God Himself steps in to give the account of His redemptive work. He speaks of His people being surrounded by a strange nation, speaking a strange language. The Egyptian people were not in a special covenant relationship with Him. Incensed to see His people enslaved by this evil empire, God flies in to rescue His people from this evil condition. But why is God so concerned about this problem of their slavery when we know that He is most concerned with redeeming His people from sin? It is because God does not separate these things. If He will redeem His people from sin, He will redeem them from bond-slavery as well. The Apostle Paul drives this point home hard in 1 Corinthians 7:21–23 when he tells the Corinthian saints, "Be not the slaves of men, for you are bought with a price." If Jesus Christ spilled His blood for our redemption from sin and human slavery, it would be a shame for Christians to support the slave-based systems that disregard the blood of Christ. Therefore, Christians will always fight slavery of every form, whether it be chattel slavery or slavery to big governments. Even as God redeemed His people from slavery in Egypt, He redeems us by the blood of His Son from the slavery of sin as well as from the slavery of tyrannical slave masters and governments.

Verses 8–10. Here Yahweh lays down the terms of the covenant. He did not deliver His people so that they would return to the bondage of serving the false gods of the nations around them. It is the same with us. He did not save us from our sins that we would continue to live under the bondage of sin! For the children of Israel, the deliverance from Egypt was a picture of God's redemption from sin. If they could not by faith receive God as Savior, they would not by faith receive Him and serve Him as their God.

Verses 11–16. Sadly, this people did not have the faith to embrace the One Who delivered them from the most powerful empire on earth. They quickly rebelled against Him and stubbornly refused to obey His commandments. They ignored His law and followed after their own independent course. Our people are not much different from these people in the Old Testament. They receive the baby in the manger, and they might even receive the Christ on the cross. But they would never receive the Lamb on the throne and submit themselves to His commandments. They don't mind hearing the story of redemption, but they are reticent to obey the commandments of the One Who provided them this redemption. A great many professing believers would gladly receive the salvation story, but they do not want to keep God's commandments in their economics, family life, and civil government. They would much rather follow the economics of John Maynard Keynes, the politics of Karl Marx, and the family principles of Dr. Benjamin Spock and other humanists than the books of Deuteronomy and Proverbs!

The psalm ends with a promise: if these people will receive Yahweh as their God, then He will deliver them from the hand of their enemies, both physical and spiritual. That nation which will serve Yahweh will be blessed with the finest of wheat as well as God's peace and protection! Although many of the Western nations quickly abandoned God's Word in their belief system and ethics in the 1600s and 1700s, America maintained strong allegiance to God's Word for many generations (from 1620 to 1880). This nation and its many churches enjoyed God's manifold material blessings over those many years. We would do well to heed the warnings of this psalm and its promises!

How do we apply this psalm?

1. We live in a sinful world filled with rebellion and apostasy. We are saddened to see friends and loved ones join this apostasy over the years. But this does not prevent us from expressing joy over God's redemptive work. Our feast of remembrance takes place on the Lord's Day when we celebrate His resurrection and His victory over sin and death at the cross with the Lord's Table. It doesn't matter how much unfaithfulness we find around us; our focus is on God's faithfulness to His covenant and His powerful redemption in Christ. Obviously, we cannot rejoice in the record of a rebellious people, but we can always rejoice in the faithfulness of God to His covenant people despite their wayward actions.

2. If God has delivered us from the dragons of sin and death by His Son, then of course we should love the Lord and walk in His ways. This would be a natural response to our receiving of the love of God poured out upon us. As a kind Father, God loves to pour out His blessings upon His children who will walk in His ways.

How does this psalm teach us to worship God?

1. However depressing the spiritual decline and temperament of a nation may be, there will always be a remnant who will worship God with expressions of joy. Worship is joyful. Biblical

worship is reverent but not necessarily quiet, subdued, and serene. Musical instruments of different kinds are employed, and that adds to the exuberance of this expression of praise (verses 2–3).

2. As part of our worship, it is also appropriate to recount God's faithful works in history both from the Scriptures and from our own experiences. For example, God has blessed our nation in many ways ever since the early American colonies covenanted to walk in His laws. But now we have strayed far from the commandments of God, and God has "given us over to our stubborn hearts."

Questions:

1. Which of the Old Testament feasts is mentioned in the psalm? What is the special feast we celebrate in the New Testament church?

2. What are the two major themes of the psalm?

3. From what did God redeem His people in the Exodus? From what does God redeem us (according to Paul in 1 Corinthians 7:21–23)?

4. How can we sing for joy when we know that God's people are in rebellion against Him?

5. Are musical instruments appropriate for worship? Why or why not?

6. Give several examples of Praise Psalms.

Family Discussion Questions:

1. Are we joyful in our worship? What are the things that quench our joy? What are the things that inspire joy in us? How do we express this joy? Do we ever shout for joy?

2. In what ways have we seen God pour out blessings on our family as we have walked in His ways?

PSALM 82

Category: Didactic ～ Occasion: Failure of Civil Rule

Author: Asaph

1 God standeth in the congregation of the mighty; he judgeth among the gods.
2 How long will ye judge unjustly, and accept the persons of the wicked? Selah.
3 Defend the poor and fatherless: do justice to the afflicted and needy.
4 Deliver the poor and needy: rid them out of the hand of the wicked.
5 They know not, neither will they understand; they walk on in darkness: all the foundations of the earth are out of course.
6 I have said, Ye are gods; and all of you are children of the most High.
7 But ye shall die like men, and fall like one of the princes.
8 Arise, O God, judge the earth: for thou shalt inherit all nations.

The Point:

God instructs the judges of the earth to execute justice by His standards, as they too will one day stand before the judgment bar of God Himself.

How do we feel in the recitation of this psalm?

Our hearts are overcome by a holy reverence for the absolute sovereign rule of God over all the kings of the earth. We are somewhat impressed by the power of presidents who have authority over one billion people. Yet, as somebody once noted, even the most powerful men in the world put their pants on one leg at a time. That is, they are all mere men, and one day they will all stand before the judgment seat of God. The same cannot be said of God, Who is the absolute Sovereign. In the words of another Psalm, the kings of the earth had better kiss the Son lest He be angry and they perish from the way (Ps. 2). Whenever we recite this psalm, we send a grave warning to those judges in our countries and states who refuse to acknowledge the law of God as the standard of all justice.

What does this psalm teach us?

Verse 1. The psalmist pictures God presiding in judgment over all the gods of the earth. The use of the term "gods" should not confuse us here. When the Bible refers to "a god," it speaks of an authority. In one sense, there are many authorities or "gods" in the earth. But in another sense there is one Ultimate Authority over all, and He is the One the Scriptures reveal as "Almighty God." Those God-ordained authorities, such as fathers and mothers or judges and presidents, may be referred to as "gods" or "powers" over some region or sphere. Yet all are accountable to the God of heaven because He is over all spheres, and He will certainly judge every judgment they have made.

Verses 2–5. Now comes the exhortation for these judges, many of whom have refused to judge righteously according to the laws of God. They have exonerated the wicked and condemned the righteous in their courts. It is rare to find a judge or a legislator who will even confess to fear God in our day. So it should come as no surprise that most political authorities act in complete disregard of the law of God (which delineates between that which is righteous and that which is wicked). But pretending that God does not exist will not relieve a judge of the problem of God's existence and His judgment over all the "gods." Most certainly, God takes note of every judge who confiscates land from an innocent man, every legislator who condemns an innocent baby to death, and every president who signs a budget providing millions of dollars to abortionists.

In verses 3 and 4, God Himself instructs the judges of the earth to defend the cause of the weak and the fatherless. At the very least, these judges should repudiate the killing of orphans and unwanted children and do what they can to prevent the confiscation of the property of those poor widows who cannot afford onerous taxation imposed upon them. God is teaching these judges that His standard of justice is defending those who cannot defend themselves.

Some will take this to mean that the government must assume control of charity for the poor, making their healthcare decisions for them and redistributing the wealth from the rich to favor the poor. But the Bible clearly disallows any redistribution of the wealth as Karl Marx and other humanists have advocated. God's standard of justice is clear: "You shall not countenance a poor man in his cause" (Exod. 23:3, 6; 30:15). God calls for the same justice for the rich as for the poor. When taxation on property, income, and purchases are so high that they force widows into bankruptcy and reliance on welfare (government-based slavery), this is nothing less than oppression of the poor. When a legal system favors the defendant with a gaggle of expensive attorneys over the poor man who cannot afford a competent defense, the government has fallen into the hands of the wrong people. When a legislative body is largely controlled by high-dollar campaign donations and well-endowed lobbyists, the citizens will be oppressed and the government will be utterly corrupted. According to God's standards, a poor man should not receive a whit less justice in court than a rich man. Biblical law requires equal taxation under the law. Certainly, the wealthy should not benefit from collusion with powerful governments. Big farming should never receive subsidies from redistributed wealth. Neither should the poor receive subsidies by the forced redistribution of the wealth. In the present system, it is usually the middle income taxpayers (who do not have the opportunity to collude with big government and big banking), who bear the brunt of the taxes. The lobbyists who benefit the most from government contracts and programs usually contribute the most to the political campaigns of the legislators or presidents who favor them. Such are the injustices of present-day systems that oppress the poor.

Speaking of wicked unjust judges, the psalmist says in verse 5, "They know nothing… they walk about in darkness." Without the light of God's law, they have no basis whatsoever for the ethics they propound. Their ethical judgments are reduced to arbitrary, random, contradicting notions of kindness. They usually think very highly of themselves and their "liberal" causes, but in the end they enslave the poor, shred the integrity of the family unit, create monopolies, tyrannize the populace, and bring more evil into the world. After a society is ruled for one hundred years by this wickedness, it is reduced to chaos. The wicked gradually forfeit their right to rule the nation as they progressively abandon God's law. The people resort to more anarchy, which is the breaking of God's law by the individual, and tyranny, the breaking of God's law by the body politic. Anarchy results in more tyranny, which produces even more anarchy, until the entire system breaks down. That is why every humanist empire collapses, just as the Greek empire, the Roman empire, the Spanish empire, the French empire, and the English empire collapsed. This is what the psalmist means when he says, "All of the foundations of the earth are out of course." When civil leaders give up on justice, all bets are off for salvaging that civilization.

Verses 6–8. As the psalm ends, God reminds judges that they are mere men and will die like every other man who has ever lived. All men in all positions may be considered sons of the Most High in that they have been created by God Himself and have an obligation to obey Him. When men are caught up in the euphoria of power and money, they have a hard time humbling themselves long enough to consider their own mortality. Any person in a position of power who has a modicum of wisdom would do well to heed this exhortation. In essence, the psalmist says, "Mr. Judge, you sit in judgment today. But one day you too will stand before the judgment seat of the Judge of the whole earth. Acknowledge this Judge today and adjudicate your cases according to His standard of righteousness."

In the last verse, the psalmist calls on God to rise up and judge the earth because all the nations of the earth belong to Him. This is the heart cry of every saint who loves God's righteous law and sees men violating these principles all over the globe. May God's standard of justice and the blessing of liberty prevail everywhere!

How do we apply this psalm?

1. Men often get carried away by their own power and greatness. This is especially true in countries of great wealth and affluence. They forget to fear God, so they ignore His law. But every great empire of man comes down, and every powerful judge will be judged by Almighty God. The most wealthy and the most powerful man in the world will die, and what good will his riches do for him then? What is the use of living life without acknowledging God? Wise men will always take into consideration their fundamental duty, which is to fear God and keep His commandments in every area of life. "For God will bring every work into judgment" (Eccles. 12:13–14). Whether we exercise a little power or a lot of power, whether we are judges, legislators, or just voters, we ought always to follow God's standard of righteousness, contained in His holy law, in every one of our decisions.

2. One practical thing we can do to follow the exhortation contained in verses 3 and 4 is to defend the lives of millions of babies—usually fatherless—who die each year by the hand of the abortionist. We can do this by supporting godly candidates who commit to making this issue a high priority in their service in civil government. Also, we can support ministries that work hard to rescue babies from these clinics.

How does this psalm teach us to worship God?

Worship provides an opportunity to prophetically declare God's absolute authority over every earthly power, including legislators, judges, and other civil authorities. In doing so, we call them to submit themselves to God's righteous law. Occasionally, these prophetic warnings should play a part in psalm-singing, prayers, and sermons when we gather to worship God.

Questions:

1. What is meant by the use of the word "gods" in this psalm?

2. How does one defend the poor in judgment?

3. What happens to every human judge in the end?

4. What is another psalm that instructs the judges of the earth to humble themselves before God?

5. In what sense is every judge a son of God?

6. Give several examples of Didactic Psalms.

Family Discussion Questions:

1. How does pride blind us from recognizing God's authority?

2. How can a judge defend the rights of a poor widow in our day? What can we do to defend the rights of the poor and the oppressed in civil government or in other areas?

PSALM 83

Category: Imprecatory ~ Occasion: Church Under Siege

Author: Asaph

1 Keep not thou silence, O God: hold not thy peace, and be not still, O God.
2 For, lo, thine enemies make a tumult: and they that hate thee have lifted up the head.
3 They have taken crafty counsel against thy people, and consulted against thy hidden ones.
4 They have said, Come, and let us cut them off from being a nation; that the name of Israel may be no more in remembrance.
5 For they have consulted together with one consent: they are confederate against thee:
6 The tabernacles of Edom, and the Ishmaelites; of Moab, and the Hagarenes;
7 Gebal, and Ammon, and Amalek; the Philistines with the inhabitants of Tyre;

8 Assur also is joined with them: they have holpen the children of Lot. Selah.
9 Do unto them as unto the Midianites; as to Sisera, as to Jabin, at the brook of Kison:
10 Which perished at Endor: they became as dung for the earth.
11 Make their nobles like Oreb, and like Zeeb: yea, all their princes as Zebah, and as Zalmunna:
12 Who said, Let us take to ourselves the houses of God in possession.
13 O my God, make them like a wheel; as the stubble before the wind.
14 As the fire burneth a wood, and as the flame setteth the mountains on fire;
15 So persecute them with thy tempest, and make them afraid with thy storm.
16 Fill their faces with shame; that they may seek thy name, O LORD.
17 Let them be confounded and troubled for ever; yea, let them be put to shame, and perish:
18 That men may know that thou, whose name alone is JEHOVAH, art the most high over all the earth.

The Point:

We pray that God will destroy the enemies of His church.

How do we feel in the recitation of this psalm?

We feel as if we are in a city that is under siege. The crushing feeling of impending doom hovers over us. The enemies are fierce and formidable. Weary day after weary night, the siege continues. In such a case, what is there to do but to cry out to God for deliverance? Some are uncomfortable with the prayer, "Oh, God, destroy these enemies that have come out against us!" But what other prayer could be prayed under such circumstances? Considering the potential damage these enemies could bring upon our loved ones, we cry out in desperation to God for His mercy and protection.

Moreover, if the inhabitants of this city are really a special group of people in relationship with God Himself, wouldn't it be a terrible affront to God if enemies attacked the city? Fathers who love their families will fight for them. You would think that God would do the same for us!

What does this psalm teach us?

Verses 1–8. From the outset, the psalmist is most concerned about the enemies of God. They express their antipathy towards God by setting themselves in opposition to His covenant people.

Would the Apostles in the New Testament read this psalm and find application in the early church? In the words of Hebrews 12:22, we have also come to Mount Zion, the heavenly Jerusalem which is the "church of the first born." Also, passages like Hebrews 8:10 refer to those who are included in the better covenant with Christ as the people of God. In reference to the terms of the Abrahamic covenant in 2 Corinthians 6:17, Paul also conveys these same promises to a little church in Corinth. The Apostle quotes God's Word to His people in the Old Testament as he writes, "They shall be my people. I shall be with them and dwell in them." Also, the Apostle Peter speaks of those who have embraced Jesus Christ as the people of God (1 Pet. 2:10). Then finally, the church in the consummated kingdom of God is presented as both the bride of Christ and the covenant people of God in Revelation 21:1–4.

Now do you see how this psalm has a relevant message for our own situation? The enemies of the church of Christ are very real, and they take "crafty counsel" against the precious people of God. At this point, they have "lifted up the head," a figure of speech that suggests that the wicked have gained the upper hand in the conflict. As Paul tells us in Ephesians 6, our enemies are not mere flesh and blood, but principalities and powers; the flesh within, the prince of the power of the air, divisive spirits, deceptive heresies, and persecuting powers all work to tear apart the church of Christ. To make matters even worse, they conspire together against God's people. The world plays on the flesh. Sometimes the devil uses believers to his own ends. Our Lord noted this in the life of Peter, and still today the devil will sift our brothers like wheat in an effort to impair the body of Christ. Make no mistake about it. The church of Jesus Christ continually faces ferocious opposition from the powers of evil.

Verses 9–18. Now the psalmist calls for a complete annihilation of these enemies. He proposes a total demise in the tradition of Sisera, whose death was sealed by a large tent peg pounded through his head, or like Zeeb and Oreb who lost their heads to the men of Gideon. There was no going back for these men who had set themselves against the people of God. Their end was sealed.

Very often in the psalms, the wicked are compared to dust in the wind or a "wheel" or "tumbleweed" that quickly blows away. Despite the evil wrought by men who oppose God's people, the powers of these evil men quickly dissipate. For the brief period that they employ their persecutions, the church really suffers. But looking back at these wicked men some 30–40 years later, we are amazed at the brevity of their lives and the severity of their end. Even the persecutions of Nicolae Ceausescu of Romania lasted a mere 30 years before he was executed on Christmas day of 1989. The true church of Christ is gaining a foothold in Russia today after the quick demise of men like Stalin and Lenin. Inevitably, the church emerges from these persecutions stronger for the wear, while those who tormented the church rot in the grave.

The imprecatory pleas of the psalm are moderated somewhat in verse 16 as the psalmist prays that these men would lose nerve in their persecuting zeal and be reduced to shame. Then he takes the prayer a step further. He prays that in their humiliation they would begin to seek God Himself and be found of Him! However, in the case that they do not repent, Asaph continues to pray for their ultimate destruction.

The final verse proclaims the purpose of their destruction: all of this must come about for the glory of God! In the end, all men must know that God is absolutely sovereign over the entire world, and nobody or nothing will ever counter His purposes. Whether in this life or in the life to come, every knee will bow and confess Jesus Christ as sovereign King!

How do we apply this psalm?

If you do not consider the church of Jesus Christ and the relationships between brothers and sisters in the church to be very important, you will not fully appreciate the passionate pleas contained in this psalm. The psalmist has a vested interest in the church, the assembled people of God. The church does take the brunt of many attacks and will continue to feel these attacks over the years. Are we going to sit on the sidelines and watch the church get torn apart by heresies, gossip, or bitter feelings? Certainly such psalms as these should encourage us to cry out for God's intervention.

How does this psalm teach us to worship God?

Occasionally, worship calls for the severe imprecatory prayers that we find in this psalm. While these words should not come from hearts that are filled with hateful bitterness or vengeance against our persecutors, they should come from a love for God's honor and the precious church of Christ. Remember that it was the same Jesus Who spoke out strongly against the Pharisees and Sadducees but cried out at the end of His horrible passion, "Father, forgive them, for they know not what they do."

Questions:
1. Who are the people of God now? Who were the people of God in the Old Testament?
2. Who were Zeeb and Oreb? Who was Sisera and what happened to him?
3. What sort of opposition does the church of Jesus Christ face today?

4. What does the psalmist want to happen to the persecutors of the people of God?

5. Give several examples of Imprecatory Psalms.

Family Discussion Questions:

1. Do we love the church of Jesus Christ such that we would pray this prayer with the appropriate passion? In what ways is the church under attack in the present day (in our situation)?

2. How can we pray a prayer like this one without hating those who persecute us?

PSALM 84

Category: Testimony ~ Occasion: Ascent to Worship

Author: Unknown

1 How amiable are thy tabernacles, O LORD of hosts!

2 My soul longeth, yea, even fainteth for the courts of the LORD: my heart and my flesh crieth out for the living God.

3 Yea, the sparrow hath found an house, and the swallow a nest for herself, where she may lay her young, even thine altars, O LORD of hosts, my King, and my God.

4 Blessed are they that dwell in thy house: they will be still praising thee. Selah.

5 Blessed is the man whose strength is in thee; in whose heart are the ways of them.

6 Who passing through the valley of Baca make it a well; the rain also filleth the pools.

7 They go from strength to strength, every one of them in Zion appeareth before God.

8 O LORD God of hosts, hear my prayer: give ear, O God of Jacob. Selah.

9 Behold, O God our shield, and look upon the face of thine anointed.

10 For a day in thy courts is better than a thousand. I had rather be a doorkeeper in the house of my God, than to dwell in the tents of wickedness.

11 For the LORD God is a sun and shield: the LORD will give grace and glory: no good thing will he withhold from them that walk uprightly.

12 O LORD of hosts, blessed is the man that trusteth in thee.

The Point:

The soul of the godly man longs to be in the courts of God, ever praising Him.

How do we feel in the recitation of this psalm?

This Psalm is commonly referred to as "the Pearl of Psalms." In his writings on this psalm, the eminent commentator Charles Spurgeon described it as the very sweetest of the psalms of peace.

The human heart desires many things, including food, friendship, pleasure, entertainment, and love. But for the Christian there is no deeper desire than his desire for God. Within the deep recesses of our hearts, there is an anticipation that builds each week for that special time when God meets with His people. There is no place on earth we would rather be than in the courts of God bringing Him our worship. This is a heart that loves God, aches for God, desires God, appreciates God, blesses God, and faints for God. It is one hundred times greater than what you find in the heart of the man who has fallen for the woman he loves and cannot stand to be apart from her for a minute.

What does this psalm teach us?

Verses 1–4. Who is this God that the psalmist desires so much? It is "Yahweh of hosts!" This speaks of God's power, majesty, and retributive justice. It is common for people to desire a god made according to their own specifications, such as a "big teddy bear in the sky," some cheap romantic love, or a god whose chief end is to satisfy all mankind's desires. But we will glorify the God Who really is the sovereign over all, the King who demands our obedience, the mighty God Who commands the most powerful military forces in existence. This God Whom we love to worship is really God and truly worthy of our worship.

"I desire God." Here are the deepest yearnings emanating from the heart of a man who was created to live in relationship with God. To love God is to love His character, His mighty works, and His worship. It is not that this man desires God just for the fulfillment and enjoyment he gets out of God. What he says is that he is drawn to God. He finds God to be awe-inspiring, impressive, and the very essence of all that is good and praiseworthy. God is eternally worthy of our deepest meditation, wonder, and admiration. The psalmist never gets tired of God's presence. In stark contrast with the fallen man who hid from God in the garden, the psalmist rather hastens into the presence of God. He is drawn to the place where God meets with His people. He envies the sparrow that builds her nest for her young in the place of worship because she is always there in the presence of God. He would like to be as the priests who perpetually serve in the tabernacle. Clearly, the place of worship was the Old Testament tabernacle, referred to as the "house of God." In the New Testament, we find Paul instructing young Timothy concerning how to behave himself as an elder in "the house of God, which is the church of the living God, the pillar and ground of the truth" (1 Tim. 3:15). The house of God is where God lives and interacts with His family. The physical location of the tabernacle is now replaced with the gathering of God's people, which happens to be wherever the people of God meet together for worship in the name of Christ. Jesus said, "Where two or three are gathered in my name, there I am in the midst of them" (Matt. 18:20).

Verses 5–8. Evidently, the psalmist has not quite made it to the worship gathering yet. He greatly desires to be there, but he has some distance to cover before he arrives at the tabernacle. There seems to be a picture in his mind's eye of pilgrims, with hearts filled with hopeful expectation, working their way to the place where they will worship God. The way to worship is marked with trial and difficulty. They pass through the valley of tears (Baca). Nonetheless, since the object of their pilgrimage is the worship of God, even this valley is turned into a pleasant place of springs and pools. It is God that blesses us on our journey, because each week we make our way towards His worship in the company of those gathered in the name of Christ. If the object of our lives is not the worship of God, there is nothing that can turn our valley of tears into a joyful journey. If we are living for this world's cheap thrills and pleasures, our courage will flag and our strength will languish with each weary step through that valley.

Verses 9–12. The psalmist goes on to plead for God's special favor with these words, "Look upon the face of Thine anointed." While the psalmist is probably referring to David, we would take that to include David's Son as well—our Lord Jesus Christ. But why should we be desirous of God looking upon His Own Son with favor? What does this have to do with us? Consider that if Jesus is our anointed King, our Priest, and our Head, then God's favor towards His Son is akin to God's favor towards us as long as we are in covenant relationship with Christ. On account of the delight the Father takes in His Son, He also takes delight in the bride covenanted to His Son.

It seems this psalmist cannot find enough words to describe his appreciation for the worship of God. He continues, "Better is one day in your courts than a thousand elsewhere!" He would rather take the low position of a doorkeeper or a janitor in the house of God than live with the wicked. If David is the author of the psalm, the reference to "the tents of the wicked" may refer to his brief exile in the land of the Philistines. Living with unbelievers or sitting at the feet of teachers who refuse to live in the fear of God is distressing to the believer as it removes him far from the presence of God. He is refreshed when he returns to the warm atmosphere of the church, where God is not only recognized but loved and worshiped. With Christ in their midst and the Spirit of God working in their hearts, brothers and sisters enjoy a special time of communion or fellowship at the Lord's Table. For men and women of faith, corporate worship in the presence of the true God at a true church constitutes the best moments in life.

Not everybody is as keen on worship in the tabernacle as this psalmist. The last two verses provide some insight into this man's love for God. In a dangerous world filled with multiple layers of error and threats to life and soul, God provides light and protection, sun and shield. When we are taken by our own deceitful hearts, we can still trust in God's truth to straighten us out. God also showers us with gifts and honor while we live. All good gifts come from above, from the Father of lights. He gives us hope that our work is not in vain. As we walk uprightly, He showers us with His good gifts. When we don't, He chastises us back into the way. Finally, the psalm ends with another reference to the powerful, sovereign Captain over the armies in heaven. The Lord blesses those who trust in Him, but those who doubt His goodness have every reason to fear His judgment. We need not fear judgment because we trust in Him as children would trust a father. He is the terrifying Captain of the hosts of heaven. But He is also a tender Father and a powerful Savior to those humble saints who trust in His goodness and greatly desire to be in His presence.

How do we apply this psalm?

This psalm will come across as strange or meaningless for those who are unsure of the existence of God, or for those who consider God insignificant and unimportant. In a man-centered world where children have been trained for 12–16 years in a godless, materialistic worldview, people cannot understand this yearning for something immaterial and spiritual. Why this strong desire to be in the worship of God? Why this strong desire for God? We have lived too long in the tents of the wicked if we do not desire God very much. May God help us to worship Him every day with our families and every week in the assembly of the saints. If we find worship boring and unfulfilling, then we must be finding God to be boring and unfulfilling, which means we have yet to find God. If such is the case, let us cry out to God to melt our hard hearts and show us the complete delight of knowing Him and walking with Him. As the final verse of the psalm reminds us, it is only those who trust in God who live the blessed life, even as they traverse the valley of tears.

How does this psalm teach us to worship God?

Picture the betrothal or engagement of a man and woman. After a time apart from one another, their reunion is always a time of joy, a fulfillment of great anticipation. They only have eyes for each other. No diversion could distract them from each other in this reunion. In like manner, corporate worship with God's people should pattern this reunion, a meeting in the presence of the living God. If God is Who we say He is, if He is our chief desire, and if He has showered us with blessings, then our worship will not be humdrum. It will be focused, fulfilling, and full of vibrant life and joy.

Questions:

1. How does the psalmist refer to God in the psalm?

2. What are some of the illustrations the psalmist uses to demonstrate his longing to be in the worship of God?

3. Where are the people headed on this pilgrimage?

4. What is the valley of Baca?

5. Why do those who are traveling through this valley gain strength as they go?

6. Whom is the anointed One referred to in verse 9?

7. What does God do for His people, according to the psalm?

Family Discussion Questions:

1. What are you living for? Are you living more for the pleasures of this world than for the worship of God? Would you rather be in a movie theater or listening to your music on an iPod than

worshiping God in the congregation of the saints? Do you long to be in the worship of God? Why or why not?

2. Have you dwelt too long in the tents of the wicked? What would dwelling in these tents look like for somebody living in our day?

PSALM 85

Category: Deliverance ～ Occasion: A Backsliding People

Author: Unknown

1 Lord, thou hast been favourable unto thy land: thou hast brought back the captivity of Jacob.
2 Thou hast forgiven the iniquity of thy people, thou hast covered all their sin. Selah.
3 Thou hast taken away all thy wrath: thou hast turned thyself from the fierceness of thine anger.
4 Turn us, O God of our salvation, and cause thine anger toward us to cease.
5 Wilt thou be angry with us for ever? wilt thou draw out thine anger to all generations?
6 Wilt thou not revive us again: that thy people may rejoice in thee?
7 Shew us thy mercy, O LORD, and grant us thy salvation.
8 I will hear what God the LORD will speak: for he will speak peace unto his people, and to his saints: but let them not turn again to folly.
9 Surely his salvation is nigh them that fear him; that glory may dwell in our land.
10 Mercy and truth are met together; righteousness and peace have kissed each other.
11 Truth shall spring out of the earth; and righteousness shall look down from heaven.
12 Yea, the LORD shall give that which is good; and our land shall yield her increase.
13 Righteousness shall go before him; and shall set us in the way of his steps.

The Point:

God will restore His disobedient people as they cry out to Him for mercy.

How do we feel in the recitation of this psalm?

We are suffering under the displeasure of God, and this is an extraordinarily uncomfortable position for us. Sometimes when a child is disciplined, there is a short period of time in which he is out of fellowship with Dad and Mom and the rest of the family. Being out of fellowship is a miserable condition for the little one. As a child who loves his father cannot endure the displeasure of his father for long, even so we cannot continue under the anger of God towards us. God's eternal justice demands a severe, fearful punishment for our sins. Justice cries mightily for death and eternal hell. But we are relieved to discover that mercy and peace intervene in our behalf. By the end of the psalm, we will express faith in the covenant promises of God. This brings a great relief to our souls, and we are confident that God will give us what is good.

What does this psalm teach us?

Verses 1–3. How many times will God restore His people when they rebel against His law and reject His Word? With the Jews, that rebellion occurred almost continually over a period of 1,500 years—in the wilderness, in the time of the Judges, in the time of the Kings, and in the time of Christ. During His ministry, our Lord Jesus accused the Jews of partaking with their fathers in the murder of the prophets of God. In His words, they were about to fill up the measure of their forefathers (Matt. 23:30–36). What Christ is up against is an age-old pattern of rebellion, punctuated with periods of repentance and mercy. For the first three verses, the psalmist reviews God's record of mercy and forgiveness. And it is on this basis that he steps in to plead for God's mercy again.

Verses 4–7. Like the little boy who has been disciplined and now seeks his father's forgiveness and restoration, the psalmist prays that God would put away His anger towards His people. But two things need to happen to restore this covenant relationship with God. Verse 5 elucidates that God must turn both our hearts back to Him and His heart back to us. The one will not happen without the other. So the psalmist speaks on behalf of the entire congregation when he prays for a revival in the hearts and lives of the people. When relationships are broken down in the family, there will be no happiness in the home; the same thing applies in God's relationship with His church. God must soften our hearts and turn us back to Him, and then we are back in His communion. If God does not show His mercy to us by working in our hearts through His Spirit, then we are doomed. There will be no salvation for the church and no salvation for His people.

Verses 8–10. The very beginning of the restoration of our relationship with God happens when we listen to the words of God and hide them in our hearts. Faith begins when we hear the promises of God and cling to them. What are these words that we must cling to? With the coming of Jesus, the Messiah, God promised peace to men. As the man of faith reads the words, "Being justified by faith, we have peace with God through our Lord Jesus Christ," he takes God at His word and knows that he has peace with God. These words produce immeasurable comfort in him. It is interesting that verse 8 includes another quick warning that we not return to folly. How quickly children raised in Christian homes wander away from the truth of God's Word as they are drawn to the empty promises offered by the gods of this world!

Salvation is near to those who fear God. Even before we hear the Word of God, we must fear the God of the Word because the beginning of all knowledge and wisdom is the fear of God. A good way to understand this is to use an analogy of a Christian running the bases on a baseball diamond each time he gets into the Word. First base is always the fear of God. Without fear of God in the recognition of His power, His law, and justice, nobody will ever make it to second base, which is faith. The base-runner receives God's salvation by faith, and then of course he moves on to love because it is impossible to receive God's love without loving Him in return. Those who love God will naturally keep His commandments, and with that, he will have run all the bases!

Verse 10 provides a beautiful description of the salvation of God. The covenant of salvation that God has drawn up for His people is made up of truth and love. It is both a written compact and a relationship. When either one of these is absent, then we have something less than a saving relationship. A marriage of a man to a woman must consist of both objective vows and a relationship of loving and caring for one another. Suppose someone was to say, "Of course I'm married! I took the vows twenty years ago, and I have a ring, but—I have never kissed my wife. I have never told her that I love her. In fact, I have never spent a single minute cultivating our relationship in love." What could we say about this marriage? It could hardly be considered a true marriage. On the other hand, if a man was living with a woman in an attempt to cultivate a marriage relationship—but without a commitment of vows or a ring—there would still be a problem with the relationship. The same problem can exist in one's relationship with God. Some desire a relationship without the law of God and the truth of His Word. Others may unduly emphasize the law of God and preach His truth without an equal emphasis upon a relationship based in faith, love, and joy. This same imbalance can happen in how someone may view his relationship to the church. While some want a church relationship without a commitment to membership, others demand a commitment to membership but do little to cultivate the love of the brotherhood. Either perspective produces an unbalanced view of the Christian life.

God's salvation is presented in verse 10 as a beautiful picture of justice and peace kissing one another. But how can this be? If the justice of God cries out for the punishment for our sins, how could we ever be reconciled to this justice? Of course, it is God who provides the solution to this great conundrum. It is only through the sacrifice of His own Son that He may be both Just and the Justifier of those who come to Christ by faith (Rom. 3:26).

Verses 11–13. The psalm began on a negative note, but it ends on a strong note of optimism. God's truth springs out of the earth and righteousness prevails. Although He must work with a consummately rebellious people, He will make them righteous. He will set them in the way of His steps. It is a gradual process of sanctification that consummates in final glorification, but the faithful will trust in the faithfulness of God to pull it off. With every seed of faith that sprouts in the hearts of our children, and with every soul that is saved, we see the goodness of God. The Christian merely opens his eyes and witnesses the goodness of God all around him! With every generation, the righteous rule of Christ spreads from shore to shore. With every family that walks in God's laws and every nation that roots itself on the principles of God's Word, we see the fruits of righteousness spring up in the earth. This is God's doing. Let us celebrate the goodness of God as He brings righteousness to this sin-enslaved world!

How do we apply this psalm?

1. Attempts to separate the fear of God from the Gospel message have been devastating to untold numbers in our day. If you are going to be saved, you must first fear God. You will never be able to believe the Word that is taught unless you honor the God Who reveals it to you and honor those who teach it by listening attentively. It takes faith to listen to the Word, to then believe its importance and relevance for you, and to finally believe in it for your own salvation.

2. There are secular schools that teach the Bible as "literature," but they warn their teachers not to teach it dogmatically as if it were true. "Teach it with scientific objectivity and proud skepticism," they say. This is a wrong-headed way of looking at the Bible. If the beginning of knowledge is the fear of Yahweh, certainly no one should ever approach the Word of God without fearing God! Salvation is far from a people who

refuses to fear the Creator, who have not been taught that the beginning of wisdom and knowledge is the fear of God.

3. There are thousands of denominations and splinter groups in the Christian church, and thus there is very little unity in the church today. Ultimately, these divisions result from a failure to understand the truth, or from a failure to use love, joy, peace, longsuffering, and meekness to resolve differences. When men fail miserably at keeping "the unity of the spirit in the bond of peace," there must be either a lack of commitment to the truth or a failure to love. May God help us to love His truth and love one another!

How does this psalm teach us to worship God?

Congregational worship provides a great opportunity to cry out to God for reformation of the church. The church is weaker today in Western countries than it has been in many years because of a lack of love of God, His truth, and His people. Are we that much different from the wayward people of Israel who lived from 1400 B.C. until the time of Christ? We should be able and willing to pray these sorts of prayers in the congregation of the saints, calling out to God for His mercy upon His church as it weakens from generation to generation in Europe and America.

Questions:

1. Describe the pattern of rebellion found in the nation of Israel from the time of Moses until Christ came.

2. What are the first steps towards spiritual renewal outlined in this psalm?

3. What are the two things that constitute a marriage relationship and that constitute our relationship with God?

4. How do Righteousness (Justice) and Peace kiss one another?

5. In what spirit does the psalmist end the psalm? How did he begin the psalm?

6. Give several examples of Deliverance Psalms.

Family Discussion Questions:

1. How careful are we to listen to the words of God?

2. Do we love both God and His truth in His Word? Do we communicate the truth in love?

PSALM 86

Category: Deliverance ～ Occasion: Dangerous Men Threaten

Author: David

1 Bow down thine ear, O LORD, hear me: for I am poor and needy.
2 Preserve my soul; for I am holy: O thou my God, save thy servant that trusteth in thee.
3 Be merciful unto me, O Lord: for I cry unto thee daily.
4 Rejoice the soul of thy servant: for unto thee, O Lord, do I lift up my soul.
5 For thou, Lord, art good, and ready to forgive; and plenteous in mercy unto all them that call upon thee.
6 Give ear, O LORD, unto my prayer; and attend to the voice of my supplications.
7 In the day of my trouble I will call upon thee: for thou wilt answer me.
8 Among the gods there is none like unto thee, O Lord; neither are there any works like unto thy works.
9 All nations whom thou hast made shall come and worship before thee, O Lord; and shall glorify thy name.
10 For thou art great, and doest wondrous things: thou art God alone.
11 Teach me thy way, O LORD; I will walk in thy truth: unite my heart to fear thy name.
12 I will praise thee, O Lord my God, with all my heart: and I will glorify thy name for evermore.
13 For great is thy mercy toward me: and thou hast delivered my soul from the lowest hell.
14 O God, the proud are risen against me, and the assemblies of violent men have sought after my soul; and have not set thee before them.

15 But thou, O Lord, art a God full of compassion, and gracious,
long suffering, and plenteous in mercy and truth.
16 O turn unto me, and have mercy upon me; give thy strength unto
thy servant, and save the son of thine handmaid.
17 Shew me a token for good; that they which hate me may see
it, and be ashamed: because thou, LORD, hast holpen me, and
comforted me.

The Point:

Amid the dangers and threats of this world, the believer prays
to God for His deliverance, comfort, and strength in the life
of faith.

How do we feel in the recitation of this psalm?

Some little boys are very proud of their fathers and love to speak
of them in glowing terms to their friends. When a bully picks
on the boy, he might point that out to his father who typically
would have compassion and intervene on behalf of his son.
In a similar sense, the psalmist boasts about God here. David
hangs everything on his relationship with God. He is "on the
right side" of God, and he wants to stay that way. If you are a
member of the family of God, then you could not have a better
Father. But your relationship with your Father is important.
As you identify with the psalmist, you will experience a strong
sense of security, knowing that the Creator of the Universe is on
your side. This is very important, especially when the powerful
forces of darkness reject God's law and make no bones about
taking His Name in vain and persecuting His people.

The psalmist feels a closeness to God such that he communicates
directly and honestly to Him. He gladly confesses his own
weaknesses and testifies to his reliance on God for protection
and guidance down this dangerous journey we call "the
Christian life."

What does this psalm teach us?

Verses 1–7. This is an individual testimony of faith and a cry for personal salvation. It is a "Me" psalm. The psalmist introduces himself with two descriptive words, both of which describe a believer in relationship with the true and living God. He is holy and needy. "Holy" does not mean sinless perfection; otherwise, why would David need God's mercy and forgiveness (verses 3 and 5)? To be holy is to be set apart for a special relationship with God. In the Old Testament, this relationship was marked out by circumcision. This was an external indication of a relationship (like a wedding ring for a married couple). Circumcision did set David apart in a special way to God, but he still had the problem with his sins. That is why David still must cry out to God for mercy, deliverance, forgiveness, and joy.

It is interesting that David requests the gift of joy in verse 4. Effectively, the joy of God's salvation (Ps. 51:12) is the bottom line metric for the life of true faith. It is the one thing that can be measured in the faces and lives of our brothers and sisters in Christ. At the end of the day, at 11:59 and 59 seconds, if we have not experienced that joy, we have not yet internalized the grace of God in redemption.

This special relationship allows David to cry to God for His protection and deliverance in the day of trouble. Why would God cast away one who trusts in Him for salvation? What sort of God would do this, especially if He promises to save all those who trust in Him? Why would He break His promise? David is certain that Yahweh will hear and save him—the man who has called out to God for help twenty times a day for the last five thousand days.

David also prays this prayer on the basis of God's character. If our God was stingy or disinterested, then we could hardly expect Him to act in salvation. But this is not the case at all for Yahweh, our God. He is kind and forgiving, pouring out His love on those who call on Him in faith (verse 5).

Verses 8–13. Now David takes a moment to speak of the mighty works of God in his own life and among the nations. God has delivered him from the depths of eternal death and hell (verse 13). Even those nations that have created other gods will one day bow the knee to the true and living God, Yahweh. As history plays out and the empires of men come and go, God will see to it that He is glorified in the nations of men. If there were some other competing god in the mix, Yahweh would have to share His glory with another, and His law would not be ultimate. But there is no other god. Therefore, the psalmist commits himself to Yahweh, the God of Israel. In verses 11 and 12, he makes four commitments for his daily walk with God: to receive the truth of God's Word, to walk in that truth, to praise God with all his heart, and to glorify His name forever.

David also asks God for an undivided, steady heart that continually walks in the fear of God, living in the ever-abiding consciousness of God's reality. To know that God is real and to affirm His true sovereignty, power, and righteousness is to fear Him. These things cannot be separated. The problem is that we do not live in this constant awareness of God's true reality all the time. When we do not fear God, of course we will sin. James says that the double-minded man is unstable in all his ways, and this is because his basic worldview perceptions flip-flop constantly between the fear of God and the fear of something else. If we are constantly fluctuating from the fear of God to the fear of circumstances or the fear of men, we will not experience joy in trials and steady courage in the day of adversity.

Verses 14–17. Returning to the underlying theme of the psalm, David prays for deliverance from the hands of enemies who are bent on destroying his life. Life is dangerous, especially when we experience the battle between good and evil to some extent or another. How do you recognize those who are on the side of evil in this battle? David points out that these men have no interest in God. He doesn't see these men standing in the worship of God and lifting up holy hands on Sabbath morning. He doesn't see these men kneeling before God in their living rooms on Monday morning, worshiping God with their families. He doesn't see these men taking an interest in the law of God or quoting chapter and verse in the halls of the legislatures. If these men oppose God, then God must and will oppose them (unless they repent).

In verse 15, David contrasts these violent men of malicious intent with God Himself, Who is abundant in love and mercy to those who cry out to Him in faith. Then David goes on to pray for God's mercy and strength. Courage in the battles we wage will either come from faith in ourselves or faith in God. Even a great warrior and king like David would not dare to rely upon his own strength in the day of battle. David reveals his heart in the psalms, and it is clear that he lives by faith. He battles by faith, and we witness him continually crying out to God for His mercy and strength.

Finally, David prays for a visible sign of the goodness of God in the midst of conflict. He may be thinking of the plagues in Egypt, the hailstones that fell on the Amorites, or the halting of the sun that enabled Joshua to gain the edge in battle. Such demonstrations of God's power frighten the enemies of God's people. For a brief, terrifying moment, they realize they are up against the God who has sovereign control over everything, and they do not have an iota of a chance in this war against God and His people.

How do we apply this psalm?

1. Verse 11 speaks of walking in truth. God's Word must never be construed as mere propositions to which we give tacit assent. It is more than that. We walk in truth. For example, we believe that God is both triune and sovereign, and these should not be dry, sterile doctrines that sit in theology books to be pulled out from time to time for some theological debate with those who disagree. Rather, they should frame the way we live every moment of the day. Because God is sovereign, we should trust in His sovereign hand even when He leads us through the valley of the shadow of death! If we really believe that God

is triune, this should keep us from absolutizing the individual on the one hand or the collective body on the other hand. We must live each moment by faith in God's truth.

2. Secondly, this psalm impresses on us the importance of walking in the fear of God all day long. What strength this would give to us if we consistently lived in the rock-solid fear of the true and living God! When we fear God, we never fear the enemies working to destroy us.

How does this psalm teach us to worship God?

We enter worship with a sharp sense of the reality of war. The battle lines are drawn in worship. Either men fear God or they will have no regard for Him. Either men have an interest in a right relationship with God, or they do not. It is a dangerous battle we fight, and we must regularly issue these cries for deliverance. As we sing these psalms, hear exhortations based upon them, and meditate on the Lord's faithfulness, compassion, and strength, we gradually gain a renewed confidence in God and courage for the battle.

Questions:

1. How does David try to persuade God to help him in this psalm?

2. What are the mighty works of God mentioned in this psalm?

3. What does David commit to do in verses 11 and 12?

4. Give several examples of visible signs of God's goodness, in the history of the people of God, that put the enemy to shame.

5. Give several examples of Deliverance Psalms.

Family Discussion Questions:

1. Where do we get courage for the battle? Do we have that undivided heart that lives in the fear of God?

2. How do we know that we are "on God's side"?

PSALM 87

Category: Didactic ～ Occasion: Internationality of the Church

Author: Unknown

1 His foundation is in the holy mountains.
2 The LORD loveth the gates of Zion more than all the dwellings of Jacob.
3 Glorious things are spoken of thee, O city of God. Selah.
4 I will make mention of Rahab and Babylon to them that know me: behold Philistia, and Tyre, with Ethiopia; this man was born there.
5 And of Zion it shall be said, This and that man was born in her: and the highest himself shall establish her.
6 The LORD shall count, when he writeth up the people, that this man was born there. Selah.
7 As well the singers as the players on instruments shall be there: all my springs are in thee.

The Point:

We are blessed to be born and reborn in the church of Jesus Christ, and many shall enjoy this privilege from every corner of the globe.

How do we feel in the recitation of this psalm?

We feel blessed to be part of a City whose builder and founder is God—a City where God dwells and the one place that is closest to the heart of God. Moreover, our hearts leap to give God the glory for the great expansion of this city into every nation around the world. The unity of the church across national boundaries is far more substantial than the cheap unity provided by the man-centered United Nations, and we delight in this unity! The psalm ends with voices blending and multiple instruments joining in to give joyful praise to God, the Source of all blessings.

What does this psalm teach us?

Verses 1–3. There is a special place in society that God calls home. While the Bible maintains that God is omnipresent (Ps. 139:7ff) and that nobody can ever escape the presence of God, still His special presence in society is found only among His people. In the days of Old Testament Israel, God was found within the walls of Jerusalem, and He made His residence in the temple there. Those who came to worship Him there received a special blessing from Yahweh their God (Ps. 24:3– 5). Indeed, "Yahweh loves the gates of Zion more than all the dwellings of Jacob!"

The first verse gives the history of this special City, when Yahweh Himself laid its foundations. It was His plan to build a congregation for Himself. Speaking to the woman at the well, Jesus said the hour would come when men would no longer go to Jerusalem to worship the Father (John 4:21). Also, Jesus told his apostles that where two or three of them were gathered, there He would be in the midst of them. From these and other texts, we conclude that the special presence of God is shifted to wherever His people gather in the assembly of the church. This makes the city portable, not unlike what we find with the tabernacle in the wilderness. The church is the City of the living God, the great heavenly Jerusalem, the general assembly and church of the first born (Heb. 12:22–24).

According to verse 3, this City has a great reputation! Glorious things are said of this City! Of course, this is not true of the apostate church, the compromised church, the schismatic church, the unloving church, or the church that refuses to preach the truth against the world. But where there are brothers willing to die for each other and for the truth, there is a City that will never pass away. Today, these churches assemble on the first day of the week all over the globe. Millions of people hear the Old and New Testaments preached and respond to the Word in powerful ways. The living God is praised in these public worship services. God is praised with more genuine fervor than all the other gods of the heathen receive from their devotees. What a contrast from A.D. 30, when only a handful recognized the all-sovereign God of Israel Who created heaven and earth! Tribes that once engaged in cannibalism and human sacrifice now accept the single sacrifice of a Savior, gratefully receiving His cup of *koinonia* (communion) in their convocation on the first day of the week.

Verses 4–6. These verses speak prophetically of the great expanse of the City of God throughout the world. Even those from Egypt to the south (Rahab), Babylon to the east, and Ethiopia (Cush) to the far south will acknowledge the God of Israel. The Lord will record their names as those born in Israel, as those who have been grafted into the covenant body of God's people. Those born into a godly family are in a sense already part of the kingdom of God (verses 4–5). Paul speaks of the household of Narcissus which is "in Christ," in Romans 16, and he elsewhere speaks to a local church at Thessalonica which is "in Christ." The kingdom of God is made up of individuals, families, and churches. Contrary to the pure individualist view of human society today, the Bible teaches that families and local churches, as corporate bodies, are part of the kingdom of Christ. Thus, when a child is born into a godly family which happens to be a part of a godly church, there is a sense in which he is already part of the city of God. He is born into the kingdom of God. Jesus said of nursing infants (*brephos*), that "of such is the kingdom of God" (Luke 18:16). Of course, these children must learn to walk in faith and give testimony to that faith by confessing Christ before men (Matt. 10:32). This is an essential part of belonging to the City.

God Himself writes the names of the citizens of the City in a register. Now do you see that this City is built more of living stones than of bricks and mortar? This is how Peter refers to the City of God in 1 Peter 2:4–6. As God writes in His register the names of those who were born in Zion (those born into godly families and reborn by the saving power of the Spirit of God), the mortar between the stones begins to set, and the city walls rise.

Verse 7. Together these living stones combine to sing praises to God, Who laid the stones in place. We should also note here that few other religions actually sing praises. You will not find praises being sung among the Buddhists, the Moslems, or the Hindus. Islam repudiates music in worship. You will find no song book or singing at the mosque. What a contrast with the aesthetic beauty of Christian worship, born out of the Book of Psalms!

The psalmist ends with a powerful, poetic statement, "All my springs are in thee." The fountains that feed the deepest desires of the human soul are found right here in the church of the Firstborn. This statement is not an irresponsible over-statement concerning the importance of the corporate body of believers. An individualistic society such as ours, produced by the revivalism of the 18th and 19th centuries, can have a hard time swallowing declarations such as this. But our church fathers from Augustine to Calvin have wholeheartedly received this confession, insisting that there is ordinarily no salvation outside of the church of Jesus Christ. These forefathers knew that the normal place to find believers who are living and growing in faith is the church! The importance of the church corporate has been down played for several centuries, especially by evangelicalism. Evangelicalism's revivals produced more short-term decisions, false commitments, and shallow faith than real substantial fruit. Unless those who received the Word in a revival service were actually planted in churches, there were precious few seeds yielding fruit unto thirty, sixty, or one hundredfold.

How do we apply this psalm?

This psalm teaches us to treasure the City of God, which is the church of the Firstborn, the church of Jesus Christ. The City is God's project in history. Whereas men spend their lives constructing empires with great power centers only to watch them fall apart, the church of Christ is built on the preaching of God's truth and the love of the brothers and sisters. If God's truth and genuine love are the foundation and the mortar of the building, you know that the building can never come apart. Worldly textbooks ignore the importance of the church in history, and pessimistic theologies assume that Jesus is losing ground, but their focus is wrong and they do not look at the world through eyes of faith. However, we will delight in God's great project in history. Let us be careful not to minimize what God has accomplished over the centuries in Europe, North and South America, Australia, Asia, and Africa. God has accomplished what He prophesied in this psalm!

How does this psalm teach us to worship God?

We should occasionally speak of the church itself in worship. After all, corporate worship is the context in which the church comes together, so a little teaching on the church is always in order. While we are involved in corporate worship, we should also praise God for what He has accomplished in the church throughout the ages, delighting in the fact that we are part of this holy City that serves as a fountain of God's good gifts.

Questions:

1. What is the City of God?

2. How does Peter refer to the City of God? Of what is it constructed?

3. What does it mean to be born into the City of God?

4. Why was it such an amazing prophecy to the Old Testament Jews that there would be some from Egypt, Cush, and Babylon born into Zion?

5. How does this psalm impress on us the importance of the church?

Family Discussion Questions:

1. What kind of esteem do we have for the church of the firstborn? Do we consider it a privilege to have been born and reborn into the church of Jesus Christ?

2. Do we derive spiritual health and strength from participating in our local church? What would happen if we were to separate ourselves from the church? What would our spiritual condition look like after ten years?

PSALM 88

Category: Deliverance ~ Occasion: Death of Loved One

Author: Heman the Ezrahite

1 O LORD God of my salvation, I have cried day and night before thee:
2 Let my prayer come before thee: incline thine ear unto my cry;
3 For my soul is full of troubles: and my life draweth nigh unto the grave.
4 I am counted with them that go down into the pit: I am as a man that hath no strength:
5 Free among the dead, like the slain that lie in the grave, whom thou rememberest no more: and they are cut off from thy hand.
6 Thou hast laid me in the lowest pit, in darkness, in the deeps.
7 Thy wrath lieth hard upon me, and thou hast afflicted me with all thy waves. Selah.
8 Thou hast put away mine acquaintance far from me; thou hast made me an abomination unto them: I am shut up, and I cannot come forth.
9 Mine eye mourneth by reason of affliction: LORD, I have called daily upon thee, I have stretched out my hands unto thee.
10 Wilt thou shew wonders to the dead? shall the dead arise and praise thee? Selah.
11 Shall thy lovingkindness be declared in the grave? or thy faithfulness in destruction?
12 Shall thy wonders be known in the dark? and thy righteousness in the land of forgetfulness?
13 But unto thee have I cried, O LORD; and in the morning shall my prayer prevent thee.
14 LORD, why castest thou off my soul? why hidest thou thy face from me?

15 I am afflicted and ready to die from my youth up: while I suffer thy terrors I am distracted.
16 Thy fierce wrath goeth over me; thy terrors have cut me off.
17 They came round about me daily like water; they compassed me about together.
18 Lover and friend hast thou put far from me, and mine acquaintance into darkness.

The Point:

The believer cries out day and night to God, even when he is emptied of all strength, tangible hope, comfort, and support from loved ones.

How do you feel in the recitation of this psalm?

There are times when your trials become so heavy that you are left without strength to carry on. Perhaps you have been abandoned by your friends, or you have been adjusting to the death of a loved one. Each day is one long, weary, uphill struggle. You are completely overwhelmed. The bitter gall of the trial lingers long and hard on the tongue. You can feel the sand grinding between your teeth as you drag yourself across the hard, dry desert floor. At this point, death appears to offer the only possible relief to your predicament. Even prayer does little or nothing to lessen the blow of the trial, but you pray anyway. This psalm presents the worst possible condition for the believer, who is in almost constant throes of depression. This psalm is unusual in that, by the end of it, there is no perceptible change in the mood. If the psalm is of any comfort at all, it is merely from the fact that you are still in communication—although in limited communion—with the God of all comfort.

What does this psalm teach us?

Verses 1–2. The only indication that the psalmist has not given up all hope is found in his willingness to continue crying out to God. He may be on the very threshold of death, but even in this state he will continue mumbling his prayers to God as best as he can. In fact, nearly all he does is cry out for God's salvation. Day and night, he continues this prayer. All comfort, strength, and encouragement have vanished. But he still continues his prayers to the only One Who can possibly save him. This psalm is not the absence of faith; it is the ultimate display of faith! When the props are removed and all other comforts are taken away, the man of faith will turn to God, in Whom alone there is still the possibility of salvation. Even though that salvation may seem remote, true faith will not let go of the distant possibility that God may still intervene and save.

Verses 3–8. In these verses the discouraged psalmist describes his condition in weary word after weary word. Seven times he refers to death, the grave, the pit, and the darkness to which he draws near. He professes to have no strength. When discouragement has gotten the upper hand, one typically loses the motivation and strength to continue on with life. Such is the case with the poor soul here. Through it all he can sense the strong displeasure of God with him. He suggests that God is as far from him as He is from the poor soul who is in the lowest hell. Such confessions remind us of the pitiable cry of the Son of David and the Son of God at the cross, "My God, my God, why hast thou forsaken me?" Of all the horrible suffering that visits the children of God, none can possibly supersede that which Christ suffered on the cross. No separation from God will ever be so sharp, so painful, or so real as that which the Son of David suffered there. Therefore, any believer cast down to the lowest point of his life can still look down even lower and see the Author and Finisher of his faith in the midst of His passion, Who was "at all points tempted as we are" (Heb. 4:15).

In true form with almost every other psalm that registers such severe troubles, the psalmist here assigns the cause for his condition to God. He is careful not to impugn Him with evil or injustice but only to acknowledge His absolute sovereignty.

It is God who has laid him in the lowest pit. It is God who has distanced him from his friends. It is God who has seen fit to take his close friend. It is possible that this refers to the death of an intimate relation. If this be the case, then he must humbly submit to this bitter providence as well. It is God's wrath that stands hard against him. The Psalmist recognizes that all the problems that a man experiences in his life must not be reduced to mere happenstance. Problems do not arise from an environment gone awry, and neither are they some evil to be subjectively recognized by man alone and solved by man alone. Rather, all of man's problems (either corporately or individually) are linked in some way or another to a broken relationship with God Himself. This psalm therefore forces a man to face His Creator and his relationship with Him.

Verses 9–14. Now this section constitutes a plea for deliverance, a cry of faith, and a series of well-prepared arguments designed to secure the mercy of God. The psalmist, Heman, speaks of his incessant weeping and his constant petitions to God, day and night. It has not been for lack of importunity that this man fails to penetrate the heavens of brass. He presses the argument. If God has created him for His worship and praise, he argues, what does God profit by his death in the grave? What dead person has ever raised his hands in worship and lifted up his voice in a song of praise? Such arguments are persuasive indeed.

We must still insist that God is both just and wise in withholding His mercy from His people. Yet it is appropriate for the psalmist to continue his plea for mercy. It is appropriate to come on the basis of the mercy of God and the redemption of Christ, pleading the merits of His work. There is nothing essentially wrong with asking God why He withholds His mercy in spite of all the pleas of His saints. He may not answer the question. He doesn't have to. Nevertheless, asking this sort of question is important for a son who appeals to his father's love for him. These prayers are important because we are sons of the living God, and we know that when the deliverance finally comes, it is marvelous. It is eternally glorious.

Verses 15–18. The psalm ends with a return to the description of the terrible afflictions suffered by this saint. Evidently, the condition of the psalmist has not changed at this point. He is still overwhelmed. He is still abandoned by friends. He is still alone, afflicted, and wishing to die. He continues to suffer under the trying hand of an offended providence. But this in no way minimizes the importance of this prayer. The important thing is that he is still praying.

How do we apply this psalm?

1. There is never a time when a Christian should stop praying. Though our situation may have reached the depths described in this grim psalm, we must never stop praying. To stop praying is the final abandonment of all hope. Even as we walk through the final hours of our death, such prayers are of great value to us. The psalmist is right about this matter of death. Without the resurrection, we could never praise and worship God again as His creature as we have done many times in our worship, and that would be unacceptable for God who insists on that worship!

2. While it is true that the dead cannot praise God, we are still alive! As long as we are alive, we can declare the faithfulness and loving-kindness of God. On the other hand, if we were to spend a lifetime neglecting the worship of God, why should God raise us from the grave and hell to worship Him at the end? Let us worship him while we are alive. While we have breath, let us praise the Lord! (Psalm 146:2; 150:6).

How does this psalm teach us to worship God?

1. Keeping in mind that this is an "individual" psalm intended primarily for personal worship, it would be appropriate to use it to that end. Psalms like this teach us how to suffer, but more importantly they teach us how to worship God in times of suffering. This may be the psalm to memorize when you are going through the most severe trial of your life. Pray this psalm to God in the midst of deep suffering.

2. While this psalm is more fitting for private worship, yet the church may choose to recite or sing it during times of great loss and trial within the body of the church. It is comforting to know that we are not the only ones who suffer intensely since the fall of man in the garden. Sharing in the sentiments and the faith of the psalmist can build our faith.

Questions:

1. Who brought the suffering upon the psalmist?

2. In what ways could this psalm reflect the testimony of Jesus on the cross?

3. How do we know that the psalmist has not completely abandoned hope?

4. What sort of pronouns does the psalmist use in the psalm? Is it a corporate or an individual psalm?

5. Give several examples of Deliverance Psalms.

Family Discussion Questions:

1. Have you ever lost a friend in death or separation? How did you feel when this happened?

2. Have you ever felt as if God were very distant from you? What was the lowest point in your life? Did you continue to pray during those times?

PSALM 89

Category: Faith ～ Occasion: Unfaithfulness of God's People

Author: Ethan the Ezrahite

1 I will sing of the mercies of the LORD for ever: with my mouth will I make known thy faithfulness to all generations.
2 For I have said, Mercy shall be built up for ever: thy faithfulness shalt thou establish in the very heavens.

3 I have made a covenant with my chosen, I have sworn unto David my servant,
4 Thy seed will I establish for ever, and build up thy throne to all generations. Selah.
5 And the heavens shall praise thy wonders, O LORD: thy faithfulness also in the congregation of the saints.
6 For who in the heaven can be compared unto the LORD? who among the sons of the mighty can be likened unto the LORD?
7 God is greatly to be feared in the assembly of the saints, and to be had in reverence of all them that are about him.
8 O LORD God of hosts, who is a strong LORD like unto thee? or to thy faithfulness round about thee?
9 Thou rulest the raging of the sea: when the waves thereof arise, thou stillest them.
10 Thou hast broken Rahab in pieces, as one that is slain; thou hast scattered thine enemies with thy strong arm.
11 The heavens are thine, the earth also is thine: as for the world and the fulness thereof, thou hast founded them.
12 The north and the south thou hast created them: Tabor and Hermon shall rejoice in thy name.
13 Thou hast a mighty arm: strong is thy hand, and high is thy right hand.
14 Justice and judgment are the habitation of thy throne: mercy and truth shall go before thy face.
15 Blessed is the people that know the joyful sound: they shall walk, O LORD, in the light of thy countenance.
16 In thy name shall they rejoice all the day: and in thy righteousness shall they be exalted.
17 For thou art the glory of their strength: and in thy favour our horn shall be exalted.
18 For the LORD is our defence; and the Holy One of Israel is our king.
19 Then thou spakest in vision to thy holy one, and saidst, I have laid help upon one that is mighty; I have exalted one chosen out of the people.
20 I have found David my servant; with my holy oil have I anointed him:

21 *With whom my hand shall be established: mine arm also shall strengthen him.*

22 *The enemy shall not exact upon him; nor the son of wickedness afflict him.*

23 *And I will beat down his foes before his face, and plague them that hate him.*

24 *But my faithfulness and my mercy shall be with him: and in my name shall his horn be exalted.*

25 *I will set his hand also in the sea, and his right hand in the rivers.*

26 *He shall cry unto me, Thou art my father, my God, and the rock of my salvation.*

27 *Also I will make him my firstborn, higher than the kings of the earth.*

28 *My mercy will I keep for him for evermore, and my covenant shall stand fast with him.*

29 *His seed also will I make to endure for ever, and his throne as the days of heaven.*

30 *If his children forsake my law, and walk not in my judgments;*

31 *If they break my statutes, and keep not my commandments;*

32 *Then will I visit their transgression with the rod, and their iniquity with stripes.*

33 *Nevertheless my lovingkindness will I not utterly take from him, nor suffer my faithfulness to fail.*

34 *My covenant will I not break, nor alter the thing that is gone out of my lips.*

35 *Once have I sworn by my holiness that I will not lie unto David.*

36 *His seed shall endure for ever, and his throne as the sun before me.*

37 *It shall be established for ever as the moon, and as a faithful witness in heaven. Selah.*

38 *But thou hast cast off and abhorred, thou hast been wroth with thine anointed.*

39 *Thou hast made void the covenant of thy servant: thou hast profaned his crown by casting it to the ground.*

40 *Thou hast broken down all his hedges; thou hast brought his strong holds to ruin.*

41 *All that pass by the way spoil him: he is a reproach to his neighbours.*

42 Thou hast set up the right hand of his adversaries; thou hast made all his enemies to rejoice.
43 Thou hast also turned the edge of his sword, and hast not made him to stand in the battle.
44 Thou hast made his glory to cease, and cast his throne down to the ground.
45 The days of his youth hast thou shortened: thou hast covered him with shame. Selah.
46 How long, LORD? wilt thou hide thyself for ever? shall thy wrath burn like fire?
47 Remember how short my time is: wherefore hast thou made all men in vain?
48 What man is he that liveth, and shall not see death? shall he deliver his soul from the hand of the grave? Selah.
49 Lord, where are thy former lovingkindnesses, which thou swarest unto David in thy truth?
50 Remember, Lord, the reproach of thy servants; how I do bear in my bosom the reproach of all the mighty people;
51 Wherewith thine enemies have reproached, O LORD; wherewith they have reproached the footsteps of thine anointed.
52 Blessed be the LORD for evermore. Amen, and Amen.

The Point:

Despite His unfaithful people, God will hold true to His covenant made with David from generation to generation.

How do we feel in the recitation of this psalm?

As this psalm progresses, we experience two sentiments simultaneously. There is a bitter disappointment with the present condition of the people of God and a hopeful confidence in God's covenant promises. Verses 37 and 38 mark a terrible transition between what we know is true by the revealed promises of God and what our eyes witness in the present reality. The psalm represents a crisis of faith, but in the last verse we confirm our faith in God one last time. We derive much security and comfort from reminders of

God's faithfulness to His covenant, but, as our eyes shift to the deteriorating condition of God's people, our hearts grow cold with discouragement. We long for the glory days of old, wondering if God will ever revisit His people again with His covenant mercies as He did in times past.

What does this psalm teach us?

Verses 1–4. This introduction sets the theme of the psalm. Ethan the Ezrahite testifies to a steadfast faith in the covenant-keeping God despite the increasing apostasy of His people. Ethan is certain that God will continue the project that He initiated during the days of Abraham and David. God will have a people, establish His King, and build His Kingdom that will never pass away. We cannot overlook the rock-solid commitment that God has made to His project—this merciful covenant. It will never be revoked. The biblical word "covenant" holds very intense connotations. When God established that covenant with Abraham, He passed between the bloody forms of dead animals cut in half. A covenant is a promise or a deal that cannot be broken. When a faithful husband promises to be true to his wife "till death do us part," he cannot even think of breaking that covenant. The covenants God makes are even more binding. Marriages may dissolve; the records of marriages may burn up when city halls burn down. But the covenant God made with David is established in the heavens where no records will ever burn. It is established forever.

The central matter of this covenant is the eternal reign of David's line. Whereas earthly kingdoms will pass from family to family, such as the English throne passing from the Plantegenet family to the Tudors and then to the Stuarts, this is not so with the kingdom of God. This throne remains in one family—the line of David. There are still some who do not realize this rule of David over the whole world. "If David is dead and gone, who is this King of Israel?" they ask. The Apostles made it clear that Jesus Christ Himself is the fulfillment of this prophecy, and His kingdom remains to this day. It subsumes all of life for both those who will recognize His kingship and those who refuse to recognize it. God has placed His Son on the throne, "far above all principality, and might, and dominion, and every name that is named, not only in this world, but also in that which is to come: and hath put all things under his feet, and gave Him to be the head over all things to the church" (Eph. 1:20–21). From this passage we can see that Jesus Christ is Head and King over more than the church. He is Head over all things—with a special interest in the provision and vitality of His church.

Verses 5–18. Faith in this covenant requires faith in the One Who makes the covenant, so the following verses describe our faithful God. This covenant is not made with some weak, vacillating god who cannot or will not keep his word. In these verses, our God is portrayed as a mighty man in battle, more fearsome than the greatest warriors in all of the annals of history. It doesn't mean all that much when some weak king shows a little mercy to his subjects. But when the most powerful Ruler of the Universe chooses to make covenant with His people to protect and defend them, it is a most fearsome, majestic, and noteworthy matter indeed! This God has absolute control over the motions of the stars and the raging of the high seas that toss aircraft carriers about like toothpicks. He took Egypt, the world's greatest empire, and snapped it in two like a twig. His is no arbitrary standard of justice. He is the source of justice and maintains the standard without compromise. While He will not bend His standard of justice, He finds a way to show great mercy in judgment.

The psalmist then describes the blessed state of those who have heard Yahweh's name and walk in His favor. What a blessing it is to be in relationship with such a One who reigns over all yet is merciful to those who come to Him in humility! His people glory in His strength. At various times in history, it was a privilege to be a citizen of a country like Rome or America, especially when those nations were in the zenith of their power. It is far more of a blessing to be identified with the God Who created heaven and earth and rules by His absolute, sovereign power through His Son Jesus Christ. He exalts the horn of those He favors, which means that He gives them the upper hand in the conflict.

Verses 19–37. This third set of verses now expands more on the covenant that God makes with His people Israel, more specifically with David. Speaking in the first person directly to David, the Lord lays out His purposes for this kingdom. He promises to strengthen David for the task. But, somewhere between verses 22 and 29, the focus shifts from David to His greater Son. For Christ would come through the line of David, and He would one day ascend to the throne. As part of the covenant, God promises to beat down David's enemies and weaken those who hate him. He guarantees that David's Son will excel in authority over all of the kings and rulers of the earth. God's merciful favor will attend Christ and His Church, while the enemies of Christ the King run for cover. There are only two or three references in the Old Testament to the Fatherhood of God, and verse 26 is one of them. Of course, the New Testament is filled with these references, especially as Jesus Christ appeals to His Father throughout the Gospels—a clear fulfillment of the prophecy contained in Psalm 89:26: "Thou art my Father, my God, and the Rock of my Salvation." This is interesting because we do not find that Abraham referred to God as "Father." But now we enjoy this privilege because we are in Christ, Who is the beneficiary of an eternal, intimate connection with the Father.

Several times throughout this psalm, the psalmist certifies the absolute certainty of this covenant. As sure as men have counted on the sun to rise by day and the moon to light the night, this covenant will remain. God has sworn to this covenant, and He cannot lie.

Verses 30–37 provide a precursor to what comes in the last, saddening verses in the psalm. God includes this important caveat so as to address the possible scenario in which David's progeny rebels against the covenant. This scenario was not just likely to happen—it was certain to happen. So what happens when David's descendants rebel against Yahweh (Rehoboam, Jehoram, Manasseh or anybody else)? Speaking in this case about the corporate body of the people of God, the Lord promises chastisement for them as a father would chastise a son should he rebel. Yet through it all He promises that He will stay true to the original covenant. This project will never fizzle out. There may be a period of time now and then where God's people will pass through dark and persistent rebellion. Yet He will never completely remove His favor from them.

Verses 38–52. As it turns out, the reference to the possibility of rebellion was not a far-fetched proviso in the covenant. For now the psalm makes the terrible transition back to the present reality. The Ezrahite must have written the psalm sometime during the period of spiritual decline in Israel, possibly even during the exile in Babylon. The relationship was broken. God had cast off His people because they were abhorrent to Him.

In 2007 a young man from a devout Christian home in Colorado cursed his parents in a public forum, rebelled against them in the most radical sense, and murdered four people in Christian ministries before he was killed by a security guard. Obviously, such wicked behavior brought great shame upon this boy's parents and family members. It made him odious and abhorrent to those who were closest to him. Imagine how his parents must have felt about this foul behavior. This is something like what has happened to the nation of Israel, God's rebellious son. The relationship has unraveled. The covenant is in tatters, and God is angry with His "anointed." He has ground the crown into the dust and turned the strongholds of David's kingdom into ghost towns. The only manifestation of God's kingdom on earth and the only people belonging to God have turned into an embarrassment to God and to the nations around them. God gave them over to be a punching bag for their enemies.

Is Ethan the psalmist accusing God of breaking the "everlasting covenant"? He comes close to saying this, but he stops short of it.

It seems that the man knows that one day God will salvage this covenant (verses 30–37), but he doesn't know how it will happen. Still he asks God how long He will withhold His mercy from Israel. He wonders out loud how God can continue to accept the reproach cast upon His people by their enemies, who have taken advantage of their weakness. So he closes the psalm with a blessing, which we take to be a vindication, a certification that God is and always will be good and true to His Word.

How do we apply this psalm?

1. This passage may apply to Jew and Gentile alike. For almost 2,000 years the Jews have suffered a great deal for their rejection of the King, and such passages as this may apply to the post-A.D. 70 Jews. But the Gentiles also were grafted into the vine of the people of God (Rom. 11), and it is appropriate to draw incisive application to other periods in the history of the kingdom. Now, the entire Western world has turned on Christ and His rule. The Presbyterian Church (U.S.A.) endorsed sexual abominations by ordaining homosexuals to the ministerial office for the first time in 2011. Former Christian territories like England and Turkey are now largely controlled by the Muslims. "Thou hast also turned the edge of his sword, and hast not made him to stand in the battle. Thou hast made his glory to cease, and cast his throne down to the ground." The church is virtually powerless to change the culture in our time because it is synthesized with the culture. Therefore, the church is failing in Europe and large parts of America—wherever the Christian church was once highly influential. The divorce rates and fornication rates in the evangelical church and outside the evangelical church are shockingly similar to each other. We are experiencing the wrath of God on the Christian church in America right now. We receive the reproach of enemies that mock the fledgling, compromised Christian church in this country. Indeed, God has turned His face from us, and we ourselves should pray these prayers for God's mercy, based upon His promise to David.

2. This promise to David has been fulfilled in the Lord Jesus Christ. In Acts 2:32–35 the Apostle Peter says that Christ must rule until He brings all of His enemies under His footstool. Taking in the worldwide view of the kingdom, we must acknowledge that God has been faithful to His promise to David. Jesus rules in the hearts and lives of millions around the world. For Ethan the Ezrahite, who saw the people of God in complete disarray but did not witness the coming of Christ and His subsequent reign, it took a great deal of faith for him to say "Blessed be Yahweh for evermore. Amen and Amen." It should be far easier for us to see the fulfillment of the Davidic covenant and say these words with all of our hearts.

How does this psalm teach us to worship God?

The covenants that God made with David and Abraham should come up in Christian worship on a regular basis because these are our covenants. We address God on the basis of the contract He made with our fathers in the faith. He promised that in Abraham's Seed all of the nations of the earth would be blessed. He promised that the Son of David would reign forever on that throne. We pray that these nations would be blessed by His rule in our day! We pray that God would take His kingdom around the globe and that Christ would reign in our hearts and in every area of our lives. We pray all of this on the basis of the covenants that He made with our forefathers in the faith.

Questions:

1. What is the Hebrew word for "covenant"? What is the etymology of the word?

2. What was the Davidic covenant?

3. How did God fulfill this covenant?

4. What does it mean to exalt the horn of a person or a nation?

5. What did God say He would do if His people rebelled against Him?

6. What was the condition of God's relationship with His people when this psalm was written?

7. Give several examples of Praise Psalms.

Family Discussion Questions:

1. How can you be sure that God will save His people from their sins? How can you be sure that Jesus Christ rules? How sure can you be that God is true to His Word?

2. Do we talk to God as one who is in a relationship with Him as the psalmist does here? Do we try to win God's favor back as a son might who has offended his father? How do our prayers use relational tones and words?

PSALMS BOOK 4

PSALM 90

Category: Prayer ~ Occasion: Assessing Life

Author: Moses

1 LORD, thou hast been our dwelling place in all generations.
2 Before the mountains were brought forth, or ever thou hadst formed the earth and the world, even from everlasting to everlasting, thou art God.
3 Thou turnest man to destruction; and sayest, Return, ye children of men.
4 For a thousand years in thy sight are but as yesterday when it is past, and as a watch in the night.
5 Thou carriest them away as with a flood; they are as a sleep: in the morning they are like grass which groweth up.
6 In the morning it flourisheth, and groweth up; in the evening it is cut down, and withereth.
7 For we are consumed by thine anger, and by thy wrath are we troubled.

8 Thou hast set our iniquities before thee, our secret sins in the light of thy countenance.
9 For all our days are passed away in thy wrath: we spend our years as a tale that is told.
10 The days of our years are threescore years and ten; and if by reason of strength they be fourscore years, yet is their strength labour and sorrow; for it is soon cut off, and we fly away.
11 Who knoweth the power of thine anger? even according to thy fear, so is thy wrath.
12 So teach us to number our days, that we may apply our hearts unto wisdom.
13 Return, O LORD, how long? and let it repent thee concerning thy servants.
14 O satisfy us early with thy mercy; that we may rejoice and be glad all our days.
15 Make us glad according to the days wherein thou hast afflicted us, and the years wherein we have seen evil.
16 Let thy work appear unto thy servants, and thy glory unto their children.
17 And let the beauty of the LORD our God be upon us: and establish thou the work of our hands upon us; yea, the work of our hands establish thou it.

The Point:

Life is fragile and fleeting, but by God's mercy our lives will be worth something for all the living we have done.

How do we feel in the recitation of this psalm?

We enter the psalm with feelings of deep awe at the permanence of God and His power in creation and judgment. There are storms on other planets where the winds blow at 600 miles per hour over land masses the size of our earth. These storms could wipe out all life on Planet Earth in 30 seconds. But God spares us for now. In contrast with almighty God stands puny man, fragile and fleeting, especially in view of God's overwhelming judgment. Feelings of futility sometimes visit those who have lived a few years and can see death approaching. Is it really worth going through all the struggles and suffering of life only to see our lifes' work burned and our bodies buried in a grave? Why bother living this life at all? These sorts of questions are not uncommon for adults in their 40s and 50s as they begin to reflect on the net value of their lives. But these feelings of futility are quickly replaced with feelings of deep fulfillment in the heart of a true believer because his life is blessed in God. He knows that his life is worth living because God will make something of eternal value out of what he has done with his life.

What does this psalm teach us?

Verses 1–5. The first half of the psalm contrasts the stability and eternity of God with the fragility and vulnerability of man. Earthly relationships come and go, men are disloyal to one another, and then they all die and their memory disappears into the fading marks on a gravestone. But God is always here. There may be people who have been a part of your life for a long time. Maybe your father and mother have been with you all of your life. They are regular fixtures in your world. But this will not last forever. If it has not already happened, there will come a day when you will no longer be able to return home to visit your father and mother because they will be gone—buried deep under the soil. This is not true for God, however. He is always home, and it doesn't matter whether we are speaking of Abraham in 1600 B.C., the Apostle Paul in A.D. 60, or the rest of us in the present day, we can always count on God being the same Father He has always been to His people, from generation to generation.

Even after your father and mother have passed away, no doubt you will still be able to visit the Grand Canyon in Arizona or Mount Everest in Tibet. Did you know that there was once a time long ago when these "permanent" sites were not there? Before God formed Mount Everest, God was present, and after

Mount Everest burns to the ground, God will be present. This is how the psalm begins.

It is hard to say if verse 3 refers to the destruction of the rebel Israelites in the wilderness (whom God destroyed with snakes, disease, and other means) or the Egyptians who He destroyed at the Red Sea. Either way, God really brings deadly judgment on man, all the while offering opportunity for repentance. Even in His judgment, He extends mercy and calls for repentance! There is opportunity for repentance and an extension of mercy right down to the end as God rains fiery judgment upon the children of men.

Verse 4 returns to a contemplation of God. He is no slave to time, and He is in no hurry to bring about His purposes. It may be helpful to consider the other three dimensions of human existence—space. If I wanted to go to the moon, I would have to build a rocket ship and travel for many days before I could walk on the moon. But God does not have to get to the moon, for He is already on the moon. He is not subject to space, for He is sovereign over space in His omnipresence. In a similar sense, God is not subject to time. He does not have to "wait" for things to happen as we must if we are to get from the year 2011 to the year 2040. Such contemplations are beyond all comprehension!

We look at the last thousand years since the beginning of the apostasy in the West as a very long, arduous process. However, God says that a thousand years for us is only a day from His perspective. Let's try to look at it from His perspective for a moment. Christianity's influence peaked in the 1500s, which was by about noon in God's timing. The Renaissance, the universities, and the Enlightenment philosophers did their damage, and the Reformation was a meager attempt to salvage Christianity's inevitable drift towards the humanist apostasy. Then the missionary movement took the Gospel to every corner around the world between 1700 and 2000. The influence of Western Christianity received a little burst in the founding of a Christian nation on the shores of New England in the 1600s and

1700s (at about 2:00 PM in God's timing). By the 1800s and 1900s (or 4:00 PM in God's timing), an extraordinary number of Jews turned to the Christian faith. The destructive influences of national socialism, communism, scientism, ungodly uses of technology, materialism, existentialism, and nihilism brought about the virtual annihilation of entire cultures and civilizations in the 20th and 21st centuries. By 5:00 PM in God's timing, the Muslims began displacing Christian apostates (humanists) in England, Germany, France, Switzerland, and Canada. Now the Christian influence continues in small nooks and crannies throughout the Western world as it spreads to other continents around the world. All of these events are interconnected and play a part in God's plan for one single day! It seems like a long arduous process for us, but it is only one day in God's "Day Planner"!

Verses 6–11. These six verses contrast puny man with almighty God, Who is eternal and sovereign over space and time. Man is like grass that is here today and gone tomorrow. Who would bother writing the life history of some stem of grass growing in the backyard? If you did record the history of a clump of grass, I doubt that you would find anybody who would be interested in reading it. The lifespan of a blade of grass may be a year or two, and a human might live a little longer than that. But this is nothing in comparison to the immortality and eternality of God! Of course, man's problems are even deeper. He has the problem of sin, and he is subject to God's judgment for sin. In verses 7–9, the psalmist expresses deep wonder at the swift and complete destruction God brings upon the sinner.

Grass will get a year or two, but man gets seventy to eighty years to live. In one way or another, either directly or indirectly, every man suffers the effects of the wrath of God every day of his life. Moses' prediction for longevity is as accurate today as it was when he wrote it some 3,500 years ago. Life was hard then, and it is just as hard today (even with improved medical technology). Although Christians may enjoy a little redemptive restoration here and there, all the pain, tribulation, suffering, the sorrow, broken relationships, diseases, and death are evidences of the burning wrath of God against this world of sin. Life is really hard, and then you die.

Verse 11 magnifies the problem even more with a contemplation of the anger of God in the execution of His judgment. As the popular aphorism goes, "Life is the pits, and then you die." But what happens after you die? None of us has seen first-hand the powerful anger of God evidenced in the fires of hell. Truly, the sight of it must be overwhelming and must inspire the ultimate fear of the Almighty!

Verses 12–17. Following this sober contemplation, Moses presents his major point:

> "Teach us to number our days, that we may apply our hearts unto wisdom."

This powerful admonition calls for a sober reflection upon the days of our lives. Although many young people want to think they will live forever and the elderly do not like to think about their impending death, Moses insists that we should live with our death in view. How we spend the time that God gives to us in this life is important, and we should redeem the time by applying our hearts to wisdom. Keeping the commandments of God is the definition of wisdom, according to Deuteronomy 4:6. Paul instructs us to "redeem the time for the days are evil." Not much has changed since Moses and Paul wrote these words. However, the temptations to waste time with foolishness, vain pursuits, games, internet activity, and other pastimes are one thousand times more prevalent today than they were just two hundred years ago!

The last five verses of the psalm contain a prayer for God's mercy as we apply our hearts and lives to wisdom. Of course, we will never be able to apply our hearts to wisdom without the grace of God working in us. Moses prays that God will return to us because we will not return to Him (verse 3) unless and until God returns to us and shows His favor to us. The earlier God visits us with His mercy, the more we will rejoice in this life of suffering. All around us is this ugly world of sin. In our natural state, we are ugly. If we will be beautiful, if there will be any beauty, it will be found where Emmanuel, the Son of God is present. May we be found in Him.

In these last verses Moses also grapples with the problem of true fulfillment in life. If we are just cosmic dust floating around in a chance universe, there can be no satisfaction in life. Or, if we are in rebellion against God and refuse to serve Him, our lives on earth are nothing but a miserable introduction to a miserable eternity in hell. What possible satisfaction can anyone get out of either of these two scenarios? Indeed, the only possibility for any real satisfaction and joy in life must be found in the God Who Himself is eternally self-sufficient, eternally glad, and eternally fulfilled in His ultimate purpose (verses 1 and 2). Only God can satisfy us in His mercy. Only God can make us joyful in the afflictions and misery of the life we live and the death we will die.

Moses prays for a vision for the work that God is doing in this world. Only God's work will amount to anything significant. Only the Kingdom of Jesus Christ will stand the test of time since it is God's project. There is plenty of work that is done in this world that will burn. The empires that men build will go up in smoke, proving that their work was for naught and all of their commitments were useless. Who wants to see their lives account for nothing at the end? Moses, above all people, should have considered his life's work important. After all, he delivered a million people out of enslavement to the greatest empire of the day. He successfully led the people of God to victory in battle and prepared them to take the Promised Land. But even this great man understood that all of these efforts would amount to nothing unless God established the work of his hands.

How do we apply this psalm?

1. The entire psalm is an application. We are encouraged here to maintain the right perspective concerning life because our days are numbered. Walk in wisdom. Walk in God's truth. And

this truth includes all the revelation of Scripture concerning the nature of God, the nature of man, God's provision of redemption, God's righteous laws, and everything found in His Word. It is more than to hear the Word and know the Word. We must, by His Spirit, apply the Word to our thoughts, words, and actions—all the while being absolutely reliant upon the mercy of God.

2. Sometimes older people look back on their lives with regret. It is sad that they did not turn to wisdom sooner and soberly reckon the shortness of life. They wasted away much of their lives. In keeping with the prayer of verse 13, we pray that God would visit our children with His mercy early in life. Then they will be able to serve Him all their days rather than wasting their lives in the service of the devil.

3. Often, we take great satisfaction in a sense of accomplishment. Whether we achieved some material success or even a spiritual conversion through the witnessing of the Word, we like to think that we did something important, that our lives are worthwhile. But all of this is for naught if God does not bless the work in His eternal kingdom. In all that we do, let us look to God for His blessing. Let us not rest content in the accolades of men and the subjective feelings of self-satisfaction. Let us pray that He would take these meager efforts we have exerted in building homes, churches, and businesses, turning them into something that will shine for eternity.

How does this psalm teach us to worship God?

Worship includes prayer to God. This prayer of Moses' contains the deepest reflections of the soul of a very wise man. It is the only psalm of Moses recorded in Scripture. What we find here is somewhat comparable to the thoughts of Solomon in the Book of Ecclesiastes. This prayer sets a realistic and humble assessment of human life against the backdrop of God's eternal and infinite nature. Primarily, it is a prayer for God's mercy upon His people, imploring that He would save them and that He would establish them, their work, and their families forever.

Questions:

1. Who is the author of Psalm 90?

2. What two things are juxtaposed in this psalm?

3. To what is man compared in the early verses of the psalm?

4. What appears to be the condition of God's people when the psalmist wrote this psalm?

5. What is the major point contained in verse 12?

6. What makes our lives worth living?

Family Discussion Questions:

1. Do we feel as though our lives are worthwhile? Are we doing anything that will have lasting value for eternity? If so, what makes it of lasting value?

2. Do we soberly consider the fact of our certain death even now? If we were to live considering the shortness of our days, would we be so likely to waste our time in sin and foolishness? How would this affect the way we lived? Would we be sober or somber? Would we be joyful?

3. How do we apply our hearts and lives to wisdom today?

PSALM 91

Category: Faith ~ Occasion: Fearful Times

Author: Unknown

1 He that dwelleth in the secret place of the most High shall abide under the shadow of the Almighty.
2 I will say of the LORD, He is my refuge and my fortress: my God; in him will I trust.
3 Surely he shall deliver thee from the snare of the fowler, and from the noisome pestilence.
4 He shall cover thee with his feathers, and under his wings shalt thou trust: his truth shall be thy shield and buckler.

5 Thou shalt not be afraid for the terror by night; nor for the arrow that flieth by day;
6 Nor for the pestilence that walketh in darkness; nor for the destruction that wasteth at noonday.
7 A thousand shall fall at thy side, and ten thousand at thy right hand; but it shall not come nigh thee.
8 Only with thine eyes shalt thou behold and see the reward of the wicked.
9 Because thou hast made the LORD, which is my refuge, even the most High, thy habitation;
10 There shall no evil befall thee, neither shall any plague come nigh thy dwelling.
11 For he shall give his angels charge over thee, to keep thee in all thy ways.
12 They shall bear thee up in their hands, lest thou dash thy foot against a stone.
13 Thou shalt tread upon the lion and adder: the young lion and the dragon shalt thou trample under feet.
14 Because he hath set his love upon me, therefore will I deliver him: I will set him on high, because he hath known my name.
15 He shall call upon me, and I will answer him: I will be with him in trouble; I will deliver him, and honour him.
16 With long life will I satisfy him, and shew him my salvation.

The Point:

With a loving God as your refuge and strong fortress, you have no reason to fear the most dreadful evil possible.

How do we feel in the recitation of this psalm?

We feel completely secure in the arms of God. Though surrounded by thousands of enemies, we feel as though we have an impervious shield around us. We are invulnerable. But all of this is because we trust in God and love Him above all else. Everything hinges on this love for God as we implicitly trust in His protection.

What does this psalm teach us?

Verses 1–4. This psalm is a three-way conversation that takes place in the congregation of the saints. When you first read it, the psalm may be a little hard to follow. But if you read the psalm as you would a dramatic dialogue in a play script, this will enhance the message communicated. Throughout the psalm, you will find a mix of faith testimonials, exhortations, and comforting promises.

In verse 1, the speaker begins addressing another person (or persons or perhaps an entire congregation of saints). He testifies and exhorts at the same time.

He is probably a pastor or elder in the church whose job is to lead the people to believe in the Lord. If the leader has no faith, how can he exhort others to faith? Hence, the speaker begins with this powerful, personal testimony, "I will say of the LORD, He is my refuge and my fortress: my God; in Him will I trust."

He speaks to those who are abiding in the secret place of the most High. This is a special place where God loves His people, and His people love each other. The Bible never separates the love of God from the love of brothers (John 15:10; 1 John 3:14). Is there any other place where Christ meets with His people as He does in the church—where two or three are gathered together in the name of Christ?

But this faith is far more than a corporate faith. It is also an individual faith, for the speaker announces to all that he is trusting in God for his salvation. Then he describes the blessings that come to those who always look to God for salvation.

At the foundation of why we need the salvation and protection of God is the fact that we have an enemy. The devil is real, and the world opposes us at every turn. Certainly, most of us are aware of the physical dangers that confront us every day, whether they are potential car accidents, poisoning, fatal viruses, etc. But our existence is made up of more than the physical world. The spiritual world is equally—if not more—dangerous, and our enemies are invisible and often hard to ascertain. We live a very dangerous life. We are constantly threatened with deceitful temptations and evil calamities. The former draw us into sin, and the latter produce much suffering in our lives. So we are realistic about our situation, but we are not fearful or cast down. That is because we are absolutely confident that God will deliver us wherever we happen to be along this "dangerous journey."

In verse 4 the preacher compares the Lord God to a mother hen that protects her chicks under her wings. This tender picture is repeated throughout the psalms (Psalm 36:7, 61:4, etc.), and Christ our Savior uses similar language in Matthew 23:37. There is a natural instinct within the hearts of parents that rises up to protect their children when danger threatens. Since the Author of this instinct must be God Himself, we know that He will be the best Protector for His people, and He will protect His own children from deadly harm.

"His truth shall be thy shield and buckler." Surely, there is nothing that protects us more from the evil that threatens our hearts and lives than the Word of God itself. That is why those who forget to read God's Word over a period of weeks and months open themselves up to the worst attacks of the devil. The greatest protective force for the people of God comes from the faithful, truth-filled preaching of the Word in the congregation because God's Law-Word identifies sin. God's truth identifies error. It is corrective and carefully cuts the fleshly and worldly influences away from our hearts and lives. It rips the pretty face off of the hypocrisies that corrupt the people of God, and it identifies the deceptive temptations of the evil one.

Verses 5–8. Now comes a litany of more blessings that visits those who dwell under the shadow of the Almighty. First, that enslaving, torturous fear that would turn us into miserable cowards disappears even in the most harrowing circumstances. It is frightening enough to walk through a field in the daytime where the arrows are flying. At night, it is even more dangerous. Yet the psalmist wouldn't think twice about crawling through a minefield in the dark if he had to. The Christian general Stonewall Jackson, who was known for his steadfast trust in the sovereign hand of God, once remarked to an attendant, "I feel as safe in battle as in bed." We are in sovereign hands, yes. But we are also in loving hands. Thus, we have a double reason to feel impervious to the slings and arrows set against us.

When a deadly epidemic attacks a city, sometimes thousands and even tens of thousands of people succumb to the malevolent virus. Mass graves fill up with piles of dead bodies. But the man of faith walks through the city without an iota of fear (verses 6, 10). History gives us many stories of Christian missionaries and pastors who attended the sick during terrible pandemics, and God gave them strength and health to carry on. Of course, this does not mean that believers will never die or that they will never contract a deadly disease. The psalmist speaks of something far more spectacular than an occasional resuscitation or an immunity to some disease. He is alluding to Paul's bold statement in 1 Corinthians 15:55–56:

"O death, where is thy sting? O grave, where is thy victory? The sting of death is sin; and the strength of sin is the law."

Death has no sting and holds no fear for the believer. What little harm is caused by viruses, arrows, and fire is short-lived and is very soon dispelled by God's eternal salvation. The believer is absolutely safe on the battlefield because he has confidence that he is going to heaven. But this is not the case for the wicked— those billions of people who refuse to put their trust in God for their salvation—who will be destroyed in the flames of hell.

Verses 9–13. The last half of the psalm presents two characteristics of those persons who abide under the shadow of the Almighty and enjoy the privilege of His protection and salvation. In verse 9, the man is described as the one who has made Yahweh God his habitation. As did Enoch of old, this man walks with God. First, he considers himself a child of God, and then he acts like a child of God. He doesn't need to hide from God as Adam and Eve did in the garden. He talks to God in prayer, he listens to

God in His Word, and he promptly confesses his sins to God when he needs to restore the relationship.

Following this description, the psalmist lists more blessings that attend the man who walks with God. But is he overstating the case when he asserts that no evil will befall this man of God? I don't think so. There are two ways to view the adversities that come upon us. On the one hand, if an unbeliever stubs his toe, he might curse his "luck" and call it a "negative" happenstance in a random, chance universe. But a believer who stubs his toe while he walks with God can still feel his Father's hand on his shoulder. At the same time he is confident that all events are under the sovereign hand of his Father. Therefore, in the ultimate sense, he cannot consider this "adversity" as purely negative. It is intended for his correction and benefit. He knows it because he feels his Father's hand upon his shoulder. As Paul puts it in the New Testament, "All things [even adversities] work together for good to those who love God, to those who are the called according to His purpose" (Rom. 8:28).

God is particularly careful to watch over His children. He will even assign angels to attend to them, to guide and protect them. Moreover, He empowers his children to trample a lion and a dragon with their feet as effortlessly as smashing a bug on the driveway. The lion and dragon should be taken as a reference to Satan, who is the major enemy of the human soul and is compared in Scripture to a lion, a snake, and a dragon. We trample Satan and His demon minions because the Seed of the woman, Christ Himself, crushed the head of that snake at the cross (Gen. 3:15; Col. 2:15).

Verses 14–16. As the three-way conversation progresses at the end of the psalm, God Himself speaks to the preacher and to the rest of the congregation. He mentions the second characteristic that marks the man who enjoys the privileges of God's salvation in verse 14. This is a man who not only walks with God in faith but also loves God. He has a personal relationship with God, such that he can claim to know Him. The man who loves God is safe, very safe. How could a man who loves God with His heart, soul, mind, and strength ever fear the judgment of God or expect anything less than His salvation?

How do we apply this psalm?

1. You can be sure that there is not a person God has saved who does not now love Him. We must acknowledge God's sovereign grace in this relationship. It is God who gives us a heart of flesh and enables us to love. Therefore, His love must come first, which is the order laid out in John's epistle. "We love Him because He first loved us." Our loving begins with His loving, when we by faith know and trust that He loves us. It is for us, then, to love. This is the business of the Christian. We have nothing to fear as long as we are loving God.

2. We have no business fearing even the worst imaginable calamities. If we wrestle with a fear of man or a fear of circumstances, then we have moved out from under the refuge of the Almighty. Daily, heart-deep reliance upon God, as will be demonstrated in our prayer life, is essential if we are going to live this psalm.

How does this psalm teach us to worship God?

Worship builds up our faith. Confidence in the sovereign hand of God should yield a strong faith, producing testimonies and exhortations like those found in this psalm. A pastor in communist Vietnam would often exhort his congregation to faith in God while keeping a suitcase leaning against the pulpit. He had been arrested so many times that he wanted to have a change of clothing available in case the authorities threw him in jail! Do you think his congregation caught the message he preached? The man must have seemed impervious to the threats of the evil one as he cried out to his congregation, "A thousand shall fall at your side, and ten thousand at your right hand, but these communists will not halt the preaching of the Gospel of Christ in this nation!" Do you think such a message from such a man would encourage his parishioners to faith? In like manner, our faith should be bolstered each Lord's Day as

we hear the preaching of the Word of God from the lips of a
man who lives the life of faith.

Questions:

1. Who are the speakers in the psalm, and to whom are they speaking?

2. What are some of the metaphors and similes used to express God's
protection in this psalm?

3. Who crushed the head of the serpent (or the devil)?

4. What does the psalmist mean when he says that no harm will
befall the man who trusts in God?

5. What are the two things that mark the believer, according to this
psalm?

6. Give several examples of Faith Psalms.

Family Discussion Questions:

1. Do we consider God to be our refuge, our strong tower, and our
place of habitation? Are we always there, or do we wander away
from this place of refuge?

2. How much do we fear circumstances or the things that men could
do to us?

PSALM 92

Category: Praise ~ Occasion: The Lord's Day

Author: Unknown

*1 It is a good thing to give thanks unto the LORD, and to sing praises
unto Thy name, O Most High.*
*2 To shew forth thy lovingkindness in the morning, and thy
faithfulness every night,*
*3 Upon an instrument of ten strings, and upon the psaltery; upon the
harp with a solemn sound.*
*4 For thou, LORD, hast made me glad through thy work: I will
triumph in the works of thy hands.*

5 O LORD, how great are thy works! and thy thoughts are very deep.
6 A brutish man knoweth not; neither doth a fool understand this.
7 When the wicked spring as the grass, and when all the workers of iniquity do flourish; it is that they shall be destroyed for ever:
8 But thou, LORD, art most high for evermore.
9 For, lo, thine enemies, O LORD, for, lo, thine enemies shall perish; all the workers of iniquity shall be scattered.
10 But my horn shalt thou exalt like the horn of an unicorn: I shall be anointed with fresh oil.
11 Mine eye also shall see my desire on mine enemies, and mine ears shall hear my desire of the wicked that rise up against me.
12 The righteous shall flourish like the palm tree: he shall grow like a cedar in Lebanon.
13 Those that be planted in the house of the LORD shall flourish in the courts of our God.
14 They shall still bring forth fruit in old age; they shall be fat and flourishing;
15 To shew that the LORD is upright: he is my rock, and there is no unrighteousness in him.

The Point:

We have seen God's works, and we rejoice in them.

How do we feel in the recitation of this psalm?

We are glad. This is a psalm of great rejoicing over the works of God's hands. It is exactly the sentiment that we ought to feel when we sing hymns like "Great Is Thy Faithfulness." Feelings of gratitude should warm our hearts in sincere appreciation for every one of God's spiritual and physical blessings. As we consider how God has blessed us with children or grandchildren, food on our tables, happy, peaceful homes, and a church body that loves one another and feeds the orphans, we ought to look up to heaven with a huge smile upon our faces and say, "Thank you, God!"

This psalm also includes a second form of rejoicing, which we engage in when we see that justice is done and the wicked receive their just deserts. We rest in the fact that things will always work out well for the righteous and for the cause of righteousness. Every evil work will be justly punished because God is sovereign and perfect in all of His works. This is praiseworthy!

What does this psalm teach us?

Verses 1–5. What better thing is there to do in life than to give thanks? Giving thanks for the gift does more for the soul than receiving the gift. It is our highest delight, and it produces the most joy. Yet how many families fail to apprehend this vision for life, and so remain in a constant state of discontentment, misery, and conflict simply because they refuse to give God thanks? Maybe you have seen the spoiled child with a thousand toys. His fat little face is stuffed with candy, and all he can do is whine and pout over every little inconvenience. His foul ingratitude is torturous to those around him and a curse on his own happiness.

Joyful gratitude is the net sum, bottom line metric of the Christian life. Are you living the life of true faith? Have you received God's good gifts of salvation? To the extent, and only to the extent, that you have realized the goodness of God in your life, you will respond in warm-hearted, grateful praise.

Gratitude should be a daily expression in the believer's life (verse 2). If God is an everyday reality to us, and if we are beneficiaries of God's goodness every day (which we are), then we ought to speak of His faithfulness every morning and evening. Also, God has given us a wonderful form of human expression in music and song. Whether on the Lord's Day or any other day of the week, we can express our thanksgiving to God with songs played on harps, pianos, and other instruments. God is worthy to be praised! He has been good to us, and we ought to let that be known every day of our lives!

Verses 4 and 5 focus upon the works of God as the great motivation to praise. If you can see that all good things are from God and all bad things work together for good to those who love God, then you will see all things as the work of God's good hand.

Verses 6–11. Again, the psalmist raises the all-important antithesis between the wicked and the righteous in these verses. Might the works of these evil men contravene the goodness of God and frustrate His purposes? Not at all. The wicked actually fit nicely into the eternal purposes of God. Even their momentary access to power only increases the magnitude of their fall, and in the end God is glorified in it all. While the wicked wilt and die like the grass, God is still in the heavens. The important thing is that nothing will detract from God's glory, and His praise will resound through the heavens for eternity.

It is also important to remember that God will utterly overwhelm His enemies, and Christ is ruling right now until He brings all His enemies under His footstool. But He will overcome our enemies as well. This is the thrust of verses 10 and 11. You may remember from Psalm 75 that the exaltation of the horn is an age-old military practice in which the conquering army blows a triumphant blast through a horn that echoes down the valleys and over the plains. This signifies to everybody in the vicinity that the conquerors have secured the upper hand in the battle. You will not properly relate to this imagery unless you see the life you live as a great battle and recognize the ever-present reality of enemies in your life.

While it is the business of Christians to "do good to those who despitefully use" them, this does not mean that these enemies are given free license to oppress the people of God indefinitely. One day, God will bring these enemies down and execute His vengeance on them. In doing good to our enemies, we are not justifying their behavior, nor are we minimizing the wickedness of their oppression. Nor are we in any way mitigating any of our desires that they cease and desist from their persecuting ways. Yet we have no business taking revenge on those who do us wrong. We still have great confidence in the absolute sovereignty and justice of God; He will exercise perfect justice, whether at the cross of Christ or in the fires of hell forever.

Verses 12–15. Inexorably, the wicked will make their way to their final ruin. Their empires will crumble and their accomplishments will fade away. But, throughout the generations and into eternity, God will bless the righteous. He will bless their lands with life and peace, freedom and prosperity. He will sanctify their lives by His Spirit. He will bless their families with many godly children and grandchildren. Set a godly people next to an ungodly people, and immediately you will see a vast contrast. While the ungodly are steeped in sin, fornication, illegitimate births, sexually transmitted diseases, conflicts, divorce, pride, massive debt, government tyranny, and the like, the godly are blessed with joyful families, stable communities, freedom, humility, peace, and righteousness. The differences are sharp and marked.

There is nothing more beautiful than finding an elderly man or woman who is still soft to the Word of God and continues to grow in faith, love and joy. These sweet people provide an especially sharp contrast with the more typical elderly folk who just grow more bitter, ungrateful, and hopeless with age. The wicked will approach death with anger and fear, but there are many professing believers as well who in their later years seem to reach a plateau in their Christian walk and cease to grow in love and knowledge of God. They are not willing any more to repent of their sins or humble themselves before God. However, this is not the case with the blessed man of verse 14! This blessed man is one who continues to bear fruit in his old age. This old saint retains a robust health. He is "fat and flourishing" in his soul despite the inevitable process of decay that consumes his body with age. Even as death is attacking his body at the end of his earthly existence, life continues to fill his soul!

The psalm ends with a contemplation of the God Who is behind all of this. He will judge the earth because He is the

Judge of perfect justice, and He will save His people because He is the Rock of their salvation.

How do we apply this psalm?

An "attitude of gratitude" must pervade the Christian life. Our prayers, conversations, and songs should be filled with gratefulness to God for the good things that He has done. If a day goes by in which we have not felt warm sentiments of gratitude, we have failed to catch the vision of this psalm. Moreover, if we fail to see God's hand working in the minute details of our lives, chances are that we will not be able to lift our voices in praise of God's works.

Let us be thankful for everything, whether it is large or small, consequential or inconsequential. Praise God for the gift of Christ Who saves us from hell! Give Him thanks for the gift of fingernails that are good for an occasional back scratch. Whether it is the blessing of a juicy strawberry that God appointed for our enjoyment or the challenge of a flat tire on the freeway, let us learn to respond to all things with gratitude. As a family, we must cast the worrisome, discontented, grumbling life aside and embrace this life of gratitude!

How does this psalm teach us to worship God?

Our worship must include thanksgiving for God's works. Even in our prayers, as we bring our petitions before the Lord, we must not forget to include an offering of thanksgiving (Phil. 4:6).

Questions:

1. Why is thanksgiving important for the believer?
2. What are the things that warm the heart of the psalmist to gratitude in this psalm?
3. What is one good way to express warm gratitude to God?
4. Why does God empower the wicked?

5. What does it mean to "lift up the horn"?

6. Who must exercise judgment on our enemies?

7. What does it mean for an elderly person to be "fruitful, fat and healthy?"

8. Give another example of a Thanksgiving Psalm.

Family Discussion Questions:

1. Are we a thankful family? Is thanksgiving a regular practice in our home? How often do we give thanks?

2. Quickly, let us list fifty things for which we are very thankful.

Suggested Activity: Consider having each family member pray a prayer of thanksgiving for at least one of God's blessings. In these prayers, do not ask God for anything. Simply praise Him for His goodness.

PSALM 93

Category: Praise ~ Occasion: Turmoil

Author: Unknown

1 The LORD reigneth, he is clothed with majesty; the LORD is clothed with strength, wherewith he hath girded himself: the world also is stablished, that it cannot be moved.
2 Thy throne is established of old: thou art from everlasting.
3 The floods have lifted up, O LORD, the floods have lifted up their voice; the floods lift up their waves.
4 The LORD on high is mightier than the noise of many waters, yea, than the mighty waves of the sea.
5 Thy testimonies are very sure: holiness becometh thine house, O LORD, for ever.

The Point:

The Lord reigns in heaven, and nothing can possibly move Him from His position as absolute Ruler of the universe.

How do we feel in the recitation of this psalm?

Imagine what it would be like to stand at the surf of an ocean bay as a fifty-foot tidal wave gathered force and crashed with a mighty blow upon the shoreline! When this happens in the vicinity of seaside communities as it did in Sendai, Japan in 2011, entire cities were flattened in mere seconds. But that was only one wave. Suppose that a second wave rolled in with a one hundred-foot crest, and then a third wave hit the shore with a two hundred-foot crest and one hundred times the destructive force of the first wave. The crashing of the waves would be deafening, and the effects would be utterly terrifying! With each successive wave, hour after hour, day after day, there is an increase in the intensity of force. In the face of such devastating energy, the pride of man melts into oblivion. Who can stand in the face of such power? Yet these natural disasters are only material forces. Behind them is an infinite, spiritual Power far and away greater than any physical force we experience on earth. Yahweh in the heavens merely speaks a word, and these angry waters cower in fear. Galaxies halt in their courses and stand in awe of Almighty God. Now, what about you?

What does this psalm teach us?

Verse 1. The psalm intersperses prayers of praise to God with public declarations concerning Yahweh, the King of the earth. In the New Testament, the Greek word used for preaching is *Kerusso,* which may be translated "herald." When a king has a message for the land, he sends his heralds through the towns and villages to "herald" the announcements. These men speak with authority because they represent the king himself. It is in this context that the preacher stands up and proclaims the grand statement found in verse 1: "Yahweh reigns!" Now this pronouncement defines God's relationship with all of the cities, towns, and countries around the world. Whether or not all men acknowledge His Kingship, the Lord reigns over all the earth. It is true that many today wish to think of God as being distant and disengaged from His creation. Such pipe dreams may do a little to quiet a disturbed conscience here or there, but the Christian faith repudiates this altogether. We believe that God is very much involved in every detail of His realm, for He fills the role of King of the World.

Two things distinguish a king who is over a given realm. First, the king has authority to establish law and require the obedience of his subjects. This is no empty authority because the rightful king also bears sufficient power to ward off any would-be competitors who would attempt to usurp his power. Second, he maintains a system of oversight, enforcement, and justice that ensures that his agenda is accomplished over the entire expanse of his dominion. Earthly kings are always limited by their own weaknesses, inconsistencies, and failures, but God is the unfailing, absolute, and majestic King of all the earth. His law is certain and nobody breaks it with impunity. Nobody can ruin His plans, trash His planet, or bring His kingdom down.

"The world is established, that it cannot be moved." If God was not King of the earth, then the fate of the world would be in the hands of men or in the hands of random chance. This is the worldview of the materialistic naturalists who deny the possibility of a supernatural Being that has anything to do with our world. As they become more self-conscious of their worldview perspective, they live in an almost constant fear that man will destroy the planet or that some random asteroid will careen into the orbit of the earth and wipe us all out. If God is King of the earth, then of course He is both wise and powerful enough to create and preserve a robust earth that can withstand the destructive efforts of sinful man. Certainly, He can control the flight path of asteroids and comets. We should be far more concerned about violating the moral laws of the King Who made this earth than about puny man destroying God's earth.

Verse 2. Shifting from preaching to prayer, the preacher turns to God and cries out, "Your throne is established of old. You are from everlasting!" Here is the reason why we need not fear the effects of some random chaotic events in a universe of pure chance. We can count on the regularity of nature in Creation and a world with established physical laws and patterns because the God who created it is the same from everlasting to everlasting! His throne existed long before the world was ever created, and His rule has never been challenged, nor can it ever be challenged.

Verses 3–4. Although we need not fear that the world will disintegrate at the whim of chaotic destructive forces, there are still mighty forces at work by nature and human design that threaten the peace and security of those who dwell on the earth. We may suffer a hurricane, a tornado, or the detonation of a nuclear armament in our cities. As we face these mighty waves and contemplate their potential destructive force, we cry out to God, "The floods have lifted up, Oh Lord!" But instantly, we realize that God is greater than these puny forces. He is worthy of our worship and awe. The tidal wave that ruined Japan in 2011 was the most expensive natural disaster since the worldwide flood. The images of whole cities, roadways, and buildings swept away in the flood will reside in the minds of that people for generations to come. For months and years afterwards, the Japanese will fear another earthquake or tidal wave. But God is a billion times more powerful than these little tidal waves, and He is capable of bringing a judgment much more severe upon Japan or any other nation on the earth. Oh, that men would fear the true and living God!

Verse 5. There are so many things in life on which we cannot rely. Economies collapse. Earthquakes and tornadoes destroy villages. Friends grow distant or pass away over the years. But there is something that is certain and immovable. We would do well to keep our eyes fixed upon this certainty. The testimonies of God never change. With all the uncertain vicissitudes of life—the tragedies, the broken relationships, the failures, the unfulfilled dreams, and the dissolution of our greatest endeavors—there is still something we can count on. The testimonies of Yahweh are sure, rejoicing the heart. In addition, the dwelling-place of God will never be desecrated. It will continue to remain holy and pure, beautiful and majestic, most fitting for the holy God who dwells therein.

How do we apply this psalm?

Do we order our behavior more by the ideas of men, powers of government, and fears of natural disasters or economic calamity than by the unchanging laws of God? If the laws of God take second fiddle to the dictates of men, then we certainly do not live the spirit of this psalm. If God is King over the whole earth, He really ought to be treated as such. Therefore, we will not fear natural forces but rather serve the sovereign King. We should be more interested in studying God's commandments than following the paths of dangerous hurricanes on the Weather Channel.

How does this psalm teach us to worship God?

This psalm is a wonderful illustration of the weaving together of two aspects of worship. The worshiper talks about God (preaching), and then he talks to God (prayer), in what is called preaching and prayer. While talking to God, he may mention the trials and tragedies that befall men, but inexorably his contemplations concerning God Himself will dominate his meditations.

Questions:

1. What two forms of worship are interspersed in this psalm?
2. What is a king?
3. How does God compare to other earthly kings and rulers?
4. How does this psalm address those who concern themselves with the possible destruction of the planet?
5. In a world of change, what are the things that do not change?
6. Give several examples of Praise Psalms.

Family Discussion Questions:

1. How do we react during times of chaos and tragedy? Do our thoughts run according to the pattern of this psalm?

2. Do our hearts long for something good that will not slip out of our hands? How does God meet this particular longing of our souls?

PSALM 94

Category: Imprecatory/Exhortation ~ Occasion: Murder of Innocents

Author: Unknown

1 O Lord God, to whom vengeance belongeth; O God, to whom vengeance belongeth, shew thyself.
2 Lift up thyself, thou judge of the earth: render a reward to the proud.
3 LORD, how long shall the wicked, how long shall the wicked triumph?
4 How long shall they utter and speak hard things? and all the workers of iniquity boast themselves?
5 They break in pieces thy people, O LORD, and afflict thine heritage.
6 They slay the widow and the stranger, and murder the fatherless.
7 Yet they say, The LORD shall not see, neither shall the God of Jacob regard it.
8 Understand, ye brutish among the people: and ye fools, when will ye be wise?
9 He that planted the ear, shall he not hear? he that formed the eye, shall he not see?
10 He that chastiseth the heathen, shall not he correct? he that teacheth man knowledge, shall not he know?
11 The LORD knoweth the thoughts of man, that they are vanity.
12 Blessed is the man whom thou chastenest, O LORD, and teachest him out of thy law;
13 That thou mayest give him rest from the days of adversity, until the pit be digged for the wicked.
14 For the LORD will not cast off his people, neither will he forsake his inheritance.
15 But judgment shall return unto righteousness: and all the upright in heart shall follow it.

16 Who will rise up for me against the evildoers? or who will stand up for me against the workers of iniquity?
17 Unless the LORD had been my help, my soul had almost dwelt in silence.
18 When I said, My foot slippeth; thy mercy, O LORD, held me up.
19 In the multitude of my thoughts within me thy comforts delight my soul.
20 Shall the throne of iniquity have fellowship with thee, which frameth mischief by a law?
21 They gather themselves together against the soul of the righteous, and condemn the innocent blood.
22 But the LORD is my defence; and my God is the rock of my refuge.
23 And he shall bring upon them their own iniquity, and shall cut them off in their own wickedness; yea, the LORD our God shall cut them off.

The Point:

God's sense of justice is 10,000 times keener than our sense of justice, and He will most certainly destroy those who deny His relevance as He defends the soul of the righteous.

How do we feel in the recitation of this psalm?

How would you feel if you witnessed a wicked brute stabbing a poor helpless child on a street corner? What if you were powerless to intervene? If there was a single merciful bone in your body or the slightest sense of justice in your heart, you would cry out to God for His swift intervention! We do experience a sense of relief as we consider that God is far more interested in every injustice that has ever been committed in this world than we could ever be. Even when it appears that the political trends ever and increasingly oppose the cause of righteousness at every front, we are confident that God will vindicate His Own Name and save His people from ruthless tyrants.

What does this psalm say?

Verses 1–7. To understand the sentiment of the psalm, you need to picture the psalmist having just walked out of a legislative committee hearing that approved the legalization of infanticide for children born with birth defects like Down's Syndrome. He is devastated to learn that the bill was overwhelmingly approved by a vote of 33 to 2. He feels beaten by the powers of darkness. It seems that all the institutions of higher learning, all the major media voices, and all the political forces are against him. The wicked triumph.

Both the psalmist and the apostle Paul are careful not to countenance any inclinations towards taking personal vengeance. "Vengeance is mine, I will repay, saith the Lord" (Rom. 12:19). This means that all vengeance belongs to God. That's His business. Still this does not preclude our invoking God's attention to the matters at hand. While we may be thankful for the mercy God extends towards us, we should also grow weary of the injustices we see around us. It is important that Christians retain a healthy commitment to justice as defined by God's laws, especially where gross injustices become the order of the day. This commitment is what impels the psalmist to pray these imprecatory words.

The root issue with the wicked is their pride. When they build their "impregnable" towers of tyranny and injustice, they use the concrete blocks of pride. It takes a trillion tons of this stuff to build these towers. Whether these empires are large or small, a malevolent fiefdom or modern socialist power state, you can be sure they are using pride for their building blocks. Often the construction begins in their academies and then is institutionalized in businesses and politics. For hundreds of years, these institutions labor under the work of these proud men, and one proud generation gives birth to an even prouder generation. First the Renaissance produces the humanist Enlightenment and the French revolution. After another hundred years or so, the Enlightenment gives birth to the brave atheism of post-modernism. As we follow the morality of this once-Christian nation, we watch the youth move from courtship, to dating, to "shack-ups," to hook-ups, to an enthusiastic endorsement of homosexuality—all within a period of 100 years. How long will God permit moral anarchy in the bedroom and institutionalized atheism in the classroom? Will we have to wait until the year 2600 before He intervenes? Doubtful.

Verses 4–7 sketch a profile of these wicked men. As the godly continually give God the glory and the credit for all good things, the wicked are busy congratulating themselves for their creations. They glory in the accomplishments of men. If you read their newspapers, you know that they are far more interested in rendering glory to famous politicians, actors, sports figures, and businessmen than to God the Creator of heaven and earth. Proudly, they asserted in the first Humanist Manifesto (1933) that "Man is at last becoming aware that he alone is responsible for the realization of the world of his dreams, that he has within himself the power for its achievement." To this we say, "How long shall they utter proud things? God is the source of all power and authority, not man!"

Their arrogance will lead them to the greatest miscalculation of all, which would be the affliction of the people of God. For thousands of years, we have seen civil governments and anarchical bands murder the precious saints of the living Christ. After the Roman persecutions came the rising tyranny of the European empires. This brought about bloody purges such as the Saint Bartholomew's Day Massacre (1572) and the persecution of the Scottish Covenanters at the hands of the Stuarts (1680s). Following the reformation period, worldwide persecutions began with renewed vigor to result in the weakening of Christianity in the West, and the growth of materialistic atheism—through the modern totalitarian state— and the growth of Islam in the 20th and 21st centuries. Whether this persecution came under the cloak of religious or political motivations, suffice it to say that tyrants like to kill God's people. They have been doing this since Cain killed his brother because Abel offered a more acceptable sacrifice (Heb. 11:4).

These wicked people go after the widow, the stranger, and the orphan. When the Rwanda political leaders organized the slaughter of over 800,000 Tutsis over a period of 100 days in 1994, the true colors of wickedness became clear to the world. As in this case, sometimes the hatred of cultural aliens or strangers gives way to full-fledged genocide. But the most egregious forms of murder take place in the slaughter of babies by abortion and infanticide. When Senator Barack Obama voted against the Illinois Born Alive Infants Protection Act in 2003, he became the most powerful American politician to ever publicly endorse infanticide. What makes abortion all the more grievous is that it is usually recommended for babies whose fathers commit fornication with the mother and refuse to provide for the child. Therefore, it is often fatherless children who are oppressed far more than any others. God uses strong language against the oppression of fatherless children in Exodus 22:22–23.

Verse 7 gives a little more insight into these men. They are not atheists *per se* because they still acknowledge God's existence. In fact, they still recognize the covenant name for God, since they refer to Him as "Yahweh." Chances are, these are not the Moabites or the Philistines. These are men who have been taught something from God's Word, and they obstinately rebel against it. Effectively, they are what we call "deists." As the Western world apostatized from the faith in the 1700s and 1800s, the road they took was "Deism Avenue." These apostates concocted a god who was distant from his creation, somehow disconnected from the little planet floating around in the Milky Way Galaxy. Deists do not want a real God who is truly omniscient and maintains the most absolute standard of justice. The god they prefer may have set a few laws in motion billions of years ago, but he has lost interest in his world today. Conveniently, this view of God enabled modern man to overcome his guilt complexes and sin with impunity.

Verses 8–11. The Psalmist responds to these deist rebels by calling them fools and "brutish"; they are animal-like in their stupidity. Of course, God is very much connected with every action, every word, and every thought of men. To think for a moment that God is blind to anyone's actions is sheer irrationality. I recall one family who forbade their dog from entering the carpeted area of the house, but they allowed him to occupy the kitchen. On occasion, as the family sat in the living room, the dog would put his paws over his eyes and slowly elbow his way on to the carpet. The way the dog figured it, if he could not see his master, he assumed in his animal brain that his master could not see him! How are these brutish men any different in their thought processes from this dog? It is impossible to escape God's all-seeing eye and all-hearing ear. Doesn't it make sense that the God Who created trillions of eyes for men, dogs, and flies should have eyes Himself with which to monitor every scene and every event that occurs in His universe? All knowledge is derived from God anyway. If men have learned a few billion things, doesn't it follow that God knows far more than what men have picked up from Him? Clearly, God is defined in this passage as the Source of all reality and all true knowledge.

Verses 12–15. In this section, the psalmist lays down the lines of demarcation between the righteous and the wicked. The truly blessed man is the one who is in relationship with God. It is a father-son relationship, where the father is willing to chasten the son and train him in how to live life (Heb. 12:6–13). The righteous man is a learner. He knows that he has not achieved sinless perfection, and he cheerfully submits to God's training in order to learn to live life in accord with the laws of God. Throughout history the days of adversity always came. Empires fell and men's hearts failed them for fear. But the righteous men were always well prepared for these judgments, both temporal and eternal. We see that those who live in covenant with God and have been trained in God's laws will prosper through times of severe trial.

When the wicked appear to have the upper hand, we must believe that Jesus Christ is still over all things to the church (Eph. 1:21). God is sovereign. He commands all men everywhere to repent. His temporal judgments may delay for a couple hundred years but never for a thousand years. God will not abandon His heritage, and He will call the nations to account.

Verses 16–23. This is where the psalm gets personal. Since the wicked now control almost every important government system today, and since the Christian church is persecuted, despised, or ignored in most countries around the world, who will stand against these wicked men? Who will defend the innocent? Who will protect the righteous? Since 1997, seventeen additional countries endorse abortion by "liberalizing" their abortion laws (including Cambodia, Columbia, Ethiopia, Iran, Portugal, Switzerland, and Thailand). More Christians died for their faith in the 20th century than in all the previous nineteen centuries combined. From all reports, the 21st century will be even worse. Everywhere around the world, we find Christians shot, burned, hanged, tortured and even stuffed into metal shipping containers or septic tanks. Either by anarchical forces or by governmental decree, Christian clergy become targets for assassination. Organizations like Voice of the Martyrs collect many reports of Christian churches, along with scores of homes and businesses owned by Christians, being burned to the ground. Dozens of nations across the globe have now passed strict anti-conversion laws in an attempt to stifle the spread of Christianity. At one time, Christian missionaries enjoyed the protection of "Christianized" governments in London or Washington D.C., but not any more. Who will rise up for us against the evildoers? We have to believe that the Lord's attention is riveted to what is going on here. If He is truly sovereign, and if He really sent His Son to die for His church, would He desire to protect and defend His church through the ages? Yes. This is His promise and commitment. We must let meditations on God's covenant mercies and justice sustain and comfort us through the wild revolutions and violent persecutions of the day. As men and women of true faith, we ought to spend more time dwelling on God's nature than reading news reports concerning the latest achievements of the wicked. Here is another reason why it is so important to study the psalms: these words bring us back to reality, God's reality, God's perspective, which will make us less deistic in our thinking and more God-centered.

"Shall the throne of iniquity have fellowship with you?" (verse 20) This helps us to understand the relationship of civil government to the true and living God. Some governments are in covenant with God, and some are out of covenant with God. At the beginning of this country, the governments of the colonies desired a right relationship with the true and living God (as evidenced by their early charters, their days of fasting and prayer, and their godly leaders). In some of the colonies, those serving in political office would even take an oath of allegiance to the God of the Old and New Testaments. But as time went on, this nation forgot God. In the year 1967, Colorado became the first state in America to "frame mischief by law" by legalizing abortion. Ironically, John Love, a Republican governor, signed the abortion bill into law.

Either our states will meet with God's approval, or they will face his judgment. As Jesus Christ rules supreme on the right hand of the Father, the judges of the earth would do well to "kiss the Son, less they perish from the way" (Ps. 2:12). It will not be long before God will cut them off in their wickedness. These persecutions of the innocents will not continue forever; they may perhaps continue another thirty or forty years. This is the perspective of the psalmist.

How do we apply this psalm to our lives?

1. As long as the innocents suffer at the hands of wicked men who reject Gods laws, the faith of God's people will be tested. For over forty years now, abortion has remained a legal right in the United States of America. Do we really believe that God is in the heavens? Will He ever take vengeance on nations and/ or individuals that defy His rule? As we meditate on God's Word and God's work in history, these precious truths should buttress our faith.

2. Let us also be careful not to fall into the perspective of the deist ourselves. Whether we recognize it or not, God is very much involved in our lives. Either we are in right relationship with Him, submitting ourselves to His chastening hand, and learning to live life according to His rules in His household, or we are not in right relationship with Him. Our business is to get right with God, and we do this through faith in Jesus Christ, His Son.

How does this psalm teach us to worship God?

1. Worship is about restoring a right perspective of God. In reading and teaching God's Word, we remind ourselves of God's holy character, and then we consider our own relationship with Him. We also consider the state of the wicked around us. We look at those institutions and governments that increasingly oppose Christ and His righteous law. With confidence, we call them to repentance, for God's judgment is certain. We know he will act in His perfect timing. Before the worldwide flood, Noah must have witnessed a great amount of evil for a very long time. There must have been millions, if not billions, of deists who confidently asserted rebellion and formed great institutions opposing God and His law, and God waited… for a thousand years. Then the first drop of rain fell out of the sky, and it was over. God acted in judgment on the unbelievers and at the same time saved Noah and his family in His mercy.

2. Occasionally, worship might also include a call for God's judgment upon His enemies. This is an affirmation of God's judgment, not ours.

Questions:

1. What is the difference between God's vengeance and our vengeance? How can we cry out for God's vengeance without giving way to taking personal vengeance against our enemies?

2. How does this psalm describe the wicked?

3. How does the psalm describe the righteous man?

4. Give several examples of how the wicked persecute the righteous and murder the innocents today.

5. What is "deism"?

6. Give several examples of Imprecatory Psalms.

Family Discussion Questions:

1. Do we ever turn into little "deists" ourselves and pretend that God is not watching us? How might we avoid this deceptive perspective on reality?

2. Are we generally optimistic or pessimistic as we look at history? How does this optimism or pessimism affect our day-to-day walk in faith? Do we really believe that God will curtail the acts of wicked legislatures that "frame mischief by law"?

Psalm 95

Category: Praise/Exhortation ~ Occasion: Hardness of Heart

Author: Unknown

1 O come, let us sing unto the LORD: let us make a joyful noise to the rock of our salvation.
2 Let us come before his presence with thanksgiving, and make a joyful noise unto him with psalms.
3 For the LORD is a great God, and a great King above all gods.
4 In his hand are the deep places of the earth: the strength of the hills is his also.
5 The sea is his, and he made it: and his hands formed the dry land.
6 O come, let us worship and bow down: let us kneel before the LORD our maker.
7 For he is our God; and we are the people of his pasture, and the sheep of his hand. To day if ye will hear his voice,
8 Harden not your heart, as in the provocation, and as in the day of temptation in the wilderness:
9 When your fathers tempted me, proved me, and saw my work.

10 Forty years long was I grieved with this generation, and said, It is a people that do err in their heart, and they have not known my ways:
11 Unto whom I sware in my wrath that they should not enter into my rest.

The Point:

We call God's people to worship Him, but before this can happen, it is critical that they come with the right heart-attitude.

How do we feel in the recitation of this psalm?

Waves of joy sweep over us as we contemplate the power of God's creation and His covenant love towards His people. Reverently, we kneel before the Lord Who is both a King and Shepherd to us. As we read verse 7, we are shocked a little by this exhortation that comes directly from God Himself. Instead of congratulating us for the worship we render to Him, He firmly warns us against unfaithfulness and grumbling.

What does this psalm say?

Verses 1–2. Our psalm begins with an invitation to sing God's praise, but we must sing with rejoicing. How many Christian sects spend excessive quantities of time defending a certain music style or some form of psalmody? Then, when they finally manage to force the congregation into this form, have they really succeeded at what God wants in their music? While it is important to replicate God's truth in our singing, it is also crucial that we express the sanctified emotional tone found in the psalms. GOD STILL WANTS REJOICING! It is possible to sing the most glorious lyrics ever written, words that express the most powerful human emotions, without feeling a shred of that emotional tenor or even comprehending the meaning of the words. May God forgive us when this happens! In a real sense, the kind of tunes used are not of primary importance. We ought to employ the best music we can find to appropriately meet the meaning and emotion of the psalms and hymns written from Scriptural truths. But at the end of the day, it is the hearts of those singing the songs that really matter. Are they singing because that's what everybody is supposed to do? Or are they expressing true joy in the salvation of God, the Rock of their salvation? We have great cause to be thankful, especially if God has redeemed us from sin, death, and hell forever!

Verses 3–5. The following verses provide reasons for our rejoicing and praise: God is great and God is powerful. These words help to bolster the idea of rejoicing. For many today, rejoicing is the emotion expressed over such superficial things as eating a sweet dessert or receiving a compliment. But biblical rejoicing includes the sentiment that the children of Israel experienced as they watched Pharaoh's army flailing about in the mighty waves of the Red Sea. Creation also provides great testimonies of God's might. Thanks to powerful telescopes, we can see the power of God in billions of galaxies burning with trillions of gigantic nuclear fusion reactors.

The reference to "gods" in verse 3 alludes to authorities over which God is the ultimate authority. There is no competition with God's authority anywhere in the universe or outside of the universe. He is King over all gods.

If you were to stand upon the mountains or the great deep valleys in the oceans, you would find them to be breathtakingly large and deep. It is extremely difficult for a man to climb Mount Everest or descend 36,000 feet into the depths of the Marianas Trench. Many men have lost their lives in deep waters or on the high mountains, all of which speak to the breathtaking power of God's creation. But we also observe God's wisdom and intention in the formation of the world. He is no distant God. His hands formed the dry land, both by His works of creation and by the worldwide flood that reordered the earth's crust. There are no accidents, and nothing is left to the mechanisms of impersonal laws. What we see in nature is exactly what God intended to bring about through His works of creation and providence.

Verses 6–7. Here is the second reason for praise and rejoicing: we are in relationship with God. By the mere fact that He is our Creator, we owe Him our allegiance (verse 6). But He is more than a Creator for us. He is the Shepherd for us. At the final judgment, Christ will say to some, "I never knew you." Yet in John 10:14 we find that the good Shepherd knows His sheep. There must therefore be some who are not in the shepherd-sheep relationship with the living Savior. If this is the case, then this psalm must apply only to those who are in covenant relationship with the living God.

Verses 8–12. Abruptly, the worship psalm grinds to a halt. Out of the blue, the psalmist shifts from worship to exhortation and warning. Though it may seem odd, it shouldn't. Actually, men and women who sit in worship services can develop callused hearts towards God as the people of Israel did in the wilderness. Children who grew up in church services forget why they are there. Within a generation or so, they grow indifferent towards God and the mighty works of God in salvation. They yawn through the worship services. They might even demand more of God's blessings or more miracles before they will agree to believe in God.

This warning is real and relevant to those who sit in church, for there were some who participated with the church in the wilderness (Acts 7:38) but never quite made it to the Promised Land. In like manner, there are some who participate in the church of the New Testament. They eat of the spiritual meat (1 Cor. 10:3–4, 16–17), and they taste of the spiritual gift (Heb. 6:4). But they harden their hearts to the grace that is given them (Heb. 3:13–15), indicating that they were never truly regenerated in heart (Matt. 13:20–21; Heb. 6:9). It is not enough to sit in church worship services, listening to the Word preached week after week. By faith, we must receive the truths of God's Word. By faith, we ascertain that the worlds were framed by the word of God. By faith, we must call to remembrance His mighty acts of deliverance at the Red Sea and at Calvary. And we must never cease to be amazed at His great and powerful works. When we fail to see the hand of God in history, that is the point at which we cease to wonder, and we fail to give Him the praise that is due Him.

How do we apply this psalm to our lives?

The children of Israel did not enter into God's rest in the Promised Land, though it was only a temporal rest. Let us carefully assess our own hearts, lest we are hardened as well and forfeit our eternal rest. Indications of hardness of hearts include a failure to recognize God's good gifts, a lack of trust in Him during times of trial and difficulty, and a coldness to the Word of God as it is preached.

How does this psalm teach us to worship God?

Without daily exhortation in God's Word, we may begin to see the hardening of hearts towards the things of God in our own households. As a plant withers when it receives no water over two or three weeks, so hearts will harden when there is no daily exhortation in our homes. This is the thrust of Hebrews 3:13ff. That the Lord would include this strange exhortation in the middle of a praise psalm should be of no surprise to us. Men's hearts usually harden, whether there are a million people in the wilderness or one hundred fifty people in a little community church in Tucson, Arizona. Therefore, worship leaders should not think twice about stopping a service in the midst of a time of praise in order to warn the congregation about hardening their hearts. Maybe the songwriter sensed that minds were wandering and distracted within his own congregation even as they sang this psalm of praise. Singing such majestic lyrics out of mere rote may amount to dishonoring the name of God. At the very least, this mindless rote is incompatible with the holy exercise of worship in which we purportedly engage.

Questions:

1. What does God want from us in our singing, according to this psalm?

2. How do we know that God was intimately involved in the formation of this world's valleys and mountains?

3. How does this psalm speak of our covenant relationship with God? Does everybody enjoy this relationship with Him?

4. Who is the good Shepherd, according to the New Testament?

5. What did the children of Israel do to tempt the Lord in the wilderness?

6. Give several examples of Exhortation Psalms.

Family Discussion Questions:

1. Over the last ten years, have we seen our hearts harden or soften to God's Word? What is the general spiritual trend in our home? What is the spiritual condition of our church?

2. Do we experience joy when we sing at home and at church? Is it important that we rejoice in every song that we sing? What sorts of songs might commend more rejoicing?

PSALM 96

Category: Praise ~ Occasion: Multi-National Gatherings

Author: Unknown

1 O sing unto the LORD a new song: sing unto the LORD, all the earth.
2 Sing unto the LORD, bless his name; shew forth his salvation from day to day.
3 Declare his glory among the heathen, his wonders among all people.
4 For the LORD is great, and greatly to be praised: he is to be feared above all gods.
5 For all the gods of the nations are idols: but the LORD made the heavens.

6 Honour and majesty are before him: strength and beauty are in his sanctuary.
7 Give unto the LORD, O ye kindreds of the people, give unto the LORD glory and strength.
8 Give unto the LORD the glory due unto his name: bring an offering, and come into his courts.
9 O worship the LORD in the beauty of holiness: fear before him, all the earth.
10 Say among the heathen that the LORD reigneth: the world also shall be established that it shall not be moved: he shall judge the people righteously.
11 Let the heavens rejoice, and let the earth be glad; let the sea roar, and the fulness thereof.
12 Let the field be joyful, and all that is therein: then shall all the trees of the wood rejoice
13 Before the LORD: for he cometh, for he cometh to judge the earth: he shall judge the world with righteousness, and the people with his truth.

The Point:

God is worthy to be praised in the presence of the heathen, and true believers will glorify Him by advocating His Lordship over all.

How do we feel in the recitation of this psalm?

Jealousy for God's praise wells up within us, especially when we see men serving false gods that wrest worship away from the true and living God. Whether it is Americans skipping worship for professional ballgames or pagans bowing before idols of wood and stone, we cannot help but point out the vanity of their worship. It is both stupid and wicked. Why do they insist upon worshiping the mere creations of men, when they ought to be worshiping the Creator of heaven and earth? This psalm calls for bold worship and bold preaching! There is no doubt or hesitation here. We exalt in our God before men and declare His kingship over all the earth.

Towards the end of the psalm, we rejoice in the expectation that God will finally come to judge the earth. Any and all injustices suffered will be put right in the end. Our hearts rest in this truth. While others may walk around with furrowed eyebrows, stressing out over the injustices in the world, we are absolutely confident that God will see to it that every wrong will be set right at the final judgment.

What does this psalm say?

Verses 1–2. Is there ever cause to write new music for God's praise, or should we use the same words and tunes used over thousands of years of church history? Because every culture and every generation expresses itself differently, there will always be new expressions of praise in the worship of the true and living God. This should not change the basic content of worship or the emotional fabric of worship. As Jesus instructed us in John 4, we must worship God in spirit and truth, and this framework of spirit and truth is rightly defined for us in Scripture, especially in the Psalms. Yet still, God gives His people the liberty to develop new forms of praise for use in worship. When men impose a certain form over thousands of years and disallow any development in music across cultures, they curtail Christian liberty and human expression. For our singing to be acceptable to God, we must express God's truth in music that is actually believed in our hearts. We should also use the emotions, tones, rhythms, and tunes that best accommodate the truths expressed. When Ambrose (A.D. 400) or Bernard of Clairvaux (A.D. 1130), or Charles Wesley (A.D. 1760) writes a hymn that powerfully expresses the deep truths of the incarnation, the atonement, or the resurrection of Christ, the hearts of God's people are refreshed in adoration and praise. They feel the passion of the words. They agree with the words in faith. And they join in unison with millions of others throughout the entire world to lift a new song of praise to God above!

Note also that God wants His people singing everyday. Three times the psalmist repeats the command to sing. Singing ought to be the warp and woof of our daily life. While most world religions do not teach their followers to sing, this ought to be a basic constituent of every Christian church. As early as eight or nine years old, children should be able to sing in tune, even in parts. When families sing God's praises throughout the day, their children will grow up in an environment of godliness.

If not the primary theme of our songs, God's salvation for His people is of central importance in our music. While the pagans sing their mournful ballads and meaningless chants, our lyrics are filled with hope in God's salvation. The heathen sing of drunkenness, death, and hopelessness, but we sing of resurrection. They mourn over lost love, but we exalt in the love of God that will take us to glory!

Verses 3–6. Some have thought that the Old Testament Jews neglected the call to missionary service, but this is not true at all. The Jews did proselytize among the heathen, and some did come to know the true and living God through this early missions work. This psalm speaks to these early efforts, and at the same time calls us to declare His glory among the heathen. Under the old covenant, the messages of salvation may have reached an occasional Ruth or Rahab. But now, all nations need to hear of the glory of God's redemptive plan fulfilled in Christ. By God's grace, they respond and millions are joining the songs of praise.

There are several things to declare, the first of which are God's mighty wonders. These may include blessings of healing that God has brought about in the lives of our family and friends but should especially include the greatest of God's works wrought in history—works of redemption and deliverance at the Red Sea and at Calvary. Good preaching will also include comparisons between the gods of the people and the God who created the heavens. Let's face it; the gods of the Greeks, the demon gods of the pagans, and the money god of the modern state never created anything! What is more, the gods of the pagans and humanists are made to look like men—fallible, puny, and something less than sovereign. We need to mock these gods, even as we speak of the God Who created heaven and earth in His sovereignty and orchestrates all things according to His perfect plan. Every great pagan empire has collapsed along with its "great" god-like leaders. It is for us to preach these things with boldness before the nations!

Among earthly kings, we know something about these characteristics of "honor and majesty." When earthly kings are honorable men and take positions of power, they command respect from their people. But no one deserves honor more than the one absolute Authority over heaven and earth, revealed to us in the Scriptures as Yahweh God. If the president of the United States is on the tenth level of authority, God takes a position 10,000 times higher than this mere man. Angelic beings created to be even higher than man surround His throne in glory. Ten billion galaxies stand between our little globe and that exalted throne of Divine majesty!

But the text also refers to "beauty and strength" in his sanctuary. Combining these two words presents a truly awe-inspiring vision of our God. Beauty is one thing. There are very beautiful, intricate, and expensive vases, but they are fragile things. On the other hand, the largest dump trucks in the world can haul 400 tons of rock, but they are not beautiful. God, however, brings beauty and strength together in perfect combination. Nature itself proves this point. For what are the stars themselves but hundreds of billions of nuclear fusion plants that form a gorgeous backdrop for God's sanctuary? What are sunsets but two hundred mile-long murals, powered by a sun that yields 3.34×10^{34} Joules of energy every day? (That's 33,40 0,000,000,000,000,000,000,000,000,000,000 Joules.)

Verses 7–10. After preaching to the nations concerning God's great works, we command them to fall on their faces before the true and living God and give Him appropriate worship. Does God deserve some credit for His great works? If you came into the presence of the doctor who found the cure for cancer and immediately delivered you and your loved ones from this dreaded disease, would it be appropriate to completely ignore his contribution? While in his presence, you might recognize the achievements of a kid who combed his hair and a woman who dresses herself well. But wouldn't it be awkward if you ignored the significant contributions of the good doctor? Hopefully, we are not so self-centered that we fail to notice anybody else's honorable achievements and worthy accomplishments! God deserves the credit for everything, for every act of creation, for every act of judgment and mercy, and for every single act of providence ever recognized by men.

God requires worship from all "kindreds," or families. These are people who live in the same house together. Wherever there are people living in the same home (typically fathers, mothers, and children), they should render tribute to their God as a group. Every family has a religion of some sort and a god that is worshiped and served. This was Joshua's confession when he announced to Israel, "As for me and my house, we will serve the Lord" (Josh. 24:15).

Verses 11–13. As the psalm crescendos into its finale, we call all creation to combine in joyful praise to God the Creator. The joyful expectations sounded by God's creation have been tied to the groaning and travailing mentioned by Paul in Romans 8:19ff. All of the troubles in the world, including the corruption, death, and decay plaguing every element of creation, has come about because of the fall of man into sin. When God comes to judge the world, He will set all things right, and creation will finally be released from this bondage. Cruelties, injustices, tyranny, disease, and environmental disasters (whether they come by accident, negligence, or intention) will come to an end when all things are made right at God's great judgment day. We can count on this happening. All creation, including the birds, fish, beagles, trees in the forests, and oceans, greatly anticipate the final day of Judgment. The way thing are right now is not the way they should be. There is something terribly wrong with our world. But all of creation retains this tremendous, cosmic hope, joyfully expecting that God will make everything right in the end.

How do we apply this psalm to our lives?

Certainly, we have a duty to worship God each day in our homes. For any God-directed family, worship ought to be a regular occurrence. This should happen in both formal and informal contexts. We may worship at a given time each day, but when we happen to see a beautiful sunset, why not fall on our knees together right then and there and give God the glory for His beauty and strength?

How does this psalm teach us to worship God?

1. Worship includes an occasional new song with new tunes and new lyrics. While we want to be careful not to rebel against the musical forms of our parents or reject the spirit and truth directed by Scripture in worship, it is refreshing to express ourselves with new prayers and new songs. Our hymns and spiritual songs should include teaching and prayers set to melody. Whatever music we use in worship, we need to be sure that we sing with all our hearts and with true rejoicing, overwhelming awe, and warm gratefulness to God. If we sing out of sheer habit and rote, we often jettison all emotion and heart commitment to the words. This form of singing serves as a sad caricature of worship and amounts to taking God's name in vain.

2. These worship psalms commend our rejoicing in expectation of God's judgment. The desire to see everything "made right," ought to be nurtured within us in our worship. While injustices should cause us to cringe and mourn, worship brings us back to hope in God's final judgment making all things right.

Questions:

1. Name several godly songwriters who have written new songs in the history of the church.

2. Is there a difference between mission outreaches to foreign nations during the Old Testament era and those in the present New Testament era? If so, how are they different?

3. What exactly do we want to declare to the heathen nations?

4. Give examples of some things that are both strong and beautiful.

5. Why should creation be joyful concerning the fact that God is coming to judge the earth?

6. Give several examples of Praise Psalms.

Family Discussion Questions:

1. What is the mix of old songs and new songs in our worship? How long has it been since we have written new music that reflects the creativity and passion of our hearts properly aligned with Scripture?

2. Is there a jealous desire in your heart to see others worshiping God? Does it bother you when you see people serving idols instead of serving the true and living God? How do you react to this?

PSALM 97

Category: Exhortation ~ Occasion: Temporal Judgment

Author: Unknown

1 The LORD reigneth; let the earth rejoice; let the multitude of isles be glad thereof.
2 Clouds and darkness are round about him: righteousness and judgment are the habitation of his throne.
3 A fire goeth before him, and burneth up his enemies round about.
4 His lightnings enlightened the world: the earth saw, and trembled.
5 The hills melted like wax at the presence of the LORD, at the presence of the Lord of the whole earth.
6 The heavens declare his righteousness, and all the people see his glory.
7 Confounded be all they that serve graven images, that boast themselves of idols: worship him, all ye gods.

8 Zion heard, and was glad; and the daughters of Judah rejoiced because of thy judgments, O LORD.
9 For thou, LORD, art high above all the earth: thou art exalted far above all gods.
10 Ye that love the LORD, hate evil: he preserveth the souls of his saints; he delivereth them out of the hand of the wicked.
11 Light is sown for the righteous, and gladness for the upright in heart.
12 Rejoice in the LORD, ye righteous; and give thanks at the remembrance of his holiness.

The Point:

When God brings temporal judgment to this world, His people rejoice as they reflect on His holiness.

How do we feel in the recitation of this psalm?

From beginning to end, this psalm commends a spirit of rejoicing. It is an optimistic, victorious rejoicing based on the confidence that God is absolutely sovereign over all powers. Severe, violent happenings do not terrify the godly because they know the source of it. Actually, they rejoice to know that none of these catastrophic events are chance happenings. Every single one comes about by the full intent of a God who is in total control, and we rejoice in that. But we rejoice over Gods holiness because we know that, in the scheme of things, everything will work its way out to meet the perfect standard of His righteousness.

What does this psalm say?

Verses 1–5. The psalm begins with a basic conviction that must lie at the root of our every thought concerning reality: Yahweh reigns! But what does it mean for a king to reign? It must at least mean that He is more than a figurehead. Our God takes an intimate interest in the details of His creation. Nothing is out of His purview, and He will bring every work into judgment. When the Christian sees fossils in a rock, he trembles for just a second because he can see the fingerprints of God on that little creature. The worldwide flood was a major historical event—among the top three in history—and we have clear interpretation from God's Word concerning this. "I will destroy man whom I have created from the face of the earth; both man and beast, and the creeping thing" (Gen. 6:7). These are His words, and this flood was His doing. Truly it was God Who killed that little fossilized creature in the rock.

It may seem odd to the modern ear that this fire, lightning, and judgment is a cause for great rejoicing. But if the highest order of good is God's righteousness—and not every man's comfort and eternal bliss—then we would greatly rejoice in this good! For the Christian there is no higher blessing and no greater comfort than to know that God is in control, and even His judgments will yield glory to Him.

The reference to fire that destroys God's enemies offers a terrifying picture of death by burning. One could hardly conceive of a more horrible way to die, but this is the nature of God's judgment. God is not to be trifled with. The destruction of Pompeii by a volcano in the year A.D. 79 was this sort of judgment. Pompeii was a city given over to licentiousness. Yet men are hardly bothered today by these fires as they rely on technological advancements and their early warning systems to preserve them from the deadly effects of natural disasters. But are they preserved from the horrible potential of the nuclear warheads that are now in the hands of non-Christian nations and rogue dictators? Today, there are far more cities in the world with populations of more than 100,000 than there were a hundred years ago, and these population centers become easy targets for nuclear weapons. Proud men and women had better fear God because He has just as much control over the whims of mad dictators and communist regimes as He does over the whims of volcanoes and forest fires. In this psalm we discover that this is one way He destroys His enemies.

The melting of the hills may refer to volcanoes, and it may also speak of the massive rearrangement of the earth's crust at the time of the worldwide flood. What is described here is not some poetic reference to the random actions of a mythological mother nature as if she were to belch when she gets an upset stomach. Not at all! When you read of a volcano killing people in the newspaper, God fully intended this to happen as an act of judgment—because of the disobedience of an individual, a tribe, a nation, or an entire world.

When the president of a large country appears before his people in great fanfare, the military sounds off 300 pounds of ordnance. But when our God appears, 60 billion-ton mountains melt in His presence. God draws close to His people for either of two purposes—to redeem or to judge. This psalm is focusing on His work of judgment, and it warns that the day is coming when He will burn up this world by fire. The hills will melt, and men's hearts will fail them for fear as they are ushered into final judgment forever.

Verses 6–7. The psalmist here answers a common question: how can God judge a people who have no knowledge of Him or His standards of righteousness? How can this be just? Questioning the justice of God is risky business. Nevertheless, the Bible offers answers to questions like this. According to Psalm 19, the heavens declare the glory of God. Paul says that the creation itself declares the power of God (Rom. 1:20), and this psalm even claims that the heavens declare His righteousness. Therefore, according to the Apostle, they are "without excuse" for their stubborn rebellion against God. But that still leaves some question as to how the heavens declare the righteousness of God. After all, one cannot read the Ten Commandments written in the sky. Back in the second verse, the psalmist virtually equates God's righteousness with His judgment. When the pre-flood people rejected Noah, a true preacher of righteousness, they turned away from a declaration of the righteousness of God. But, as the very first rain drops began to fall, they received another important message of righteousness in the form of the righteous judgment of God. Think of what a shock it must have been to those people when the torrential rains came for forty long days. Many of them probably began to think, "Maybe that old preacher of righteousness had it right?" As the storms raged on, they realized they were subject to the terrible, mighty judgment of a righteous God. For so many years they had scoffed at the judgment of God. "Where is the promise of His coming?" they asked (2 Pet. 3:3). With every raindrop that pounded on their rebellious heads, those men received the preached Word of righteousness descending from the heavens.

The psalmist goes on to challenge the nations. "Where are the gods they have served so fastidiously over the centuries? Where are the pagan gods? Where are the gods of science? Where is the god of money? What about the god of the state upon whom they have relied for their protection and salvation for hundreds of years? Where is the Federal Reserve Board? Where are the welfare programs? Will their National Aeronautics and Space Agency save them from the judgment of God by diverting some asteroid careening towards the earth at 40,000 miles per hour?" The time will come when men will finally realize that their gods are all useless. They will beat on their own heads and rue the day that they gave themselves over to those stupid gods. Therefore, the psalmist says that NASA, the Federal Reserve Board, the proud scientists, and all other worshipers of false gods had better be worshiping the true and living God NOW!

Verses 8–12. Abruptly then, this psalm shifts focus from the idolatrous nations back to Zion and the state of the righteous. Standing by and watching the mighty works of God in judgment, even the women of Zion rejoice greatly over what they see. If you were to witness the terrible judgment of God upon a wicked city like Sodom, what would you say as you watched men and women literally burning to death? Would you ask why God makes people suffer in this way? Would you tell Him that He is being mean and unkind to those poor souls? Of course, God's people should never impugn God with maliciousness. Neither would they want to gloat and rejoice out of some sense of personal vindictiveness against those taking the brunt of God's judgment. Yet, such a sight of God's fiery justice requires some sort of emotional response. The focus does not rest on the subjects of God's judgment, nor does it rest on us (who may have been offended by those receiving that judgment). The focus is on God. The daughters of Zion rejoice over God's sovereignty over all power and authority. They rejoice and give thanks "at the remembrance of His holiness" (verse 12). To know that God maintains His absolutely pure standard of holiness is a great comfort and joy to true believers. The burning of Sodom and its residents is not the essential thing. It is only a consequence of the holiness of God.

Contrasted with God's judgment upon the wicked is the blessed state of the righteous in verses 10 and 11. They are clearly defined as the ones who "love the Lord and hate evil." It is a matter of values. When push comes to shove, what do you prefer in your life? Are you more drawn to the things of the Lord, or are you drawn to fornication, lying, and idolatry? Thankfully, our salvation (both temporal and eternal) is in the hand of God in the ultimate sense. "He preserves the souls of His saints." He brings us to the truth and enables us to enjoy Him. In many ways, joy is the bottom line and net sum of a believer's life. Faith, love, and hope produce the fruit of joy. Every year, a new crop of faith, love, and hope in our lives ought to yield new measures of joy especially as the Word is continually received into our lives through preaching and Bible study.

How do we apply this psalm to our lives?

1. What are the things that elicit responses of great joy from the average person? Good food, entertainment, and children can be the source of much joy. But it takes maturity to rejoice in the most substantial things, and there is nothing more substantial than the holiness of God. When a believer can rejoice in everything because he has a vision for the holiness of God, he has achieved some maturity in his Christian life.

Is it all that important to us that God is holy and that He is the great, sovereign Judge of the earth? Intuitively, we all know that there can be no more important aspect to our reality than this, but our minds are easily taken up by less important things. Thus, we must call ourselves back to substantive contemplation on the deep things of God.

2. If God is holy, and if we love God, then it stands to reason that we should hate that which is evil (verse 10). This should also mean that we hate when good is called "evil." Sadly, a great deal of media and music affirm the breaking of God's commandments, whether by promoting fornication, violent vengefulness, or the taking of God's name in vain. This is what we hate.

How does this psalm teach us to worship God?

Worship is giving thanks at the remembrance of God's holiness. To worship is first to be struck by something that elicits awe and wonder. What more striking reason is there for worship than God's judgment, which is a manifestation of His holy character? We ought to be filled with rejoicing and gratitude, but only if we stand in right relationship to the *holiness of God!* If we love the Lord and stand in the blood-bought salvation of Jesus Christ, then and only then may we rejoice in the holiness of God made manifest to us by His holy judgments.

Questions:

1. What does it mean for a king to reign?

2. How can Paul say that men who are in rebellion are without excuse before God?

3. How do the heavens declare the righteousness of God?

4. What is the response of God's people when they view His judgments? Why do they respond in this way?

5. Provide several examples from history where the nations experienced the temporal (earthly) judgment of God.

Family Discussion Questions:

1. What are the things that bring the greatest joy to our lives? In what situations might we contemplate the holiness of God and find great joy?

2. How do we react when we happen to observe that which is evil?

PSALM 98

Category: Praise ～ Occasion: Temporal Deliverance

Author: Unknown

1 O sing unto the LORD a new song; for he hath done marvellous things: his right hand, and his holy arm, hath gotten him the victory.
2 The LORD hath made known his salvation: his righteousness hath he openly shewed in the sight of the heathen.
3 He hath remembered his mercy and his truth toward the house of Israel: all the ends of the earth have seen the salvation of our God.
4 Make a joyful noise unto the LORD, all the earth: make a loud noise, and rejoice, and sing praise.
5 Sing unto the LORD with the harp; with the harp, and the voice of a psalm.
6 With trumpets and sound of cornet make a joyful noise before the LORD, the King.
7 Let the sea roar, and the fulness thereof; the world, and they that dwell therein.
8 Let the floods clap their hands: let the hills be joyful together
9 Before the LORD; for he cometh to judge the earth: with righteousness shall he judge the world, and the people with equity.

The Point:

God marvelously delivers His people in the sight of all the nations, and this inspires great rejoicing from His people.

How do we feel in the recitation of this psalm?

This psalm inspires great rejoicing! It carries the feeling one gets after winning a pivotal battle. Most of us have never been in real battle, so we do not fully appreciate the danger and discomfiture experienced by those immersed in bloody warfare. But think about how nations in history have centered their days of celebration around military victories. Nothing unifies a nation more than winning a war against some terrible, vicious enemy. There is no more important cause for celebration and rejoicing than a monumental military victory.

In this psalm we rejoice in the victory God has won over the enslaving powers of sin, the world, and the devil. It is a rejoicing attended by loud shouts, clapping, and fanfare. In the previous psalm, we rejoiced over His judgment and His holiness. In this psalm we rejoice over the salvation He bestows on His people as well as His righteous judgment.

What does this psalm say?

Verses 1–3. Several times throughout the psalms thus far, the psalmists encourage us to "sing a new song to the Lord" (Ps. 33:1, 96:1, etc.). Whenever God performs His great and wondrous works in the redemptive history of the church in the Old and New Testaments, His people sing a new song to the Lord. If Christ, the Son of God, is the long-awaited Messiah, and if He conquered the enemies of the devil, death, and hell at the cross, then you would think that such deeds call for some great new songs! If Jesus Christ rose from the dead, an event far more significant than the victory at the Red Sea, then it would be well to sing of it. Indeed, the Red Sea experience was an awe-inspiring redemptive work of God, and the psalmists rightly refer to this memorable event in the Old Testament Psalms. They did not write songs referring directly to the resurrection of Christ because it had not happened yet! Whenever we witness powerful works of God at the Red Sea, at Calvary, or in our own lives, we are impelled to sing a new song to the Lord. Joyful Christians can not help but respond in joyful, creative praise for God's mighty work of salvation!

The salvation of Christ and His righteous reign are inescapable. Even the heathen witness God's righteous law overwhelming the pagan practices on this world's continents. The death cry of the pagan Roman Emperor still resounds through the centuries, "Oh Galilean, thou hast conquered!" Even if some pagans gaze longingly back to the days of human sacrifice, gladiatorial killing games, widow burning, infanticide, cannibalism, and other demonic exercises, the world will never return to those dark days because "His righteousness He openly shows in the sight of the heathen!" The righteous reign of Christ will continue unabated until the final consummation.

True to His promises, God unfailingly delivers His salvation for His covenant people. In fact, this psalm speaks of it as if it were an accomplished fact. The salvation of Israel was as good as done, even though this psalm was written about 1,000 years before Christ came. Now, 2,000 years later we can sing this psalm with even more faith and certainty because God fulfilled His promises in Jesus Christ.

Verses 4–9. The remainder of the psalm calls for joyful worship from all creation because of the judgment of God. Again, we rejoice over God's salvation *and* His judgment. Typically, these two acts of God come hand in hand. When the Gospel is preached, some are saved while others are hardened for judgment. When the children of Israel were saved at the Red Sea, that redemption was attended by a severe judgment upon the Egyptians, whose hearts were hardened against God. The cross is salvation for believers, but the cross is judgment too. Jesus Christ suffered the judgment due for our sins on the bloody cross. Therefore, when we praise God for His work of redemption, we cannot remain quiet and noncommittal about His acts of judgment. To question God's justice is to deny the true meaning of His redemption. Both redemption and judgment call for enthusiastic, joyful praise.

When men reject God's salvation, and when they harden their hearts against God, it is wrong to think of God as the loser in the issue of their salvation. Plainly, God will be glorified in His perfectly just judgment, and we can rejoice in this.

In verses 7–9 we call upon all creation to join with us in this joyful worship. We interpret the crashing waves and the wind blowing through the trees as sounds of worship as well. If God created trees, then every tree and everything that trees do will give glory to God. They are doing what God created them to do, and so all of God's creation speaks of His power, wisdom, and justice.

How do we apply this psalm to our lives?

When you are completely convinced that the entire natural world is the work of the Creator, then you will interpret everything that happens in the natural world in the right way. Crashing waves on the seashore, cats giving birth to kittens, and falling stars in the sky are declarations of praise to the Creator. God programmed the natural creation to give Him glory. However, His human creatures give Him praise and glory as an act of the will. Giving God glory is as much our purpose as it is the purpose of the rest of creation. The difference is that we are self-conscious of what we are doing, and we do it willingly!

How does this psalm teach us to worship God?

1. We worship in response to the mighty works God has accomplished in history. There can be no doubt that both God's judgment and His redemption are important bases for worship. It is for us to strike a balance between these two works of God's hands, and the psalms help us to do that wisely.

2. This psalm also argues for appropriate worship, containing many voices and instruments. While some of our worship is quiet and contemplative, that is not the tenor of this psalm. This is a psalm for the whole congregation, and it calls for volume and instrumentation. Drawing from the corpus of biblical references to worship music, it appears that singing is a very

important element for God's people. But psalms like this one include stringed and brass instruments in the worship service.

Questions:

1. What event in history was far more significant than Israel's deliverance at the Red Sea?

2. How has God shown His righteousness to the heathen?

3. What other psalms call upon nature to rejoice in the judgment of God?

4. How did God's redemption and judgment both appear at the Red Sea? At Calvary?

5. Give several examples of Praise Psalms.

Family Discussion Questions:

1. How well do we balance praise for God's judgment and praise for God's redemption in our worship?

2. How well do we balance the volume of victorious worship with that of quiet, contemplative worship?

PSALM 99

Category: Praise ~ Occasion: A Disobedient Church

Author: Unknown

1 The LORD reigneth; let the people tremble: he sitteth between the cherubims; let the earth be moved.
2 The LORD is great in Zion; and he is high above all the people.
3 Let them praise thy great and terrible name; for it is holy.
4 The king's strength also loveth judgment; thou dost establish equity, thou executest judgment and righteousness in Jacob.
5 Exalt ye the LORD our God, and worship at his footstool; for he is holy.

6 Moses and Aaron among his priests, and Samuel among them that call upon his name; they called upon the LORD, and he answered them.
7 He spake unto them in the cloudy pillar: they kept his testimonies, and the ordinance that he gave them.
8 Thou answeredst them, O LORD our God: thou wast a God that forgavest them, though thou tookest vengeance of their inventions.
9 Exalt the LORD our God, and worship at his holy hill; for the LORD our God is holy.

The Point:

We exalt the Lord our God because He is the "thrice-holy God," and this is evidenced in His violent hatred towards idolatry and sin.

How do we feel in the recitation of this psalm?

We feel the hot breath of God's vengeance blazing against idolatry. The fire from God burns away our fleshly idolatry and grinds it to powder, and the hair on the back of our hands may get singed a little. The cross is where we sense most vividly the violent justice of God against sin by way of the death of His only begotten Son.

We tremble before the Lord, but not because God is coming to throw us into the pit of hell forever. We know that He casts others, body and soul, into hell, but we shudder now because His transcendence, majesty, and holiness put Him in a whole different league. If we might be a little nervous while meeting the president of the United States, we will shake visibly and our voices will quiver even more when we come face to face with this thrice-holy God.

What does this psalm say?

Verses 1–3. The psalm is divided into three sections, each of which ends with a declaration of the holiness of God. In Isaiah's vision of the throne room of God, the seraphim cover their faces and feet as they cry out "Holy, holy, holy!" The Bible never repeats a phrase more than three times in a row so as to avoid vain repetition and exaggerated, feigned emphasis— which, interestingly enough, is commonly used in modern musical forms. Here the triple emphasis provided by the angels is enough to make the point in the strongest possible form. God is holy; He is above everything in all of reality in heaven and in earth. This is the over-arching theme of this psalm.

This first section of the psalm focuses on the nature of God as He sits in sovereignty, reigning over all reality. While the Lord is with His people and "dwells between the cherubim" in the tabernacle, He is also "high above all the people" (verse 2). God is with us, but He is also far above us. At the very least, His people should be overwhelmed with the greatness of God, even if the rest of the world ignore Him and take His name in vain. Even God's name is considered "great and terrible," according to the King James Version rendering of the verse. These words denote something majestic, potentially dangerous, and very powerful. A reference to God's name points to His reputation. When we listen to a Bach cantata or gaze upon a spectacular skyscraper, we learn something of the reputation of great artists and architects. But what do we think when we look at the galaxies about us? Or, as we look at the millions of complex elements in the inner universe of the human cell, do we pick up anything about the reputation of the designer? Actually, every square inch of reality and every single event in providential history speak of the reputation of the Great Designer and Sovereign Controller of all things. We learn about God's name and reputation every second of every day. When we catch a glimpse of the expanse of the universe and the great galaxies, and when we watch great mountains explode (as Mount Saint Helen did, sending 100 million tons of ash around the world), we know that God must be great. When atom bombs fell on Hiroshima and Nagasaki, and when a third of Europe died from the Bubonic Plague, we learned that God is potentially dangerous. When we see a sunset span the horizon, creating a 300 mile-wide mural, we know that He is supremely creative and majestic!

The only proper response to these profound considerations must be trembling. The earth shakes and the people tremble at the vision of God's transcendence and holiness. What we find in John's revelation is a great deal of "falling down" before God in worshipful fear and reverence (Rev. 1:17, 4:10, 7:11, 14:7, 15:4, 19:4). John's response was no different from Isaiah's in the Old Testament because they most certainly worshiped the same God.

Verses 4–5. At this point in this psalm, we've already affirmed the power and transcendence of God. But what import does this power have if it never really accomplishes anything? What good is a muscular man who never does anything with his great strength? However, God's power is more than potential energy. This King of the world loves to employ His power to establish justice in the earth. Elsewhere, the psalmist goes so far as to say that ALL of God's works are acts of judgment (Ps. 111:7). If you were to bring all of God's works together, you would find that they mete out absolutely perfect justice. No wicked act will escape His righteous judgment. No one can accuse God of excessive severity—or lenience—in any of his works.

This is equally true of His treatment of His own people, the children of Jacob. But why should He execute judgment and righteousness among His own people? As Peter warns of the judgment to come upon the ungodly, he includes the sober reminder that judgment begins in the household of God (1 Pet. 4:17). God purges His Own people by tribulations, persecutions, and tests. When this happens, it is a difficult time of great suffering for the church (1 Pet. 4:19), yet it is a means by which He strengthens true believers "who commit the keeping of their souls to Him in well doing." Persecution and tribulations also serve to purge the church (or the "household of God") of the thorny-ground and stony-ground hearers (Matt. 13:21–22). In this sense, these harsh and fearful events are orchestrated by God in His sovereignty, and they may be referred to as acts of judgment. They make the church more righteous, while preparing the tares for the final Day of Judgment.

If we suffer in the winnowing work of that judgment which begins in the household of God, then our response must be to stand in awe of His perfect, just, and sovereign will in all things. We exalt the Lord our God and fall at His feet in worship! For it is His holiness that demands a holy people for Himself, and He will have a holy people, whatever it takes!

Verses 6–9. Incredibly, this powerful God who maintains the highest standard of justice is also interested in establishing a relationship with a sinful people. After the fall, this godly relationship with the line of Seth is described in these terms: "Then began men to call upon the name of the Lord" (Gen. 4:26). It is the most primitive description of our relationship with God, but it is used in the New Testament as well as in the Old Testament. Calling upon God is relying upon God. Hence, true believers will call upon God on a daily basis, consistently admitting their utter dependence upon Him.

Primary among the Old Testament saints who called on the name of the Lord are Moses, Aaron, and Samuel. According to verse 7, God's people relied upon the revelation given to Moses in the cloudy pillar. They kept his testimonies, but not perfectly. This is obvious from the eighth verse. If there is a verse from the Psalms that summarizes our relationship with God, it is verse 8. Without question, God deals with sinful men. What may be referred to here is the disobedience of Aaron and the children of Israel directly after God passed down His testimonies on Sinai. As soon as God told them not to make for themselves a graven image, they promptly produced a golden calf. Of course, there was no way that God could ignore this blatant sin. So He addressed the sin by forgiving His people and by taking vengeance on their "inventions." This may sound a little like loving the sinners but hating the sin, except that it goes even farther than that. God forgave His people and destroyed their sin! But how did God take His dreadful, white-hot vengeance upon their sin if he had forgiven them? As already mentioned, His fury against sin may be seen at the cross of Christ. Every time a man is crucified with Christ (Gal. 2:20) and the body of sin is destroyed (Rom. 6:6), we will witness firsthand something of the violent vengeance of God against sin. These two elements of God's salvation must never be separated. He forgives our sin while destroying the power of sin in our lives!

All of these things serve the interest of God's holiness, which is the theme of the psalm. Appropriately, the psalm closes with a call to worship at his holy hill, "for the LORD our God is holy."

How do we apply this psalm to our lives?

We must not interpret what goes on around us without due consideration of the holiness and the judgment of God. Even as we mortify our sinful flesh, we need to see ourselves in the light of the holiness of God. Because God is absolutely holy, He cannot permit His children to continue in their sin! It would be intolerable for one of such holy character as our Father in heaven.

How does this psalm teach us to worship God?

1. Worship requires trembling. We may not visibly shake every time we contemplate God in worship; nevertheless, this text clearly commands that response. Naturally, faith in God is requisite to fear (even as fear is a prerequisite to saving faith). If you do not clearly recognize God's powerful hand in creation, providence, and redemption, you will never come face-to-face with the reality of God's holiness and judgment such that you would respond in trembling. May God give us that vision of Himself.

2. We worship at His footstool, and we worship at His holy hill (verses 5 and 9). This speaks of our position in worship. Requiring both humility and reverence of us, the text forbids both intellectual pride in worship and excessive informality.

Modern worship tends to err in either direction. On the one hand, very smart seminary graduates sometimes take the opportunity to preen their brain feathers in their sermonizing. But the other trap is to create a worship environment geared to appeal to men by its informality. Man's entertainment, man's comfort, and man's affirmation are of highest importance to these folks, and they feel that God's love transcends His majesty and His holiness. Even in the New Testament we are reminded that acceptable worship is initiated by proper reverence and godly fear (Heb. 12:28).

Questions:

1. How many times does the Bible repeat a word or a phrase (not as a chorus, but successively iterated)? What constitutes vain repetition, at least from the record of biblical writers?

2. What is the overarching theme of this psalm?

3. What is God's "Name"? In what sense might the Psalmist refer to it as "great and terrible"?

4. How does God execute judgment and righteousness among His Own people?

5. What is the most primitive description of a true believer? (Hint: look as far back as the line of Seth.)

Family Discussion Questions:

1. Have we personally witnessed the vengeance of God against sin? Provide examples.

2. Are we cultivating reverence in our worship? How are we doing this? Is our church worship becoming more reverent or less reverent?

PSALM 100

Category: Praise ~ Occasion: Induction to Worship

Author: Unknown

1 Make a joyful noise unto the LORD, all ye lands.
2 Serve the LORD with gladness: come before his presence with singing.
3 Know ye that the LORD he is God: it is he that hath made us, and not we ourselves; we are his people, and the sheep of his pasture.
4 Enter into his gates with thanksgiving, and into his courts with praise: be thankful unto him, and bless his name.
5 For the LORD is good; his mercy is everlasting; and his truth endureth to all generations.

The Point:

Our hearts warm up with gladness and thanksgiving as we meditate on God's goodness and approach corporate worship with His people.

How do we feel in the recitation of this psalm?

We feel warm sentiments of joy, gladness, and gratitude. When we really feel the true import of the words, "God is good to us," we can't help but respond in joyful praise. In a world that is lost without truth, we have found the One we can trust Who is the very paradigm of truth Himself. In a world of terrible sin and condemning guilt, we receive mercy from the God of all mercy. We are comforted to know that we are God's sheep, and He guarantees for us His feeding, protection, and salvation from the enemies of our souls.

What does this psalm say?

Verses 1–2. As you have noticed, this study guide provides a categorization for every psalm (and there are many "Praise Psalms"). Nevertheless, this is the only psalm that comes with the title "A Psalm of Praise," which is provided, we assume, by the divine author.

The psalm begins with an invitation to the whole world to join in with glad praise to Yahweh God, the Creator of heaven and earth. This is in keeping with many other psalms (Ps. 67, 96:1, 97:1, 98:4, 99:1). This psalm is part of a cluster of these "international psalms." Our God is over the whole earth, and nothing short of the whole world giving Him glory and praise is appropriate. But this is more than a general call to worship God. This is a call for "joyful" worship and glad service to God. True believers will always be "glad" servants of the Lord God. In the Parable of the Talents told by Jesus, the fellow with the single talent was condemned to hell, but why? According to his own testimony, he buried the talent in the ground because he considered the Lord a hard and unreasonable Master, "reaping where he did not sow" (Matt. 25:14–30). It was his perception of the Master that produced such miserable, unfaithful service. If we are to provide glad service to our Lord, we must first begin with a right relationship with Him. If we think of God as a slave master or a harsh judge requiring something that we cannot possibly provide Him, our service will be that of a grudging slave and a wretched, damned soul. Surely, our God is not some exacting Master and harsh Judge Who "reaps where he does not sow." In truth, He is so merciful, longsuffering, and gracious that He sent His Son in order to pay the penalty for our sins and reconcile us to Himself! As this is the case, we have every reason in the world to worship Him with gladness and enter into His courts with singing. This is why merit-based salvation schemes are so dishonoring to God. They reduce millions of people to play the part of the miserable, unprofitable servant who was given a single talent.

Verse 3. The rest of the psalm gives good reasons for our joyful worship. First, we recognize God as our Creator. We look at our hands and know that God made them for us, so we gladly raise them in worship. We think about our minds and voices, and ask, "What kind of a God would have given us these good things?" So we raise glad voices and worship the God of all goodness with the most joyful words we can find!

Not everybody will worship the God Who made them because they are in sinful rebellion against Him. Those who gather to sing this psalm call themselves "the sheep of His pasture" (see also Psalm 95:7). They identify Jesus Christ as their Shepherd (Heb. 13:20), and they confess themselves to be His sheep. They trust that He knows what He is doing as He leads them through trials and tribulations. They submit themselves to His leadership. They receive His words of promise, encouragement, and rebuke through the reading and preaching of the Word. They listen carefully for His voice, knowing that He will one day lead them to glory.

Verses 4–5. Our joyful praise is also laced with words of gratitude and sentiments of thanksgiving. Continually, we recount the good things that He has done for us. We even interpret our trials as opportunities for growth. We see every good thing as a gift coming down from the Father of lights. Is there any other way to approach His courts? Sadly, there are some who discount God's goodness and instead focus on their suffering and misery. They enter into worship more focused on themselves than on God. They cannot see that every good gift is undeserved because they do not view their own condition from God's perspective. Their fundamental assumption is wrapped up in one simple statement, "I'm not that bad!" This is a fatally-flawed assumption. In actuality, if Adam's sinful progeny receive anything better than death and hell, they are recipients of something good from a God of mercy. If they are in God's fold and yet receive chastisement from His rod and staff, there is good comfort here as well (Ps. 23:4). This is our perspective.

How we perceive God will define our relationship with Him. When Charles Darwin's daughter Annie died, this tragedy profoundly affected his view of God. He "became more willing to proclaim his theories—and his religious doubts."[1]

1 http://www.npr.org/templates/story/story.php?storyId=100597929

Nine years later he published his famous book that redirected the entire world toward a godless naturalistic materialism. If a man cannot believe that God is good, he is in covenant rebellion against Him.

But for us, God's goodness is the great presupposition of our lives. We hang all our hopes on this basic assumption. Whatever difficulties come our way, we say, "God is good." Whatever crushing loss is suffered, God is good. Whatever blessing we receive, God is good. When things are at their worst, we are still holding to this great truth. When faced with the monumental problem of evil, we will not surrender our faith in God's goodness. God is good, and we are sinners. God has a morally acceptable reason for the evil in the world because He is good. But even more importantly, God's goodness provides a way of salvation for those who recognize God to be good! When sinners finally admit that they are sinners and beg for mercy on the basis of the goodness of God, they obtain mercy from an infinite store. We also recognize the goodness of God in providing us with His truth. We rely on the light of His truth to uncover our hypocrisies, self-deceptions, and sinful behavior. We need His truth to show us who we are, and then we cry out to Him for His mercy to deliver us from our sinful condition. Without God's truth *and* God's mercy we would be forever lost. We thank God that He reveals His truth to us, guides us to Christ's cross for everlasting mercy, and then leads us on our way by the same light of truth!

How do we apply this psalm to our lives?

1. Be grateful. Be grateful. Be grateful! The *sine qua non,* or the "essential characteristic," of the wicked is their ungratefulness (Rom. 1:21). They cannot see that God is good. They eat His food and enjoy His blessings, cursing His name and refusing to give thanks. May God by His mercy keep us from this foul ingratitude! Every day, let us thank our God from the heart for His good gifts, the chief of which is His redemption.

2. May our service and worship be filled with joy. Every single person in the world serves and worships something or somebody. Other people's gods make promises in glossy brochures which they give to their followers. But we know from the Bible's promises that service to the true and living God yields the most blessing. Such a God Who is good, gracious, and longsuffering, even to those who hate Him, is worthy of our joyful and enthusiastic service today and for the rest of our lives.

How does this psalm teach us to worship God?

This is a corporate psalm, a "we" psalm. "We" gather as God's people and call ourselves "God's sheep." We do this in unity and humility. Without humility and unity in the expression of corporate joy, there is no church. May the church learn to express joy together! As the Apostle exhorts us, "Rejoice with those who rejoice!" Too often, a third of the church comes to church rejoicing, a third of the church shows up in a grumpy mood, and a third is just disinterested and bored. The goal of the church is to learn to joyfully worship—in unison.

Questions:

1. Give several examples of "international" psalms that exhort the entire world to praise God.

2. What is unique about this psalm of praise in contrast with the other "Praise Psalms" we have identified in the Book of Psalms?

3. What was the perception of the servant with one talent in regards to his Master? What is the right perception we should have of our Master?

4. What reasons does the psalm give for joyfully worshiping God?

5. Who are the ones who can legitimately worship God, according to this psalm?

6. Is this a "we" psalm or a "me" psalm? What is the difference?

Family Discussion Questions:

1. How are we aware of God's goodness? Do we mention it very often? What part do we play in worship? Are we the joyful ones, the grumpy ones, or the disinterested ones?

2. Why should we be grateful to God? Give specific reasons, specific blessings for which our family should be grateful.

PSALM 101

Category: Faith ~ Occasion: Church Discipline

Author: David

1 I will sing of mercy and judgment: unto thee, O LORD, will I sing.
2 I will behave myself wisely in a perfect way. O when wilt thou come unto me? I will walk within my house with a perfect heart.
3 I will set no wicked thing before mine eyes: I hate the work of them that turn aside; it shall not cleave to me.
4 A froward heart shall depart from me: I will not know a wicked person.
5 Whoso privily slandereth his neighbour, him will I cut off: him that hath an high look and a proud heart will not I suffer.
6 Mine eyes shall be upon the faithful of the land, that they may dwell with me: he that walketh in a perfect way, he shall serve me.
7 He that worketh deceit shall not dwell within my house: he that telleth lies shall not tarry in my sight.
8 I will early destroy all the wicked of the land; that I may cut off all wicked doers from the city of the LORD.

The Point:

Though we live in a dangerous world filled with treachery and deceit, by faith we commit to opposing wickedness and walking circumspectly.

How do we feel in the recitation of this psalm?

You may feel like you are walking through a field of land mines. You wonder whom you can trust and how you will survive. The longer you live, the more you will learn that this is a dangerous world. Sometimes it is hard to know who to trust. Deceit and wickedness proliferate. Hypocrisy is everywhere, including in the human heart. If your own heart is untrustworthy, how in the world can you discern the hearts, intentions, and actions of others? With God's help, you must find the people of God, the faithful of the land, in order that you may "dwell" together with them. This is a song of commitment to honesty, moral integrity, and godliness.

What does this psalm say?

Verse 1. Mercy and judgment. Both are important, and both are real. Good men act justly in judgment and delight to show mercy. Since David is the author of the psalm, it is critical, in the right understanding of the psalm, to keep in mind that David is the King of Israel. Does David sing of God's mercy and judgment or his own? David probably speaks of his own, but he knows that his mercy and judgment are only replicas of the Original.

It is also important to note that David is singing of both mercy *and* judgment. To say that God only acts in mercy would be to present Him in the wrong light, for He must respect His own standard of justice even when He is merciful. Both the Old and New Testaments present ONE God Who acts in both mercy and judgment. His fiery wrath against the ungodliness of men is mentioned in Romans 1:16ff, Acts 17, Hebrews 13, and the Book of Revelation. But we also read of His mercy towards His people as well as His common mercy manifest when He sends rain "upon the just and the unjust."

David sings of mercy and judgment. If God is a God of mercy and judgment, then we will resonate with these elements of

His divine nature, exalt in them, and reproduce them in our actions. This is the theme of the rest of the psalm.

Verses 2–3. David continues the psalm with a set of four personal resolutions.

1. I will behave myself wisely in a perfect way.

2. I will walk in my house with a perfect heart.

3. I will set no wicked thing before my eyes.

4. I hate the work of them that turn aside. It will not cleave to me.

He commits himself to moral integrity first in his own heart and life and then in his family relationships. It is not uncommon for a man to act the "nice guy" in the public eye while living as a self-centered, immoral wretch before his family in his home. However, the true character of a man like this will eventually betray itself to his closest friends. His hypocrisies cannot be missed by those who know him best. That is why it is important that a man walks "in his house with a perfect heart."

With David, the true believer will make the commitment to not "set any wicked thing before my eyes." Does this contradict the Apostle Paul who finds all things lawful but not all things expedient? (1 Cor. 10:23) Of course, Paul refers to material things like food and drink in this passage. He is not encouraging any violation of the law of God (Rom. 6:1). The wicked thing David speaks of here in the Psalm would have to include idolatry, food offered to idols, and tempting influences that lead one into idolatry. Pornography, for example, leads many men into breaking God's commandments. It is a tempting influence. It speaks favorably of the breaking of God's laws. It encourages the shaming of one's neighbors, training men to exalt in the immodesty and shame of women. It presents immodesty, harlotry, and other violations of God's laws as something desirable and preferable. It invites a man into long-standing communion with the "unfruitful works of darkness." These symbols are everywhere, and they are powerful; we need to be aware of their influence. In our culture, clothing styles, icons, pictures, magazines, stories, and movies are often used as symbols, much like food offered to idols was in Acts 15:29 and 1 Corinthians 8:9–11. For example, during the latter half of the 20th century, an American company dedicated to producing licentious materials used a "bunny" to portray a fornicating "playboy" lifestyle. The identification of the black silhoutted figure of a rabbit with fornication was unmistakable to most people in Western, English-speaking nations. Of course, God-fearing Christians were hesitant to sport this symbol in their homes or on their persons. It is not that the symbol is sinful in itself. There is nothing wrong with a picture of a rabbit. Yet Christians should not be naive. We must be cognizant of what these symbols represent in the minds of ourselves and others.

Finally, David testifies to his hatred for the work of those who "turn aside." There will always be those whose walk proves to be false, wayward, and rebellious. They may be close relatives, friends, or neighbors. But as you watch them over the years, they swerve into this or that ditch. There is no keeping them on the straight and narrow because their hearts are fundamentally biased towards rebellion. Despite hundreds of hours of counseling, cajoling, warning, and rebuke, they are never convinced of truth and right. At length, godly families may have to separate from these influences in order to avoid taking on their habits of evil speaking, idolatry, or fornication. It may be wise to establish some boundaries and maintain some distance from these folks. When you see this rebellion within a family, it badly disrupts relationships especially when one part of the family is holding true to the Word of God. This is very common in the present day in the Western world, where tens of millions of people are right now in the process of apostasy against the Christian faith. Whole denominations are turning towards liberal humanist theologies or extremely destructive sins like homosexuality.

Yet from biblical records it is pretty clear that David himself did not "behave himself wisely in a perfect way." He is not alone. Regrettably, every Christian will be inconsistent to his own commitments until he is in a glorified state. While we live in a sinful world, only a life of contrition and repentance will indicate the true direction of a man's heart (reference Psalm 51). Spiritual maturity or "perfection" is the commitment of the heart of the godly man, and the important thing is that he lays out this commitment. If he never resolves anything in his heart, he will never press on to achieve it.

Verses 4–8. The remainder of the psalm follows the line of thinking contained in the fourth commitment in verse 3 ("I hate the work of them that turn aside; it will not cleave to me").

David disassociates from men who "turn aside." These men include the apostates, the divisive, or men who slander the reputations of their neighbors on the Internet or in other contexts. Disassociating from these men usually implies church discipline such as what Paul spoke of in 1 Corinthians 5. Though this process is painful and difficult, churches really have no choice in this. They must disassociate from people who make it their practice to defame others. Men and women who engage in slander are dangerous, and they upset the social order. Associations matter.

Verse 6 refers to the positive principle governing our associations. We must seek out the humble, faithful followers of Christ and associate with them. Wherever you live, whatever your station in life, you will always find the humble and the proud in and around your social situation. David's instructions are simple: look out for men and women who readily confess their sins to each other and are not caught up in academic pride, the pride of economic status, or the pride of political position, and associate with them. Associate with those who are ever and always aware of their needy position before God. They will cry out for His salvation on a daily basis, and they will prefer others before themselves.

If you find yourself surrounded by pride, slander, and rebellion, where do you turn? The solution to this predicament is found in verse 6. Find a faithful man, and keep your eye on him. Find a man who has walked the pilgrim pathway for thirty long years. Find a man, who is still humble, calling upon God for his salvation. He may not be rich or successful as the world sees it, but he is loyal to his brothers after all these years. He willingly confesses his sin and repents when he has done wrong. He still looks out for the needs of the widow and orphan. Commit to this man as a brother, and you will find the church of Jesus Christ.

Besides the sin of pride, the sin of deception may be the most devastating. If a brother will not be honest with himself or others, he will never come to true repentance. His deception will lead him to destructive ends as is seen in the case of Judas Iscariot and Absalom in the Scriptures.

The final verse might be taken by some as a little "extreme," since David commits to destroying all of the wicked in the land. Again, you should remember that David is a civil magistrate and is committed to God's system of justice, and therefore he is committed to God's definitions of right and wrong. Make no mistake; every time a murderer is put to death at the hands of the civil magistrate, the civil magistrate is destroying the wicked in the land. The word "destroy" may be interpreted "to cut off" or "to weaken" the influence of the wicked. Certainly, this should be the commitment of every influential leader in government, church, or business. Regardless of what happens in the higher positions of power, we want to see the powers of wickedness weakened in whatever purview God gives us— whether in home, business, or community. Hopefully, by the end of our lives we will look back at the small piece of the world in which we operated and find less wickedness and more righteousness!

Yet, it is not our responsibility to weed out every tare that grows among the wheat (Matt. 13:24–30). The Christian church does not believe in some sort of purifying Jihad, whereby all of the wicked are purged. Of course, murderers and rapists should be confined, executed, or extradited from a country here and there. But the major goal of the kingdom of God is not a political order whereby the sword is used liberally for every "sinner."

David ends the psalm with a reference to church discipline. When there are clear instances of "leavening" sin in the church of Christ, Paul encourages faithful churches to purge out the old leaven (1 Cor. 5:6) and to separate from brothers who are characterized by fornication, covetousness, idolatry, drunkenness, and slander (1 Cor. 5:11). Paul's commitment is the same as David's in the Old Testament. He calls for an actively engaged church leadership that is committed to cutting off evildoers from the City of God.

How do we apply this psalm to our lives?

1. Almost every word of this psalm has relevant application to our lives. All of us have fallen short of these particular commitments that David makes. Look back at verse 2. There is a quiet cry to God that He come to David's aid as he makes these commitments. Certainly, we cannot keep these commitments without God's aid, and cries of faith must always attend our commitments. For that matter, we cannot make a single commitment to do good without a constant reliance upon God for His grace to enable us.

2. The church is always beset by the proud, the deceptive, the slanderous, and the rebellious. There is no way to escape this inevitable challenge in a sinful world. Therefore, our leaders must be "on their game" all of the time. The church must be willing to disassociate or excommunicate as necessary, and the civil magistrate must not "use the sword in vain."

3. The psalm has relevant application to the individual as well. All of us should be wise in the associations we choose to cultivate. But what does a person do if the church refuses to discipline a steadfastly proud and divisive man, and he remains in the fellowship? In such a case it would come across as odd or divisive if individuals within the church community exercised their own private excommunications. This sort of thing could

result in a great deal of disorder in the church. Instead, you might moderate your associations with certain people. If you suspect a problem of pride in a brother, you have at least two options. You can overlook the problem, assume the best of your brother, and spend less time with him. Should you choose this approach, you opt for less relationship with him and thereby less obligation to his spiritual needs. Your second option is to get to know him better so that you can be in a position to correct him in the event that you find he is overcome by the sin of pride. Also, if you feel that you are spiritually immature in this area, it might be better to leave it up to an elder or one who is more qualified to correct the brother (Gal. 6:1).

How does this psalm teach us to worship God?

Making verbal resolutions or statements of commitment may serve well as an element of our worship of God. In fact, public and private worship can be the best place to commit our wills to the service of God our King. If we are engaging mind, emotions, and will in congregational worship, we should never walk out of the service with anything less than a renewed commitment to walk in obedience to our Lord. Otherwise, the worship service is nothing but empty words and emotions that may have felt good at the time but really did nothing to change the direction of our lives. God wants obedience more than sacrifice (1 Sam. 15:22) and our service more than empty promises (Matt. 21:28–32).

Questions:

1. What are the four resolutions David makes in the psalm?

2. How did David fail to behave himself in a perfect way? How does this reconcile with his commitment to do so?

3. What are the sins David uses to characterize the wicked man?

4. What is the duty of the civil magistrate in respect to the wicked?

5. What is the duty of church government in respect to the wicked?

Family Discussion Questions:

1. What are idols, symbols, pictures, or images that we might avoid bringing into our homes? Are there certain Internet websites we might avoid, for example?

2. How do we choose our associations? Are there times in which we should leave a church because of the associations?

3. Is life still dangerous for us? Do we live in a world of rebellion, deceit, slander, and pride? How might we get caught up in these things? Are we caught up in them now?

Psalm 102

Category: Faith ~ Occasion: Days of Humiliation

Author: Unknown

1 Hear my prayer, O LORD, and let my cry come unto thee.
2 Hide not thy face from me in the day when I am in trouble; incline thine ear unto me: in the day when I call answer me speedily.
3 For my days are consumed like smoke, and my bones are burned as an hearth.
4 My heart is smitten, and withered like grass; so that I forget to eat my bread.
5 By reason of the voice of my groaning my bones cleave to my skin.
6 I am like a pelican of the wilderness: I am like an owl of the desert.
7 I watch, and am as a sparrow alone upon the house top.
8 Mine enemies reproach me all the day; and they that are mad against me are sworn against me.
9 For I have eaten ashes like bread, and mingled my drink with weeping.
10 Because of thine indignation and thy wrath: for thou hast lifted me up, and cast me down.
11 My days are like a shadow that declineth; and I am withered like grass.
12 But thou, O LORD, shalt endure for ever; and thy remembrance unto all generations.
13 Thou shalt arise, and have mercy upon Zion: for the time to favour her, yea, the set time, is come.

14 For thy servants take pleasure in her stones, and favour the dust thereof.
15 So the heathen shall fear the name of the LORD, and all the kings of the earth thy glory.
16 When the LORD shall build up Zion, he shall appear in his glory.
17 He will regard the prayer of the destitute, and not despise their prayer.
18 This shall be written for the generation to come: and the people which shall be created shall praise the LORD.
19 For he hath looked down from the height of his sanctuary; from heaven did the LORD behold the earth;
20 To hear the groaning of the prisoner; to loose those that are appointed to death;
21 To declare the name of the LORD in Zion, and his praise in Jerusalem;
22 When the people are gathered together, and the kingdoms, to serve the LORD.
23 He weakened my strength in the way; he shortened my days.
24 I said, O my God, take me not away in the midst of my days: thy years are throughout all generations.
25 Of old hast thou laid the foundation of the earth: and the heavens are the work of thy hands.
26 They shall perish, but thou shalt endure: yea, all of them shall wax old like a garment; as a vesture shalt thou change them, and they shall be changed:
27 But thou art the same, and thy years shall have no end.
28 The children of thy servants shall continue, and their seed shall be established before thee.

The Point:

God has afflicted us and brought us low, so that we may see His eternal power and immutability and rejoice in the permanence of His church unto all generations.

How do we feel in the recitation of this psalm?

The range of emotions in this psalm is broad. It begins with a lonely, downcast saint who senses the opposition of enemies and the disfavor of God at the same time! Whatever the cause, his relationship with God is weak. But comfort for this poor man sweeps in as he contemplates the eternity and power of God. He draws great confidence and comfort from knowing that God will build a church, and the gates of hell will not prevail against it! As the focus shifts from himself to God and the people of God, he realizes that all is not in vain. He may not accomplish all that much in life that will abide into eternity, but there is comfort knowing that God has a project that will be brought to fruition!

What does this psalm say?

Verses 1–11. This is an unusual psalm since it moves back and forth between an individual psalm to a corporate psalm. The first eleven verses constitute the "me" psalm. Briefly, it reverts back to the personal testimony in verses 23 and 24, but the rest of the psalm may be classified as "we" material.

These are the days of humiliation for the psalmist. Nobody makes it through life on Cloud Nine, and that goes for every "great" man of faith who ever lived. Weeping, sackcloth, and ashes have become standard fare for this poor man. He is alone, oppressed, and miserable. At this point, his depression is so deep that he has lost his appetite, and he considers his life work as futile and purposeless. "My days are consumed like smoke, and my bones are burned as an hearth." Several times throughout this soliloquy, he refers to himself as "withered like grass."

Then in verse 10, he properly renders the source of his low state to the wrath and indignation of almighty God. At one point, this leader, pastor, or businessman was lifted up into a high position. Evidently, God saw fit to take him down into this present state of humiliation. Here is the difference between a true believer and an apostate. The true believer will acknowledge God as the source of all things (including the negative things that happen to him) and still maintain God's righteousness and goodness in it. He still cries out to God for salvation, though he knows this is the same God Who put him through the meat-grinder. In contrast, the proud atheist refuses to admit his own sinfulness and rebellion. He impugns God for the pain and suffering he experiences. His heart is filled with bitterness and hypocritical insincerity, and he asks, "How can a good God make me suffer like this? How can God be angry with someone as righteous as I?" The believer repudiates this foolishness. He knows that God maintains the absolute highest standards of righteousness and goodness, and He thus has every right to be angry with him.

Verse 12. Comfort seeps back into his soul as he contemplates the nature of God in contrast with his own frail, sinful, failing soul. The contrast is abrupt between the weak frailty of grass-like man and the everlasting permanence of God. While we are threatened on every side with destruction and death, God is truly above it all. His position cannot be undermined. His life cannot possibly dissipate.

The fading grass is soon forgotten. Nobody keeps historical records about every blade of grass that lived and died. Apart from God, we would all fade away and die in obscurity, and our lives would never amount to more than a hill of beans in the great scheme of things. But thanks be to God that there is a God Whose remembrance is retained unto all generations and Whose projects will retain eternal significance (because He remains throughout all generations.)

Verses 13–18. We are comforted to know that God will endure, but we are also comforted to know that something of His creation will endure as well. Men are frustrated when their great empires come to naught and their fortunes dry up. They want to believe that their lives and their work will be of some significance. But when men act alone, and when their projects are not God's project, they live in vain. God's project is His church, a people made up of Jews as well as Gentiles from every nation around the world. It is clear that the heart of the psalmist is entirely committed to this great project. All of his hopes, aspirations, and purposes hang on this worthy endeavor. Despite the fact that things are not going well for the psalmist personally, he still takes great comfort in God's commitment to Zion. He takes pleasure in her stones. He treasures the dust on the floors of this glorious edifice built by the living God!

In the year A.D. 2012, almost everybody in the entire world should have at least some vague awareness of the church of Jesus Christ. Two thousand years after Christ, the seven billion people on earth should be aware of the 2.1 billion people who call themselves Christians. Including nominal "believers," Christianity is the largest faith in the world, exceeding the #2 religion, Islam, which claims 1.5 billion adherents. The third largest religion is made up of self-proclaimed secularists (or Christian apostates) who number 1.1 billion.[2] Disregarding for a moment the fact that many have twisted biblical Christianity into their own pre-conceived ideas, and others are in the process of apostatizing away from the Christian faith, it is still amazing that so many want to associate with the name of Christ. The kingdom of God has come! Even religions like Islam and Mormonism are spin-offs from biblical Christianity. Many give lip service to the Bible, including the President of the United States. A quick survey of history shows a transformation of nations by the Gospel of Christ. In Ireland the human-sacrifices of the druids were overcome by the Gospel preaching of Patrick in A.D. 460; there are no public human sacrifices happening in Ireland today. The fear of Yahweh also fell upon the Germanic tribes when Boniface cut the great "sacred" oak tree of the pagans to the ground and built a Christian church out of it. Ancient records indicate that the Vikings in Iceland outlawed abortion around A.D. 1000, because they feared the name of Yahweh. Heathen cannibals from the South Seas received the Gospel of Christ under the indefatigable, courageous teaching

2 FN - http://www.adherents.com/Religions_By_Adherents.html

of the missionary John Paton in the 1890s. Over the centuries, the Lord has been building Zion, and the kings of the earth have seen the glory of Christ!

The kingdom of God, made up of the humble, prayerful worshipers of Yahweh, marches through time and geography—from century to century and continent to continent. On occasion, when we are faced with overwhelming discouragements in our own little world, we may forget this truth. But we need only to look at two thousand years of history, read these heartening verses before us, and know that the Lord *is* building Zion, and the gates of hell shall not prevail against it!

Verses 19–22. Our discouraged psalmist is hardly aware of his own condition any more as his focus remains upon God, His mercy, and His commitment to building Zion. Here he interprets what is going on in the earth from God's perspective. What God sees from heaven above is a world lost in sin, misery, and death. But God looks down and hears the groaning of the prisoner stuck away in the depths of some no-account dungeon. The situation feels utterly hopeless to the psalmist! As the man's life hangs by a mere thread, God enters the picture and releases him from his captivity so that he might "declare the name of the Lord in Zion!" This is an excellent picture of the church that gathers every Sunday to worship. We are the ones who have been released from captivity to shout His praise in Zion!

Verses 23–24. For just a brief moment, the psalmist reviews his case one last time. He points out that it was God who broke him down and weakened his strength, but there is no bitterness in his voice. Though at one point in time he might have been a powerful and influential man, perhaps a great preacher or a political leader, now he is a mere shadow of what he used to be. Even the great billionaires and the most powerful leaders on earth may contract Alzheimer's disease or lose the functions of their organs in their later years—and then they die. The humble believer refuses to grow bitter and angry against God. When life deals him these setbacks, he sees them as revealing the inherent weaknesses in the human frame. These things cause him to rely on God even more to make something of his life, extend his days, and provide the strength he needs to function day by day. As he experiences his own weaknesses, he can't help but contrast his finitude with God's infinitude. To contemplate God's eternity and power is enough to overwhelm his self-consciousness of his low condition.

Verses 25–28. These final verses contain some of the most astounding words in all of Scripture. Contrasting God's eternal and unchangeable existence with the temporal universe, the psalmist loses himself in these contemplations and forgets about his own finitude, demotions, and depression. The mountains have been around for a very long time. Stars have the capability of burning for billions of years. But these will perish. They will grow old like a ratty T-shirt that is tossed in the garbage and buried in the dirt. What a comfort it is to the saint to consider that God will never grow old! He will never develop wrinkles in His face or walk with a cane. When the sun, planets, moons, and stars cease to exist and must be re-formed into a new heavens and new earth, God is the same in His infinite power, wisdom, holiness, and goodness. It is only because God does not change and God is eternal that we can count on His promises and His kingdom enduring forever.

How do we apply this psalm to our lives?

1. When the church is broken down and weak in faith, how does a believer view this glorious project? While humanism compromises the truth, homosexuals control many mainline Christian churches, and pagans inherit towering cathedrals, a few faithful saints meet in warehouses and basements to worship God. How do the kings of the earth see the glory of God in this? Only through eyes of faith can the tender love of God for His church be seen. The glory of God's people is better evidenced in the faithful martyrs of China and Iran in the present day than it was when the towering edifices of the Middle Ages were built.

2. Salvation comes to us when we realize how small, weak, and sinful we really are in comparison with God's eternal power and goodness. Our confidence must be in His strength and in the endurance of His church forever. Of course, our desire is that we will play a part in this kingdom. But first we must believe in God and in His kingdom! And we must see our own poverty and weakness in order that we might seek God's salvation. "Blessed are the poor in the spirit for theirs is the kingdom of heaven" (Matt. 5:4).

3. There are no "lone wolf" Christians. Our comfort comes from knowing that God's kingdom is made up of a multitude of sinners just like us from all over the world. The "Elijah syndrome," which would complain that "I and I alone am left," is inappropriate for Christians. God will not fail with His project to build a kingdom in spite of internal compromises and external assaults on the faith. Let us not for a moment think that God's project is failing, but let us gain comfort from fellowship with other believers.

How does this psalm teach us to worship God?

Christian worship is not self-centered. It is God-centered, and this is where our comfort and joy lies. Even when we are downcast in emotional and physical distress, we still must worship. For a few moments we may consider our own condition, but the focus must always gravitate back towards God and His eternal existence. Worship relieves us of the bondage of self-consumption and returns our focus to God.

Questions:

1. Is this a "we" psalm or a "me" psalm? Explain.

2. Who brought the psalmist down to this low condition (as described in this psalm)?

3. What is the major contrast that comes back repeatedly in this psalm?

4. What is the comfort of the saint?

5. To what end does the Lord release the prisoner from his captivity?

6. Are there kings in the earth who are aware of the church of Christ? Name several kings or presidents to which this might apply.

7. Give several examples of Faith Psalms.

Family Discussion Questions:

1. What is our perspective of God's kingdom in history? Is it generally optimistic or pessimistic?

2. What are the things that comfort you when you are depressed? Is it comforting to be reminded that God cares for His church?

3. People die. Plants die. Our pet animals die. Does it help you to know that God will never die?

PSALM 103

Category: Praise ～ Occasion: Supremely Grateful Hearts

Author: Unknown

1 Bless the LORD, O my soul: and all that is within me, bless his holy name.
2 Bless the LORD, O my soul, and forget not all his benefits:
3 Who forgiveth all thine iniquities; who healeth all thy diseases;
4 Who redeemeth thy life from destruction; who crowneth thee with lovingkindness and tender mercies;
5 Who satisfieth thy mouth with good things; so that thy youth is renewed like the eagle's.
6 The LORD executeth righteousness and judgment for all that are oppressed.
7 He made known his ways unto Moses, his acts unto the children of Israel.
8 The LORD is merciful and gracious, slow to anger, and plenteous in mercy.
9 He will not always chide: neither will he keep his anger for ever.

10 He hath not dealt with us after our sins; nor rewarded us according to our iniquities.
11 For as the heaven is high above the earth, so great is his mercy toward them that fear him.
12 As far as the east is from the west, so far hath he removed our transgressions from us.
13 Like as a father pitieth his children, so the LORD pitieth them that fear him.
14 For he knoweth our frame; he remembereth that we are dust.
15 As for man, his days are as grass: as a flower of the field, so he flourisheth.
16 For the wind passeth over it, and it is gone; and the place thereof shall know it no more.
17 But the mercy of the LORD is from everlasting to everlasting upon them that fear him, and his righteousness unto children's children;
18 To such as keep his covenant, and to those that remember his commandments to do them.
19 The LORD hath prepared his throne in the heavens; and his kingdom ruleth over all.
20 Bless the LORD, ye his angels, that excel in strength, that do his commandments, hearkening unto the voice of his word.
21 Bless ye the LORD, all ye his hosts; ye ministers of his, that do his pleasure.
22 Bless the LORD, all his works in all places of his dominion: bless the LORD, O my soul.

The Point:

The contemplation of the mercy of God drives us to worship Him and bless His holy name.

How do we feel in the recitation of this psalm?

When we are overcome with a sense of the goodness of God, this is the psalm to sing. It is an effusive psalm that expresses unrestrained, heartfelt gratitude and praise in successive waves of joy. Our hearts are filled to the very brim with warm gratitude for God's never-failing mercies. By the end of the psalm, we are calling the angels together with the whole universe to praise Yahweh, the Lord.

What does this psalm say?

Verses 1–5. Since the word "blessing" or *barak* in the Hebrew, is used repeatedly in this psalm, it would be good to define it. To bless is to wish the very best for somebody or to declare that the person blessed is already occupying the blessed state. Things could not possibly go better for God. There is no way that He could improve His condition or His nature. What can man give to Him that He doesn't already have? (Rom. 11:35) That being the case, the best we can do is to declare God's state of blessedness. We exalt in God's perfections and use the most positive word we can find to indicate our approval and delight in God.

A blessing is also something that arises from the inner being of the soul—it is a strongly positive feeling towards another. Thus, the psalmist directs his soul to sound forth notes of rapturous praise to this all-blessed God. He nurtures feelings of praise to God from within his own soul. He calls every part of his inner being to the task when he says, "Let all that is within me bless His holy name!" There are various ways to distinguish the immaterial part of the man, but at the very least it includes his mind, his emotions, and his will.

What encourages the mind to initiate this praise is a remembrance of all the mercies, gifts, and benefits He bestowed upon us. As we catalog all that God has done for us, this realization presses us to reciprocate with our own blessings for Him. It is impossible to offer any thanksgiving or praise to God without constant meditation upon His good graces to us.

Verses 3 through 5 enumerate these blessings as God's merciful forgiveness, His healing, His redemption, and His lovingkindness and tender mercies. As believers, we know that God will heal all of our diseases and afflictions in His own time. This healing will not necessarily happen overnight, and we may have to wait until the final resurrection for our healing. In our lifetimes, we contract a hundred illnesses and injuries, yet somehow, by God's gracious provision, we regain strength again and again. It may not seem realistic that an 85 year-old man's youth will be "renewed like the eagle's," but this is our confident hope.

Verses 6–9. Now we move to the big-picture reasons why God is worthy to be praised. He is good to you and me, but He is also the God of perfect righteousness and judgment. In a world where there is no sovereign, righteous God ruling over all things, evil prevails and competing gods and tyrants battle it out forever and ever. But this is not our world or our worldview. Our God will execute perfect justice and make everything right, even to the point of vindicating every poor, unwanted child aborted in China and every persecuted saint who died in a feces tank in some dirty prison camp in North Korea.

"He made known his ways unto Moses, his acts unto the children of Israel." What we know about God comes from the history of the children of Israel recorded in the Old Testament, where we have records of His mighty works. When Israel witnessed these things at the Red Sea or in the Promised Land, they learned something of the nature and character of God. Other nations did not enjoy God's special attention from 2200 B.C. until A.D. 30. They were not privileged to witness God's supernatural works, and they did not have access to His special revelation.

All the blessings we enjoy come from a good God. His character is described in verses 8 and 9: He is "merciful and gracious." This gives us more reasons to bless God! He has been slow to anger with us. He does not always chastise us. Children are easily discouraged when their parents constantly correct them but seldom encourage them. This is not the way of our God. He maintains the perfect balance between correction and affection.

Verses 10–13. Returning the focus to the personal benefits we have received from the God of all lovingkindness and tender mercies, the psalmist takes a moment to speak of the forgiveness of sins. Without a doubt, this is the supreme blessing! It will take us an eternity to comprehend what God did for us when He forgave our sins in Jesus Christ. This complete absolution is beautifully described as a separation "as far as the heavens are from the earth, and as far as the east is from the west." God will not hold our sins against us.

Then, in one of the few passages in the Old Testament relating us to God as our Father, the psalmist describes God's feelings towards us. When a little four-year-old daughter contracts some horrible, painful disease and cries out to her father, it tears his heart. He would do anything to relieve the pain and ameliorate the effects of the disease. Would the God of all mercy, pity, and grace relate any differently to His children? Our relationship with the Father is only deepened by New Testament revelation, where there are one hundred times more references to God as our Father and us as His adopted children. Our father-son relationship with the Father is based in the Father's relationship with His Son, the Lord Jesus Christ.

All of this is predicated on a healthy fear of God. Many people do not see any need for forgiveness because they do not fear God or His judgment. They avoid thinking about His holiness and try to ignore His commandments as much as they can. They will never be forgiven. If they are too proud to beg for His forgiveness, they will never receive His mercy. The Lord pities those who fear Him.

Verses 14–16. The remainder of the psalm revisits the contrast made in Psalm 102 between the frailty of men and the eternality of God. For a moment men may forget their mortality as they strut around showing off their strength, power, and wealth. But constant reminders of their mortality flash into their minds as they drive past graveyards, attend funerals, contract diseases, and meet up with failure and disaster at every turn. Any work done without the Spirit of Christ, whether in economies, churches, or governments, will be consumed. It has no eternal value. It is good for us to admit our grass-like nature, and we can be comforted that God also knows we are grass!

Verses 17–22. We may be as grass, here today and gone tomorrow, but the mercy of the Lord is from everlasting to everlasting on them that fear Him. What encouragement we draw from this reminder of God's everlasting kindness to us! This grass will never wilt and die because God won't let it wilt and die. The reason He won't let it wilt and die is that He has made a covenant with this grass.

A marriage covenant includes certain expectations of a husband and wife, such as faithfulness to one another, and God's covenant is no different. What is it then to keep God's covenant? Basically, it is to walk with God in a close relationship, or as Christ put it, to "abide in the vine." Jesus said, "If you keep my commandments, you will abide in my love" (John 10:10). He practically quotes the Old Testament description of the covenant—in verse 18 of this Psalm—verbatim. Remaining in covenant with God must involve "remembering His commandments to do them." One must be careful not to take this to mean sinless perfection or a merit-based salvation. Rather, those who are regenerated by the power of the Holy Spirit will love the commandments of God and keep them. The word "keep" is used in our vernacular for "keeping a pet." When a child keeps a dog as a pet for several years, he comes to love the animal. He would know if it wandered off and was missing from the home for a day or two. The little boy might even place signs around the neighborhood alerting others to the missing pet. In a similar sense, the godly man keeps ten pets—the ten commandments of God. The covenant breaker is one who is taught the commandments of God as a child but soon lets the commandments wander away. After eight to ten years out of the home, we find him living in drunkenness, fornication, and debauchery. The commandments are as foreign to him as they were to the cannibals in New Guinea. "Whatever happened to the 7th commandment?" we ask him. He responds with a blank stare, then he laughs and says, "Oh, those old commandments?" It is plain that this man has not kept the commandments at all. He has forgotten about them. They are not even a consideration within his world. On the other hand, the godly man lives by these commandments. He takes them seriously. He is called to account for his obedience to these commandments and willingly confesses his sins when he falls short of them.

The psalm hits a majestic crescendo in the final verses, offering even more reasons to bless the Lord. God is the Ruler over the whole world. He carries ultimate authority over all, even though many will not recognize His rule. Having established God's position over the universe, the psalmist turns to the higher creation, higher than the earth and all of the rulers of the earth, and commands the angels to bless the Lord! Then he calls for all of the universe—the galaxies, the solar systems, the planets, the authorities on earth, the premier of China, all of the billions of people on earth, and all of the animal creation—to bless the Lord. Fittingly, he ends the psalm with the same call he used at the beginning, a personal directive to "bless the Lord, O my soul."

How do we apply this psalm to our lives?

1. God promises a generational blessing to our children's children, but only if we remember His commandments to do them. This repeats the addendum to the second commandment. "For I the LORD your God am a jealous God, visiting the iniquity of the fathers upon the children unto the third and fourth generation of them that hate me, and showing mercy unto thousands of them that love me, and keep my commandments" (Exod. 20:5–6). What more could fathers and mothers want out of life than God's blessing on a thousand generations after them? But it all begins when fathers and mothers remember the commandments and do them. Let us commit to keeping the commandments before us. If we post them on our walls, let us also walk in them by faith.

2. Before we keep His commandments, we must embrace the promises of God's forgiveness and salvation. To separate these

things produces a false conception of salvation that would be fatal. Only those who have been forgiven much will love much and keep His commandments (Luke 7:47–48). This psalm presents God as a merciful and forgiving God. If we accept this, then we may move on to verse 18 and keep His commandments.

3. There is warm gratefulness tucked into every word of this psalm. Does your heart become warm as you read these words? May God help us to internalize these words, that every cell in our body would render thanksgiving to God for His goodness to us!

How does this psalm teach us to worship God?

If everything that this psalm says about God is true, then He is worthy of our whole-hearted praise. Nothing less will do. We must call our minds, emotions, and wills to the task of this whole-hearted worship. Should a sermon on a Sunday morning delve into difficult biblical doctrines and go on for an hour or two, we should engage our minds with all that is in us. Our emotions should be connected to the singing of psalms and hymns as well. Some attend to the worship of God as if they were sitting in a seminary class. They do not engage their emotions. There are no tears of conviction or joy. There are never any hands raised in prayer and praise (1 Tim. 2:8). Seldom, if ever, do they shout over the victory of the resurrection of Christ! Emotions are almost entirely disengaged. Where there is no heart engaged, it will be unacceptable worship.

But what shall we say of the will? Endless lectures and emotionally-stimulated ceremonies are not enough for God. As he reminded King Saul, "To obey is better than to sacrifice." The real test of true, effective worship is what comes afterwards. If the will embraces the message, commits to more obedience and warmer service to God, and then actually follows through on repentance and obedience, then we have worshiped with everything that is in us!

Questions:

1. What are all the blessings God showers upon us, according to this psalm? Why should we bless God?

2. What does God expect of His people (reference verses 11, 13, 17, and 18)?

3. What does it mean to "keep the commandments of God"?

4. How does God compare to earthly fathers?

5. Give several examples of Praise Psalms.

Family Discussion Questions:

1. How do you know that you fear God?

2. How does this psalm comfort you?

3. Do we worship God with all that is in us? In what areas might we improve our worship?

PSALM 104

Category: Praise ~ Occasion: Walk Through the Woods

Author: Unknown

1 Bless the LORD, O my soul. O LORD my God, thou art very great; thou art clothed with honour and majesty.
2 Who coverest thyself with light as with a garment: who stretchest out the heavens like a curtain:
3 Who layeth the beams of his chambers in the waters: who maketh the clouds his chariot: who walketh upon the wings of the wind:
4 Who maketh his angels spirits; his ministers a flaming fire:
5 Who laid the foundations of the earth, that it should not be removed for ever.
6 Thou coveredst it with the deep as with a garment: the waters stood above the mountains.
7 At thy rebuke they fled; at the voice of thy thunder they hasted away.

8 They go up by the mountains; they go down by the valleys unto the place which thou hast founded for them.

9 Thou hast set a bound that they may not pass over; that they turn not again to cover the earth.

10 He sendeth the springs into the valleys, which run among the hills.

11 They give drink to every beast of the field: the wild asses quench their thirst.

12 By them shall the fowls of the heaven have their habitation, which sing among the branches.

13 He watereth the hills from his chambers: the earth is satisfied with the fruit of thy works.

14 He causeth the grass to grow for the cattle, and herb for the service of man: that he may bring forth food out of the earth;

15 And wine that maketh glad the heart of man, and oil to make his face to shine, and bread which strengtheneth man's heart.

16 The trees of the LORD are full of sap; the cedars of Lebanon, which he hath planted;

17 Where the birds make their nests: as for the stork, the fir trees are her house.

18 The high hills are a refuge for the wild goats; and the rocks for the conies.

19 He appointed the moon for seasons: the sun knoweth his going down.

20 Thou makest darkness, and it is night: wherein all the beasts of the forest do creep forth.

21 The young lions roar after their prey, and seek their meat from God.

22 The sun ariseth, they gather themselves together, and lay them down in their dens.

23 Man goeth forth unto his work and to his labour until the evening.

24 O LORD, how manifold are thy works! in wisdom hast thou made them all: the earth is full of thy riches.

25 So is this great and wide sea, wherein are things creeping innumerable, both small and great beasts.

26 There go the ships: there is that leviathan, whom thou hast made to play therein.

27 These wait all upon thee; that thou mayest give them their meat in due season.

28 That thou givest them they gather: thou openest thine hand, they are filled with good.

29 Thou hidest thy face, they are troubled: thou takest away their breath, they die, and return to their dust.

30 Thou sendest forth thy spirit, they are created: and thou renewest the face of the earth.

31 The glory of the LORD shall endure for ever: the LORD shall rejoice in his works.

32 He looketh on the earth, and it trembleth: he toucheth the hills, and they smoke.

33 I will sing unto the LORD as long as I live: I will sing praise to my God while I have my being.

34 My meditation of him shall be sweet: I will be glad in the LORD.

35 Let the sinners be consumed out of the earth, and let the wicked be no more. Bless thou the LORD, O my soul. Praise ye the LORD.

The Point:

As you meditate on God's intimate care for His creation, you respond in glorious, rejoicing praise before Him.

How do we feel in the recitation of this psalm?

As you take a bite out of a juicy peach, the rich flavors filling your mouth with delight and the juices dripping down your cheeks, your mind turns to the goodness of God. He made the peach, and He made your taste buds to enjoy the flavors of the peach. You must feel the goodness of God in the words of this psalm. In 35 verses, the psalmist will take you through the many instances of God's goodness in creation and providence, filling your mind with affectionate thoughts about a God Who is endeared to His creation. You respond in warm and glad gratitude to Him.

What does this psalm say?

Verses 1–5. The Bible does not present a god who is absent from his creation—a god the deists configured through the 1700s and 1800s. This attack on biblical orthodoxy from previous centuries was devastating to the Western Christian faith. First, they undermined the doctrine of creation with Darwin's evolutionary ideas, and then they undermined the doctrine of God's providential sovereignty. It is hard to know which was worse, but the average person today does not see God acting in history. He cannot see the fingerprints of God on every part of His creation. He does not see the little birds eating out of the hand of God or the gigantic planets directed by His omnipotent arm. This psalm stands in direct opposition to this way of thinking.

The psalmist rouses his own soul to bless Yahweh because He is very great. Quickly, he moves from the majestic nature of God Himself to the creation of the universe. From the outset, God is to be worshiped because He is the Creator of all things. First, He created light; then He stretched out the universe and filled it with stars. He created the angels and laid down the footers (or the foundations) of the earth.

God is presented here as the source of all reality. While most believers would render tacit assent to that statement, this truth does not sink into the fiber of their very being. Many have a hard time making out God's fingerprints on His creation. They look at the stars and simply see stars. They do not see God's fingerprints *on* the stars.

Did you know there are hurricanes on Neptune that blow at 1,500 miles per hour? Jupiter's major storm covers an area three times the size of our planet. Its forces exceed that of a nuclear bomb 100,000 times over. These violent "natural" forces would wipe out life on earth in a short ten minutes. But God rides on these storms like a cowboy who retains complete control over a bucking bronco.

Verses 6–9. Having established God's active involvement in the creation of the world, the psalmist addresses the next major event in history: the worldwide flood. This event is so important that every culture around the world still recognizes it in their language, folklore, and celebrations, though it is largely ignored by the proud humanist empires of the present day thanks to the high priests of the scientific community who have spent the last hundred years using futile uniformitarian assumptions to explain why sea fossils are found on the highest mountains.

In verse 5, we read that God formed the dry land (or "earth").. This had to have been a major geological event in the history of the world. Some of the fundamental structures of the earth's crust were formed at that time. But then in verse 6, God covers this dry land again with the waters "as with a garment." According to Genesis 7, the waters covered the highest mountains by about 24 feet, which would have allowed the ark to float over them without running aground.

What we see today in oceans, rivers, mountains, and valleys are mostly the geological formations produced by the worldwide flood. The psalmist plainly attributes these formations to God's intentional actions. Waterways were established by the flood, including the Colorado River which winds its way through the Grand Canyon in Arizona. There are deep valleys at the bottom of the ocean, probably formed before or during the flood. God fully intended for the ocean waters to fill these great trenches and valleys.

The ninth verse guarantees a "uniformitarian" condition until the end of the world. These waters will never again turn to cover the earth because of God's covenant promise to Noah. The ungodly have based their science on uniformitarian assumptions, claiming that the same scientific laws that govern biology, the environment, physics, etc., applied yesterday as much as they do today. But they have no basis for making such a claim! Our firm basis for science and dominion is found in Genesis 8:21–22. We hold to these uniform conditions because God made that promise directly after the flood. Our science is based solidly upon our faith in God's Word.

Verses 10–23. After addressing God's hand in creation and the flood, the psalmist declares God's providential involvement in the day-to-day operations of His creation. For the next fourteen verses, he lists the many, many blessings God pours out upon His world. All of life on the Earth is dependent upon water. This is the most basic natural resource. Plants, animals, and human beings could not possibly survive without water. If there were no water, there would be no banks, no human governments, no universities, and no economies. We would all be dead. Hence, the psalmist rightly acknowledges God's hand in providing the springs in the valleys that run among the hills, feeding man and animal alike.

Verse 15 gives the three uses of herbs, food, and drink, all of which God brings about by watering the fields that grow the crops. These plants provide wine that gladdens the heart as well as medicines and grains that provide health and strength for the body. Think of all God has done to sustain life on Planet Earth! Each and every need is provided for by the mercies of God.

To this day, most of the trees in the world were not planted by man. How did the trees in the forests of the Amazon get there? Since we reject the idea that things happen by random, purposeless chance, we must ask this question every time we wander through a forest. Who could have possibly planted all of these trees, and for what purpose? Our God of all goodness also creates a suitable habitat for the birds, the rock badgers, and the wild goats; the moon and sun contribute to this habitat (verses 19–23). Animals use their habitats and the darkness of night to protect themselves from their predators. God creates this magnificent habitat because it is His world and He loves His world. On several occasions, men have tried to create balanced, self-sustaining ecosystems—but without any real success. This should give us cause to glory in the great achievements of God in nature!

Verses 24–32. Moving from the works of God upon the earth to the other half of the creation, the next section of the psalm addresses God's providential care over the oceans. Where man can hardly survive in ships on the waves, God has created whales and other sea creatures that survive and thrive in the great waters! If you watch the fish for any length of time, you can see that they are almost constantly eating or searching for food. Again, it is God Who provides trillions of these creatures with sufficient food to sustain life.

Although the fall brought death to the animal kingdom as well as to man, God continues to replenish the earth with new life every single day. Every new life, every baby fish and baby bird derives its existence from the Spirit of God. From this we can see that God is no deist god. He is constantly engaged and intimately involved in His marvelous creation—down to every square inch of it! His involvement extends to every instance of death as well. At the moment that He chooses to withhold His breath of life, an animal here or there dies. As we consider the works of God's hands, we must cry out with the psalmist, "O LORD, how manifold are your works! In wisdom you have made them all: the earth is full of your riches!"

God's glory as revealed in Himself and His creation is an eternal reality, and the Lord also rejoices in His works. These works are seen throughout our solar system. For example, astronomers have discovered a huge volcano the size of Arizona on the planet Mars. Thankfully, the Lord chose not to put a gigantic, destructive force like this on our planet, so He chose a different planet to manifest His power and glory in such a spectacular way. The largest atom bombs created by man yield only a fraction of a percent of the power seen in God's great works. Why would He place great volcanoes on Io (one of Jupiter's moons) and on the planet Mars? Verse 31 tells us that He rejoices in His own works.

Verses 33–35. Having laid down a million reasons to glorify and worship our Creator God, the psalmist ends his song with a personal commitment to spend the rest of his life singing the praises of God. In fact, this is what he enjoys! The godly man always gravitates back to meditating upon God and rejoicing in Him.

The last verse may seem incongruous and out of order with the rest of the psalm. But when a man addresses God from the context of a sinful world filled with wicked men, it is good and proper for him to distinguish himself as a lover of righteousness. God has created the world, but God's world has been contaminated by sin through man's doing. How does the godly man view this terrible blight on God's creation? He greatly desires that the wicked will be purged from the earth— either by the blood of Christ or by the flames of hell.

How do we apply this psalm to our lives?

1. After studying this psalm, you should forever look at the world around you differently. When you view nature, you are witnessing the millions and millions of purposeful actions of the providential Sustainer of all things. Although it is easy to revert back to viewing the world as purely materialistic forces and objects, you should always use the eyeglasses of God's Word. Interpret everything through the lenses of God's Word, and you will begin to see God's fingerprints on everything!

2. The mere consideration of a creation without a Creator is dull and meaningless. However, meditating on God's Word and God's works makes everything around us shine in bright colors. Optimistic hope for the future sweeps back into our souls. These are sweet meditations, and they produce a heart of gratitude and warm blessings for the all-blessed God.

How does this psalm teach us to worship God?

1. Much of our worship begins with a contemplation of the works of God—works that unfold everyday in nature! This is a good way to enter into worship. Once we see God the Creator and Providential Sustainer working around us here and now, then we turn and praise Him for His redemptive work in history (which we did not witness with our eyes). If we can believe that God's hand is in everything around us, then we can also believe His Word concerning the plan of redemption that came about through His Son on the cross 2,000 years ago. If

we interpret our experience by means of God's Word here and now, then we will also interpret what happened 2,000 years ago by that same Word.

2. A commitment to righteousness and an opposition to wickedness are part and parcel of all godly worship. The final verse in this grand psalm witnesses to this. Practically every worship service should draw the line between righteousness and wickedness and press for commitment on the part of the worshipers. Is it your desire to eventually see Sodom wiped off the map? Some in our worship services will play the part of Lot's wife who looked back at the smoking city because she really didn't want to leave the city. Because of her lack of commitment to God's righteous agenda, He turned her into a pillar of salt.

Questions:

1. What act(s) of God formed the geological surface of the earth?

2. As Christians, what is our basis for science?

3. What do we need to sustain life here on earth?

4. How is God involved every day in the life of the animal kingdom?

5. Why did God put the volcanoes on Io and Mars?

6. What are the similarities between Psalms 103 and 104?

7. Give several examples of Praise Psalms.

Family Discussion Questions:

1. Do you find meditation upon God and His works a sweet blessing to you? What are some recent meditations from God's creation and God's Word that have given you great encouragement lately?

2. How is our view of nature different from the unbeliever's? As we study astronomy, physics, chemistry, or biology, do we experience the wide-eyed wonder of the child discovering His Father's amazing creations? Over time, do we experience more wonder or less wonder at God's creation?

Psalm 105

Category: Didactic ~ Occasion: Teaching History

Author: David

1 O give thanks unto the LORD; call upon his name: make known his deeds among the people.

2 Sing unto him, sing psalms unto him: talk ye of all his wondrous works.

3 Glory ye in his holy name: let the heart of them rejoice that seek the LORD.

4 Seek the LORD, and his strength: seek his face evermore.

5 Remember his marvellous works that he hath done; his wonders, and the judgments of his mouth;

6 O ye seed of Abraham his servant, ye children of Jacob his chosen.

7 He is the LORD our God: his judgments are in all the earth.

8 He hath remembered his covenant for ever, the word which he commanded to a thousand generations.

9 Which covenant he made with Abraham, and his oath unto Isaac;

10 And confirmed the same unto Jacob for a law, and to Israel for an everlasting covenant:

11 Saying, Unto thee will I give the land of Canaan, the lot of your inheritance:

12 When they were but a few men in number; yea, very few, and strangers in it.

13 When they went from one nation to another, from one kingdom to another people;

14 He suffered no man to do them wrong: yea, he reproved kings for their sakes;

15 Saying, Touch not mine anointed, and do my prophets no harm.

16 Moreover he called for a famine upon the land: he brake the whole staff of bread.

17 He sent a man before them, even Joseph, who was sold for a servant:

18 Whose feet they hurt with fetters: he was laid in iron:

19 Until the time that his word came: the word of the LORD tried him.

20 *The king sent and loosed him; even the ruler of the people, and let him go free.*

21 *He made him lord of his house, and ruler of all his substance:*

22 *To bind his princes at his pleasure; and teach his senators wisdom.*

23 *Israel also came into Egypt; and Jacob sojourned in the land of Ham.*

24 *And he increased his people greatly; and made them stronger than their enemies.*

25 *He turned their heart to hate his people, to deal subtilly with his servants.*

26 *He sent Moses his servant; and Aaron whom he had chosen.*

27 *They shewed his signs among them, and wonders in the land of Ham.*

28 *He sent darkness, and made it dark; and they rebelled not against his word.*

29 *He turned their waters into blood, and slew their fish.*

30 *Their land brought forth frogs in abundance, in the chambers of their kings.*

31 *He spake, and there came divers sorts of flies, and lice in all their coasts.*

32 *He gave them hail for rain, and flaming fire in their land.*

33 *He smote their vines also and their fig trees; and brake the trees of their coasts.*

34 *He spake, and the locusts came, and caterpillers, and that without number,*

35 *And did eat up all the herbs in their land, and devoured the fruit of their ground.*

36 *He smote also all the firstborn in their land, the chief of all their strength.*

37 *He brought them forth also with silver and gold: and there was not one feeble person among their tribes.*

38 *Egypt was glad when they departed: for the fear of them fell upon them.*

39 *He spread a cloud for a covering; and fire to give light in the night.*

40 *The people asked, and he brought quails, and satisfied them with the bread of heaven.*

41 He opened the rock, and the waters gushed out; they ran in the dry places like a river.
42 For he remembered his holy promise, and Abraham his servant.
43 And he brought forth his people with joy, and his chosen with gladness:
44 And gave them the lands of the heathen: and they inherited the labour of the people;
45 That they might observe his statutes, and keep his laws. Praise ye the LORD

The Point:

When teaching history lessons, true believers will teach God's redemptive plan and surround the teaching with worship.

How do we feel in the recitation of this psalm?

We are both thrilled and comforted to know that God is constantly working in, about, and through the great empires of men in order that He might nurture and grow a kingdom that will never die. He usually works behind the scenes surreptitiously, such that the ungodly have no idea what is going on! We cannot help but rejoice in God's sovereign control over all things and look forward to the inevitable success of His kingdom. Many powerful kingdoms that are built by men come and go, so there is very little that the proud humanists can say about their accomplishments. However, we Christians have one grid through which we view history, and that is what is found here in this psalm.

What does this psalm say?

Verses 1–5. It may seem strange to present this psalm as a history lesson, but that is the basic content of 39 out of the 45 verses. If any of God's people ever teaches history in public schools, private schools, or home schools, he would do well to use the inspired presentation in this psalm as a pattern! This is how it is done.

We open the history lesson with worship. This is the only proper way to talk about history because the study of history is the study of God's hand in man's reality. To ignore God in history is not only disingenuous and blasphemous, but it also ignores the "elephant in the room," especially since we know that God is the primary cause in the events of history. Thus, it should be a given that we approach history with thanksgiving and praise. Why not sing psalms to Him in the middle of a history class? Most academic institutions today would laugh at the incongruity of such an idea. What does worshiping God have to do with the academic pursuits of the minds of men? Why should men, who are used to worshiping their own minds, fall on their faces and worship the Wisdom of God? Modern man celebrates his own scientific and academic accomplishments, but he does not see that God has much to contribute to his truth and reality.

But we are commanded to study history and make known His deeds among the people. History is a required subject for every one of our children because it is the study of the wondrous works and mighty deeds of God. We would not think of teaching about the Egyptian pyramids and the feats of Alexander without referring to the judgments of God upon Egypt and Greece.

While the line of Cain builds its cities and empires, God's people are distinguished as those who "call upon His name." This is what marked the line of Seth at the beginning. They perpetually seek after God (verses 3–4). They strive to walk with Him, and they continually cry out for His salvation in faith. They refuse to forget the great works of God in history.

Verses 6–11. History is all about God's people. Those secularists who present history without God's covenant people taking a central position in the story are giving a false view. After the flood God focuses in on one of the descendants of Noah with whom He wants to establish a covenant relationship. While Egypt was building its empire, one solitary man down in Canaan was building a family altar to the Creator of heaven and earth. The Book of Genesis centers around this man and his posterity because Abraham's story is the only significant story for the first 3,000 years of human civilization on earth. Even those of us grafted into the Old Testament church find our spiritual roots in Abraham (Gal. 3:6–9, 29). What a blessing it is to be of this seed and enjoy the blessings, privileges, and salvation of the God of all history!

When an honorable husband makes a marriage covenant with his wife, he will hold true to that covenant no matter what happens. Would God be any less true to the covenant He makes with men? Not a chance! What would it take for a faithful man to break covenant with his wife? Well, God is a thousand times more faithful to His covenant than the most faithful husband who ever lived. God never walked away from His covenant. The Israelites may have hardened their necks now and then in history, but there was never a time in which there was not some remnant that carried on the heritage and the faith of Abraham.

The covenant promise included land, specifically a small portion of the earth on the eastern side of the Mediterranean Sea. It wasn't much land in comparison to the rest of the earth. But it would belong to the people of God, representing a down payment of what was to come. God's blessings are tangible and temporal as well as eternal and spiritual.

Verses 12–24. Throughout history, there have always been two cities and two kingdoms on this earth. They are the City of God and the City of Man. These two cities weave in and out of each other as they work their way through time. For some reason, God chose to work through a very small number of people after the flood. When God called Abraham out of his father's country, it was a new start for Abraham. Today, it would be like God calling a man from China to go to America, promising him the entire eastern seaboard for his inheritance. This man had no right to the land. He had no children, initially. He had no contacts, no influence, and no property of his own. But the Creator of the Universe picked Abraham to be His man, and that is all that mattered. It did not matter that Abraham was surrounded by warring kings, anarchical bands, and the great and proud empire of Egypt because several times God reproved kings who might have taken advantage of Abraham's family. Amidst thousands of wars, massacres, murders, and revolutions that occurred between 2000 B.C. and 1400 B.C. in the breadbasket of civilization, one family was immune from all of it. They enjoyed God's special protection for 600 years. History centers around the people of God. The heathen will rage. The kingdoms are disestablished. But God is in the midst of His people through every era of history.

God's sovereignty is evident again in verse 16 when He calls for a famine in the land of Egypt. For what purpose did He shake the largest empire in the world to its very core? Surely it must have been to provide a context for His people in which they would be protected, tested, enslaved, and delivered in the most spectacular way!

The story of Joseph follows in verses 17 through 22. Never mind that what is happening in Egypt is the development of the proud empire of Egypt's Middle Kingdom. Millions of people lived and died in Egypt from 2000 B.C. through 1400 B.C., but none of that matters in the scheme of things because what really matters is the story of Joseph. God delights in testing His man to humble him in some no-account Egyptian prison, and then He promoted him to the highest position in the land. God preserved Egypt through the famine mainly because He intended to preserve His people in the land of Egypt for 400 years. For a long time the Egyptians ignored this ratty group of sheepherders down in Goshen. But this despised lot was the City of God, and within a few generations these people grew into a significant, noticeable people group even stronger than their enemies, the Egyptians.

Verses 25–38. When the people of God are weak and insignificant, the City of Man will ignore them. But, if they gain numbers and strength, inevitably their enemies will turn on them. Still, all of this is within the sovereign purposes of

God. It may be hard to understand it or reconcile it, but verse 25 states clearly that God turned the heart of Pharaoh and his people against the children of Israel. The heart of the king is in the hand of God, and He turns it wherever He wishes (Prov. 21:1). In the Book of Exodus, Moses presents the tension in clear terms. Pharaoh hardened Pharaoh's heart *and* God hardened Pharaoh's heart. Two causes work simultaneously. God sovereignly ordains, while man is still morally responsible for his own hardness of heart.

As the psalmist continues with the story, God torments the land of Egypt. For their nationalistic pride, their refusal to worship and serve the true God, and their opposition to the people of God, they received the worst series of plagues any nation has ever encountered in one time period in human history. He broke the back of Egypt by killing all of the firstborn males in the land. Typically, the firstborn represents the strongest of the offspring, the one with the most potential to carry on the empire in the succeeding generation. No wonder that Egypt was glad to see the people of God leave in the end.

Verses 39–45. The story of God's redemptive work in His people concludes with a full review of His provision for them through the wilderness and all the way to the promised land. He delivered His people from Egypt, and then He gave them the cloud, the fire, and food and drink along the way. This prefigures exactly the pattern of our redemption, for God delivers us from the Egypt of our sin, baptizes us in the Red Sea, makes us part of His church, provides us with the spiritual food of the Lord's Table, and gives us direction and guidance along the way. Paul draws these comparisons in 1 Corinthians 10:2–4 and 16–17, contrasting the communion of the bread and the cup with the manna and water in the wilderness.

This history lesson ends with a word of application and an exhortation to worship. These are two critical elements in the education of a child. First of all, God expects us to integrate our knowledge into life. If knowledge does not proceed to life application, it is worthless to us. The last two verses explain why God went to all the trouble of saving them from Egypt. It was in order that His people might observe His statutes and keep His laws. Likewise, this is God's intention for His people today. Christ died that we might live for Him (2 Cor. 5:15), that He might purify a peculiar people who are zealous of good works (Titus 2:14), and that we might love Him and keep His commandments (John 14:21, 15:10; 1 John 5:2–3).

How do we apply this psalm to our lives?

1. History is about the people of God. What you have studied in this psalm will never be taught in the world history high school classes controlled by the City of Man since unbelievers never want to acknowledge the wickedness of Egypt and the centrality of God's people in history! But, as you watch world events play out, keep an eye on the church of Jesus Christ, Who is the Son of David and the fulfillment of the Abrahamic covenant.

2. This story is His Story, but it is also our story! By faith, we identify with this great story of redemption from the Old Testament. By faith we believe that God will provide us with everything we need to make it to the Promised Land, even though we are only about halfway through the wilderness journey ourselves.

3. Nations will be held accountable for the way they treat the people of God. Remember that the people of God are those who fear the true and living God and look to Him for salvation through Christ. Any "secular" nation that persecutes God's people and refuses to serve the living Christ, the Son of David, the King of kings and Lord of lords; will be destroyed. This even includes nations that have the "blessing" of the United Nations. Let us pray that our nation will serve the living Christ.

How does this psalm teach us to worship God?

1. We must not separate worship from the rest of life. There are some who feel uncomfortable with kneeling in the middle of a

history class and worshiping the sovereign Lord of history. But this should to happen from time to time when true believers teach history. You will notice in this psalm that there is praise and worship before and after the history lesson. To present God as separate from history is to teach our children the wrong view of history and the wrong view of reality.

2. Worship includes a survey of redemptive history from time to time. This does not mean that worship and preaching is entirely made up of "redemptive history." A few of the psalms really do cover the history of God's redemption, and we need to do the same thing from time to time in our worship.

Questions:

1. Why should we teach history to our children?

2. What are the "bookends" for the psalm (how does the psalm begin and end)?

3. Whose idea was it to bring a famine to the land of Egypt? Why did He do it?

4. What does God do with kings who threaten His people?

5. How would a Christian teach about the feats of Alexander and the pyramids of Egypt?

6. What did God do for His people, according to this psalm?

7. Give several examples of Didactic Psalms.

Family Discussion Questions:

1. What is the "City of Man," and how do we relate to it? Do we see God's hand of protection upon our lives as we walk through this city?

2. How do you identify with the story of redemption? What has God done for you?

PSALM 106

Category: Didactic ～ Occasion: Corporate Rebellion

Author: Unknown

1 Praise ye the LORD. O give thanks unto the LORD; for he is good: for his mercy endureth for ever.

2 Who can utter the mighty acts of the LORD? who can shew forth all his praise?

3 Blessed are they that keep judgment, and he that doeth righteousness at all times.

4 Remember me, O LORD, with the favour that thou bearest unto thy people: O visit me with thy salvation;

5 That I may see the good of thy chosen, that I may rejoice in the gladness of thy nation, that I may glory with thine inheritance.

6 We have sinned with our fathers, we have committed iniquity, we have done wickedly.

7 Our fathers understood not thy wonders in Egypt; they remembered not the multitude of thy mercies; but provoked him at the sea, even at the Red sea.

8 Nevertheless he saved them for his name's sake, that he might make his mighty power to be known.

9 He rebuked the Red sea also, and it was dried up: so he led them through the depths, as through the wilderness.

10 And he saved them from the hand of him that hated them, and redeemed them from the hand of the enemy.

11 And the waters covered their enemies: there was not one of them left.

12 Then believed they his words; they sang his praise.

13 They soon forgat his works; they waited not for his counsel:

14 But lusted exceedingly in the wilderness, and tempted God in the desert.

15 And he gave them their request; but sent leanness into their soul.

16 They envied Moses also in the camp, and Aaron the saint of the LORD.

17 The earth opened and swallowed up Dathan and covered the company of Abiram.

18 And a fire was kindled in their company; the flame burned up the wicked.

19 They made a calf in Horeb, and worshipped the molten image.

20 Thus they changed their glory into the similitude of an ox that eateth grass.

21 They forgat God their saviour, which had done great things in Egypt;

22 Wondrous works in the land of Ham, and terrible things by the Red sea.

23 Therefore he said that he would destroy them, had not Moses his chosen stood before him in the breach, to turn away his wrath, lest he should destroy them.

24 Yea, they despised the pleasant land, they believed not his word:

25 But murmured in their tents, and hearkened not unto the voice of the LORD.

26 Therefore he lifted up his hand against them, to overthrow them in the wilderness:

27 To overthrow their seed also among the nations, and to scatter them in the lands.

28 They joined themselves also unto Baalpeor, and ate the sacrifices of the dead.

29 Thus they provoked him to anger with their inventions: and the plague brake in upon them.

30 Then stood up Phinehas, and executed judgment: and so the plague was stayed.

31 And that was counted unto him for righteousness unto all generations for evermore.

32 They angered him also at the waters of strife, so that it went ill with Moses for their sakes:

33 Because they provoked his spirit, so that he spake unadvisedly with his lips.

34 They did not destroy the nations, concerning whom the LORD commanded them:

35 But were mingled among the heathen, and learned their works.

36 And they served their idols: which were a snare unto them.

37 Yea, they sacrificed their sons and their daughters unto devils,

38 And shed innocent blood, even the blood of their sons and of their daughters, whom they sacrificed unto the idols of Canaan: and the land was polluted with blood.

39 Thus were they defiled with their own works, and went a whoring with their own inventions.

40 Therefore was the wrath of the LORD kindled against his people, insomuch that he abhorred his own inheritance.

41 And he gave them into the hand of the heathen; and they that hated them ruled over them.

42 Their enemies also oppressed them, and they were brought into subjection under their hand.

43 Many times did he deliver them; but they provoked him with their counsel, and were brought low for their iniquity.

44 Nevertheless he regarded their affliction, when he heard their cry:

45 And he remembered for them his covenant, and repented according to the multitude of his mercies.

46 He made them also to be pitied of all those that carried them captives.

47 Save us, O LORD our God, and gather us from among the heathen, to give thanks unto thy holy name, and to triumph in thy praise.

48 Blessed be the LORD God of Israel from everlasting to everlasting: and let all the people say, Amen. Praise ye the LORD.

The Point:

God's people exhibited a constant pattern of rebellion in the Old Testament, but there was always a remnant among them who cried out for His salvation.

How do we feel in the recitation of this psalm?

We are horrified by the constant rebellion of a wicked, undeserving people and struck in wonder at the steadfast patience of God through it all. As in the case of the wife who has committed adultery a hundred times over and continues to receive her husband's forgiveness, we wonder why God doesn't just remove His favor from these people once and for all. We are also taken by sadness because we come to realize that this rebellious people is our people; this wayward church is our church. Then we end the psalm with a cry of faith, hoping that God will have mercy upon us even as He destroys those individuals who are steadfast in their rebellion.

What does this psalm say?

Verses 1–5. As this psalm unfolds, it contrasts the unfaithfulness of the people of God with the faithfulness of the covenant-keeping God. But for now the faithfulness of God sets the tone of the psalm. His everlasting, merciful character is rooted in His goodness and His power. God is good and God is great. How can we praise God and give Him thanks if we do not have a deep sense of these wondrous attributes? It seems this psalm may be contiguous with the previous one, for the psalmist is still reeling from his contemplations concerning the mighty acts of God. "Who can utter the mighty acts of the Lord?" Who is worthy to sing His praises with words and sentiments that fit the occasion?

As the psalmist is about to describe the unfaithfulness of God's people in the Old Testament, he takes the opportunity to call out for the mercy of God upon himself. Corporate rebellion in the church will bring the faithful remnant to the surface. That's why this psalm is couched in individualistic language. Perhaps the psalmist feels like an island of faithfulness in a sea of rebellion.

To be part of the covenant body of the church is important. God's blessings usually flow in the direction of His covenant people, and the psalmist wants to be caught up in that flow (see verse 4). "Remember me, O Lord, with the favor you bear unto your people!" Those who receive the blessings are those who love God and have respect for His commandments (verse 3). They are the ones whom God visits with His salvation (verse 4).

Verses 6–11. Now the psalm turns from the individual perspective (the "me" psalm) to the corporate perspective (the "we" psalm). Together the people of God confess their corporate sins, which are rooted in ancient times (yet seem to return from generation to generation). Sin has a cancerous element to it. Therefore, the psalmist says, "We have sinned with our fathers; we have committed iniquity."

What more spectacular event could you find anywhere in history than what we find in Israel's deliverance out of the hand of the great Egyptian empire? The ten plagues, the parting of the Red Sea, and the destruction of Pharaoh's armies were eye-popping, incomparable acts of God. Yet the people of God forgot about these mighty works within a few weeks after the great deliverance! They witnessed His wonders, but these wonders made no real impression on them.

Verse 8 provides a reason for God's saving work. He saves so as to be true to Himself and to get Himself the glory. He set out to have a people for Himself, and no earthly power could possibly annul His covenant or stymie His purposes. Yahweh God made a covenant with Abraham, and He will bring it to pass. By His acts of saving power, God humbles men and glorifies Himself. No less in the New Testament do we witness the culmination of all of God's purposes in redemption. The Apostle adds his own psalm as it were to these sentiments in Ephesians 1 as he cries out, "To the praise of the glory of His grace, wherein He has made us accepted in the beloved!" Above all others, certainly the recipients of God's powerful salvation should find profound reasons here to give God glory!

Verses 12–33. Verse 12 says the children of Israel, after witnessing the Red Sea event, believed for a little while at least and gave God praise. For the most part though, this faith was temporary and fleeting. Like the stony ground hearer in the parable, they "believed for a while," and, in time of temptation, fell away (Luke 8:15). It wasn't more than a few weeks later that they forgot His works, and they tempted God in the wilderness. (The entire journey from Egypt to Mount

Sinai took about six weeks.) To tempt God is to doubt God's faithfulness and to question His actions as malicious and unfaithful to His covenant. The psalmist says, "They lusted exceedingly in the wilderness" (verse 14). If God says, "This is what I have for you," yet you are discontented with those things and desire something besides what He has laid out for you, then you sin against Him. Accept what God has given to you with gratefulness and contentment. This is trusting, by faith, that God is good and that His gifts are good. However, the Israelites did not believe that the deliverance from Egypt and the wilderness—and the provision of the manna and the quail—were the best for them.

The following verses provide multiple instances of unfaithfulness on the part of God's people. They resisted God's appointed leaders, Moses and Aaron, by again challenging His wisdom in appointing these men. They rejected His law—the first and second commandments—by assembling the golden calf. In doing so, they reduced themselves to blind, pagan worship. Those who worship calves are nothing better than cows that graze out in the fields! Those who cannot worship an invisible God will worship stupid, visible things like cows or fallible human beings!

Verse 21 encapsulates the real issue with these people. They forgot their Savior. What a sad state of affairs! Practically everybody in the world is aware of the terrible effects of sin, which include tyranny, slavery, abuse, disease, and death. What could possibly save men from all of these tragic consequences? The answer should be obvious. A human being can save someone from drowning on occasion, but only God can save us from the deepest metaphysical needs of all! Only God can unwind the iron chains of tyranny imposed on His people. There is none other who can provide us this salvation. So when a people forgets God is their Savior, either they forget that they have to be saved from anything (which is doubtful), or they doubt God's capacity to save. Verse 24 further clarifies. They would not believe God's Word or His promises. One must believe in God's capacity to save in order to be saved. There is no essential difference between Acts 16:31 and Psalm 106:24. In order to be saved, one must believe in the Lord Jesus Christ. One must believe in the promises of God and the works of God to be saved, and that includes the works of the Son of God when He walked the earth and died on the cross for our sins.

Because they did not believe in the promises of God, they did not take the Promised Land. The situation is no different for us. If we are to be saved, if we are to live the Christian life and fight the good fight, of course we must believe in the promises of God. How can we ever get to the Promised Land if we do not believe in the power of God to take us there?

Not all of these people were faithless and rebellious. Two examples of faithfulness are mentioned. First, Moses served as the faithful leader of God's people, appealing for mercy upon these people along the way. Yet, the unfaithful majority were successful at drawing Moses into their rebel ways when he responded in anger against them and broke God's command in the process (verses 32–33). Second is Phinehas, a man with a ferocious commitment to God, who stemmed the tide of rebellion in the Baalpeor affair. This remarkable act of faith would bless many generations to come.

Verses 34–39. When God's people choose to rebel against Him, there is no telling the depths to which they will go with their wickedness. Rather than destroying the wicked Canaanites, they synthesized with their wicked ways, including such atrocities as idolatry, infanticide, and human sacrifice. There really is no neutrality when it comes to our relationship with the world. Either we will oppose it or we will amalgamate into it. Whomever is a friend of the world will be an enemy of God (James 4:4). When the children of Israel made friends with the Canaanites, they became an enemy of God.

Verses 40–46. What a tragic story! Here are the people who enjoyed great privilege, but still chose to harden their hearts against God. It is hard to imagine a father who abhors his own children, but this is the analogy used in verse 40 to describe

God's relationship with His people. Even the best of husbands eventually leaves a whorish wife, and God eventually abandons His idolatrous people to the hand of their enemies. Yet the story does not end there. When they began to cry out to God in their affliction, He delivered them. Upon the slightest movement towards repentance on their part, He turned back to them like a husband to a wayward wife as soon as she made a small effort towards returning to her husband. This demonstrates two things: the soft heart God has for His people, and the commitment He has to His covenant.

In both the Old and New Testaments, God speaks to His people as a group. He relates to them as a group. Each local church in the New Testament makes up a tiny Israel, and ᵒChrist relates to each one of them as a candlestick, noted in Revelation 2 and 3. Here again, He demands repentance of His people as a church body (Rev. 2:5, 2:16, 2:21, 3:3, 3:20), with a warning that He may have to remove their candlestick. Paul commends the repentance of the Corinthian church in 2 Corinthians 7:8–11. Of the 10 million local churches, parishes, and dioceses around the world, there are some that have provoked the wrath of the Lamb against them by their wayward pastors and defective confessions. But there are also those who humble themselves and daily seek the Lord for His mercy on them, and their candlesticks are still intact.

Verses 47–48. Some are concerned about the plight of God's people, and others are not. Those who are concerned about the demise of the faith and the weakness of the church cry out to God for His salvation. They are concerned about synthesis with the ideas and practices of the heathen. They are concerned not just for their own spiritual vitality but for the health of the body, the church. These are not "lone wolf" Christians who are only concerned about themselves and their families. They know that without the survival of a church body, there will be no individual faith fifty years hence for their children and grandchildren. They have a vested interest in the vitality of the corporate body. It is hard to separate the health of the individual from the health of the corporate body. When God refused to spare the natural branches in the vine tree and purged them, a great many Jews were consigned to blindness and rebellion for many generations (Rom. 11:21). Will a similar curse fall upon the Western "Christian" world for another thousand years or two? All we can do now is cry out with the Psalmist for God's salvation. Only God can save us from spiritual lethargy, compromise, blindness, and the tidal wave of apostasy sweeping over the West.

Whatever happens to us and our descendants, it is still our highest aim to see God praised by a multitude of people. Our salvation is not primarily for us. What we want is a people to give thanks to His holy name and triumph in His praise! Thus, it is fitting to end the psalm in a hymn of praise. And let all the people say, "Amen!"

How do we apply this psalm to our lives?

1. If you were an eyewitness of this large group of people traveling from Egypt to Sinai in 1800 B.C., would you have seen the hand of an invisible God working along the way? Or would you have provided some other explanation for the Red Sea parting and the manna falling from the sky? Would you have fallen on your face and worshiped this invisible God, or would you have struggled to provide a "scientific" explanation for what was happening? Faithless minds continue to disbelieve the God of the Exodus.

2. The faith is dying quickly in post-Christian Europe. Pollsters tell us that 50% of Americans call themselves Christians, which is down from 70% in 1970, and this trend is accelerating. Western Christianity is struggling against apostasy and synthesis with the world as Israel did for so long in the Old Testament. Even the tiniest efforts toward reformation are quickly swept aside by a hundred compromising variants. Yet it is still a worthy struggle, a critical struggle that could yield either great blessing or great devastation to millions of people in generations to come. It is times like these that call for the faith of Phinehas. One man here or there could make a significant

difference should he understand the nature of compromise, the core issues in the conflict, and at least one basic solution to stem the flow of apostasy. While we wouldn't necessarily recommend thrusting a spear into a fornicating couple, the faith and the forthright action of the man who did so in Numbers 25 are to be emulated. It is good for us to struggle mightily against the trends towards apostasy in our day. If God blessed Phinehas for generations, what mighty acts of faith might we engage that would yield tremendous generational consequences for our grandchildren and great-grandchildren to come?

How does this psalm teach us to worship God?

Is there anything more depressing than to see God's people descending into rank apostasy, child sacrifice, infanticide, and idolatry? To think that billions of people over thousands of years will harden their hearts against God and wander in darkness generates hopelessness and despair. But the psalmist is fighting for a remnant, and this is what good preaching does in the midst of wholesale apostasy. This is what the faithful few are doing in the Christian West in our present century.

Moreover, if we are going to take the time to review the gross apostasy of God's people, it should only be for the purpose of strengthening our commitment to faithfulness. What we really want to do is to bless the Lord God of Israel from everlasting to everlasting for His faithful covenant mercies. God's people may be unfaithful to the covenant, but God will ever be faithful to the covenant He made with His people, and that is what really matters to us.

Questions:

1. What aspect of God's character is contrasted with the unfaithfulness of God's people in this psalm?

2. Recount the many instances of the rebellion of God's people related in this psalm.

3. What does it mean when the psalmist says that the Israelites lusted exceedingly in the wilderness?

4. Who was Phinehas and what did he do to stem God's judgment on Israel? How did God reward him?

5. What can the remnant do in the face of serious wide-spread apostasy?

6. Give several examples of Didactic Psalms.

Family Discussion Questions:

1. How do we view the apostasy of the church in our day? Does this apostasy affect our family in any way, either now or in coming generations?

2. Are we satisfied with God's goodness to us, or do we lust after other things? What happens when we feel our hearts pulling away from God? Do we justify our apostasy the same way Israel did in the Old Testament?

Appendix A: Category & Occasion

Psalm	Category	Occasion
73	Faith	Envying the Wicked
74	Deliverance	A Decimated Church
75	Praise	Pride
76	Praise	Warfare
77	Faith	Overwhelming Trouble
78	Didactic	Family Discipleship
79	Deliverance	Persecuted Saints
80	Deliverance	Spiritual Declension
81	Praise	Day of Remembrance (Passover)
82	Didactic	Failure of Civil Rule
83	Imprecatory	Church Under Siege
84	Testimony	Ascent to Worship
85	Deliverance	A Backsliding People
86	Deliverance	Dangerous Men Threaten
87	Didactic	Internationality of the Church
88	Deliverance	Death of a Loved One
89	Faith	Unfaithfulness of God's People
90	Prayer	Assessing Life
91	Faith	Fearful Times
92	Praise	The Lord's Day
93	Praise	Turmoil
94	Imprecatory/ Exhortation	Murder of Innocents
95	Praise/Exhortation	Hardness of Heart
96	Praise	Multi-National Gatherings
97	Exhortation	Temporal Judgment
98	Praise	Temporal Deliverance

99	Praise	A Disobedient Church
100	Praise	Induction to Worship
101	Faith	Church Discipline
102	Faith	Days of Humiliation
103	Praise	Supremely Grateful Hearts
104	Praise	Walk Through the Woods
105	Didactic	Teaching History
106	Didactic	Corporate Rebellion

To order other Family Bible Study Guides,

go to GenerationswithVision.com, call 1-888-839-6132,

or send an e-mail to mail@generationswithvision.com

~ ~ ~

The Bible is the Core Curriculum in the education of a child.
If we provide our children excellent academic instruction in
mathematics, science, and grammar but neglect to teach them
Genesis, Psalms, Proverbs, and the Gospels, we have failed in
the education of our children.